POWER IN THE BLOOD

Popular culture and village discourse in early modern Germany

POWER IN THE BLOOD

Popular culture and village discourse
in early modern Germany

DAVID WARREN SABEAN
Acting Associate Professor, University of California, Los Angeles

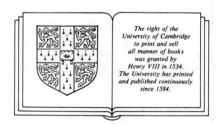

The right of the
University of Cambridge
to print and sell
all manner of books
was granted by
Henry VIII in 1534.
The University has printed
and published continuously
since 1584.

CAMBRIDGE UNIVERSITY PRESS

Cambridge
New York   New Rochelle
Melbourne   Sydney

Published by the Press Syndicate of the University of Cambridge
The Pitt Building, Trumpington Street, Cambridge CB2 1RP
32 East 57th Street, New York, NY 10022, USA
10 Stamford Road, Oakleigh, Melbourne 3166, Australia

First published 1984
First paperback edition 1987
Reprinted 1988

Printed in the United States of America

British Library cataloguing in publication data
Sabean, David Warren
Power in the blood.
1. Nürtingen (Germany) – Social life and
customs
I. Title
943'.47   DD901.N97/
ISBN 0 521 26455 3 hard covers
ISBN 0 521 34778 5 paperback

This book is dedicated

to my mother
MYRNA MAUDE DIXON SABEAN

and to the memory of my father
ELMER CLYDE SABEAN

Contents

Illustrations

Preface

The origins of this book are obscure even to myself, but the occasion of its conception I remember quite vividly. For about fifteen years, I have been piecing together all of the material I can find on the village of Neckarhausen (today part of the city of Nürtingen). The search broadened out several years ago from the rich collection of documents in the Rathaus to include the regional and state archives. About a year ago, I spent a week in the Landeskirchliches Archiv in Stuttgart reading through all of the pertinent information in the church visitation records. At the end of the week, I had three free hours before my train left, which I used to browse through the volumes of the 1580s, looking for more stories of peasant refusal to attend the sacrament of communion to match the two I had found for Neckarhausen. What I discovered makes up the first chapter in this book. It also put me on to the trail of new material to extend the questions and provide new possibilities for experimentation.

The attentive reader will see that although I skip all around Württemberg in this book, I have gained my fundamental understanding of the workings of that rural society through the patient, detailed examination of the mass of sources from Neckarhausen. I have also benefited from daily discussions over the last seven years with my colleagues in the Max-Planck-Institut für Geschichte. Especially close have been my contacts with Hans Medick, who is spending the better part of his life with his own Swabian village. Together with Alf Lüdtke, we have also been debating the exchange between history and anthropology for a long time. Little of what I have written here could have been done prior to my long 'sabbatical' in Göttingen.

Jürgen Schlumbohm read each chapter as it came fresh from the typewriter and provided me with the necessary encouragement to continue. I also argued every line with Vanessa Maher, Gerald Sider, Jonathan Knudsen, and William Reddy, all of whom brought their own work to the Institute to be discussed. They all know how much I learned from them.

An earlier version of chapter 1 appeared in the Festschrift for Rudolf Vierhaus, the Institute's director (published by Vandenhoeck und Ruprecht). His comments were valuable for revising the argument, but more important has been his continual support for my work and the superb conditions for research which he has provided.

Several people have read and commented on one or other of the chapters. Particularly helpful have been the remarks by Barbara Duden, David Cohen, Anthony La Vopa, Ivan Illich, Kenneth Barkin, Peter Reill, and Georg Iggers.

Towards the end of work on the book, I had a chance to talk with Martin Scharfe, who put me on to the trail of the broadside depicting the Beutelsbach bull sacrifice. I was received most kindly by Dr Irmgard Hampe at the Württemberg Landesstelle für Volkskunde, who gave me permission to make a copy.

In twenty years of visits to the Hauptstaatsarchiv in Stuttgart, I have spent many hours discovering things. I hope that I have been able to convey some of the excitement I have experienced reading documents. It has not always been easy for the staff to answer my needs, but they have always been helpful and encouraging. A quiet oasis in the archive landscape is the Landeskirchliches Archiv in Stuttgart, whose director, Dr Gerhard Schäfer, has arranged for me to use material from Neckarhausen and given me many useful ideas. Hermann Ott, who presides over the reading room, knows better than anyone else how to help the helpless.

During various stages of the book's production, I received important support from Brigitte Bartels and Monika Hammer, who typed the manuscript, and from Hiltrud Mintenig, who entered it into the computer. Manfred Thaller, who will play a prominent role in the introduction to the Neckarhausen book, introduced me to the mysteries of computerized text processing. The diagrams in chapter 5 were drawn by Stefan Mielke.

One night after I had hurriedly cooked a particularly depressing meal, my wife asked if I thought the peasants were worth it. Her irony has kept me sane.

Göttingen
July 1983

Introduction: Perspectives on the analysis of early modern state practice

Where there is no faith, there is no conscience but only the mark of the beast.

> Johannes Brenz, 1530

Rebellious opinion: that the external, oral preaching of the Holy Gospel of Christ is only an external action and letter, unserviceable for the inner life of the spirit.

> Württemberg Church Ordinance, 1559

Everyone babbles the words, but few obtain thereby a stronger faith.

> Johann Valentin Andreae, 1622

In our Evangelical, so-called Lutheran, churches and congregations [there is] one great defect, greater than with all other religions . . . that the majority of teachers [teach] according to the external letter.

> Georg Gottfrid Bregenzer, 1699

The freedom which you acquire today is an external freedom of your bodies . . . and not an inner freedom from your consciences.

> Superintendent Lang, 1745

The common man has . . . little receptivity for purer notions.

> Canzlei Advocat Bolley, 1796

This book is composed of a series of episodes strung out over two and a quarter centuries. All of them deal with village or small town life in the duchy of Württemberg in southwest Germany. The first chapter describes attempts on the part of magistrates during the 1580s to enforce attendance at communion, and shows how for villagers the sacrament revolved around enmity and friendship. In the second chapter, a peasant prophet appears who in 1648, the last year of the Thirty years' War,

1

met an angel in the vineyard above his village. The angel gave him a message about sin and repentance to take to the duke, but beneath the strongly encoded message there were hints of a tax revolt. The third chapter deals with an incident from the year 1683, when a thirteen-year-old girl spread the rumor that she was a witch. The metaphorical structure of her language opens up central issues about communal life and state domination. The fourth chapter deals with the career of a pastor at the turn of the eighteenth century, whom we would today probably regard as paranoid. His activities put into relief the complex problem of the relation of spiritual to temporal power. Shortly before mid century, the death of another pastor developed into a murder investigation. This story takes us into problems of kinship and conscience, local power and state ideology. The sixth chapter, taken from the very end of the eighteenth century, examines an incident involving a village which sacrificed a live bull to a cattle epidemic. The way the event was related to village discourse takes us further into problems of understanding local power and popular culture.

In every chapter, difficult problems of textual analysis confront us, and it is no simple matter to distinguish what exactly popular opinion on an issue was. Historical sources written by members of the popular classes are hard to come by until well into the nineteenth century, which gives the impression that the vast mass of the rural population remained silent witness to the progress of time. Whatever sources there are for studying peasant culture implicate in one way or another those people who to some extent exercised domination over the peasant.[1] Even court disputes between people at the local level usually involve clerks, notaries, or judges who wrote down what villagers said. What appears as direct testimony in a judicial text may well be a paragraph redaction of something that took quite a long time to say. In addition, evidence about what peasants thought or how they acted is largely anecdotal in character and subject to the distortion that story telling brings to a situation. Such evidence is often so repetitive or deals with trivial details in such a way that the historian has difficulty escaping its banality. These two problems, then – the entanglement of peasant views in sources deriving from various levels of authority and the nature of the evidence as anecdote – present issues of great importance to the student of popular culture.

We might start by pointing out that what is a fact about sources is not necessarily a weakness. Documents which perceive peasants through the eyes of rulers or their spokesmen begin with relationships of domination. After all, the notion of 'peasant' implies more than just 'rural cultivator' and takes into consideration his involvement in productive, legal, and religious relationships which dominate part of his existence. There is irony in the fact that because we cannot get to the peasant except through the lord, our evidence is often a good starting place for considering the relationships which we want to investigate. The issue is to examine the constitution of peasant notions within the dynamics of power and hierarchical relations, and the chapters in this volume are exercises in the use of sources generated by state authorities to study the peasants' view of this process.

As for the story-like character of the evidence, two kinds of narratives are presented here. Some are repetitive, such as the reports in the first chapter about people in different villages refusing to take part in communion, or the testimony in the last two, where successive villagers were questioned about matters which they all knew about or had experienced. Repetitive stories of this kind are close in form to that of peasant communication, a form which may exist in most communities with 'face-to-face' relationships.[2] This form involves concrete language of symbolic content, which constantly reiterates central aspects of social relationships. Its repetitiveness and its seeming triviality is a pointer to what in fact we want to investigate. The other forms of narrative, non-repetitive in character, lead to much the same end, for close attention to the structures of action or ideas reveals their logic and shows how the logic is remapped on to new situations or is interconnected with other pieces. We will be concerned with examining symbols and metaphors and the language of concrete experience, in order to understand ways in which villagers presented the flow of social processes and the nature of social relations to themselves and among themselves.

This book offers views into particular situations. Since the source material in one case seldom overlaps with that in another, we are confronted with disjunctions that make analysis of the same issues over the whole period difficult. Nonetheless, a goal of the book is to follow changes in village social relations and their representation over time. An issue is whether in fact there are constants in rural structures and culture based on an unchanging productive routine or the conservation of peasant thought.[3] One view seeks to find the essential peasant culture, the underground tradition, so to speak, hidden away from the lords and deeply rooted in the past. We are only offered glimpses into this world from time to time. Another position argues for relatively unchanging structures, which receive different modes of expression over time, pointing to enduring constraints and the constant reception of elements of high culture. In my view, the social relations inside Württemberg villages were constantly undergoing change during the period under consideration. Inherited items of culture continually changed shape as they were situated in new contexts. We will be taking each case separately and examining the logic of social relations and the pattern of discourse peculiar to it. We will discuss certain of the historical forces which converged at each particular point. We will also examine recurring problems and investigate some of the long term processes which brought about change.

Productive forces and social change in Württemberg

The description below is not meant to be a thoroughgoing introduction to the agrarian or economic history of southwest Germany from the sixteenth to the eighteenth century. I will pick and choose only those elements that will be helpful as background to the information and arguments in the chapters that follow. The object is to sketch some of the salient features of the social forces inside the villages of Württemberg and their articulation with the outside, stressing those particular aspects relevant to the story I want to tell. The important fact to emphasize at the outset is that Württemberg was a land of small peasant producers, although the regional towns had an active trading life as service centers for agriculture, and provided locations for professional and administrative elites. Certain areas, notably around Urach on the Swabian Alp and Calw in the Black Forest, developed proto-industrial activity, especially in the eighteenth century. However, our stories are centered mostly in villages dominated by small agricultural producers. There was no nobility as such in Württemberg, at least not after they won status for themselves as Imperial knights in the early sixteenth century. Their territories, occasionally no more than a village, remained foreign enclaves inside Württemberg and could have some importance for such matters as trading. But the nobility itself was not a class situated between the rural population and the duke. It provided no dynamic in the process of expropriation. As far as property rights were concerned, peasants held some land in private ownership, but much of the land in the territory was in a tenure arrangement with the duke of Württemberg or with some institution such as the university or one of the numerous foundations.[4] Already in the sixteenth century, the peasants, for the most part, had inheritable tenures. Tithes on grain, as well as rents, ended up in one way or another with the duke or with institutions of the territory. Taxes were levied on all land, whether owned privately or held in tenure.

It is important to understand that a large proportion of the 'feudal rent' was levied in kind in Württemberg until well into the nineteenth century. Although there were many small levies and fees, three basic forms of extraction of surplus accounted for the bulk of the approximately thirty per cent eventually taken from what peasants produced. Ten per cent of the grain harvest went for tithes (on all land – tenure and free). Approximately another ten per cent was paid for ground rents, most of which were paid in kind.[5] Both of these parts of the feudal rent did not vary significantly in proportion from the early sixteenth to the nineteenth century. The 'dynamic' element, levied in money and subject to fluctuations and long term rises, was taxes. By the end of the eighteenth century, these too amounted to a rough tenth of the agricultural product.

From the beginning of the sixteenth century, Württemberg had a higher tax burden than the neighboring territories.[6] There was an important rise at the end of the sixteenth century and another associated with the period during and after the Thirty Years' War, both involving costs of the military establishment. Taxes, of course, went directly to the state. A myriad of officials, concerned with the annual movement of considerable amounts of produce and money from villages to central institutions, determined one major way in which the villages interrelated with the state. But officials of the state were not the only ones concerned with expropriation of the peasant surplus, for at the village level the collection of all dues was mostly carried out and supervised by a set of local officials, people who were members of the village itself. A further fact important for local relations is that the pastor in a village often received the small tithe (on garden produce and the like) and was one of the few officials who dealt directly with the primary producer and enjoyed his fruits immediately.[7]

It is often stressed that in Württemberg a strong urban/rural dichotomy never developed. No large agglomeration arose with radically different modes of production or with capital structures capable of effecting transformations in the countryside. No expropriation process characterized relations with the city.[8] Even politically, villages were able to prevent a taxation structure which favored cities.[9] In the small towns, many inhabitants carried on agriculture, and artisans there were often not distinguishable from village artisans. Although town and village provided no radical disjunction, regional administrative, religious, and economic elites were centered in the towns, and wealthier town dwellers were usually a good deal richer than the wealthiest villagers. The strategy of location gave the artisanal and merchant groups of the town entrepreneurial functions with regard to building trades and the marketing of agricultural production. But probably more important was the fact that the town contained the intermediate church and state administrative officials. The latter were concerned with collecting and channeling twenty or thirty per cent of what villagers produced in agriculture to the more central state distribution centers. They also exercised judicial and political functions. Between the village chief administrative official, the Schultheiss, and the town representative of state authority, the Vogt, the social gap was considerable.

With these structural aspects in mind, we can consider some of the central facts of social and economic change over the period dealt with in this book. The sixteenth century was generally characterized by economic expansion and a rise in rural population until at least the 1580s. Although some of the population increase was absorbed by cities and armies, growth in rural areas was also considerable.[10] It brought pressure to break up the large farms formed in the late Middle Ages, a move which was successfully resisted in such areas as Upper Swabia and the Black Forest.[11] In the central areas of Württemberg, there was some division of the larger farms, but this was generally held within bounds.[12] There too a class of land poor grew up in the villages alongside peasants with relatively large enterprises. In comparison with the eighteenth century, the rise in population and the expansion in agriculture – which was driven on by an enormous rise in agricultural prices, particularly grain – were not accompanied by the growth of a village class of artisans. There were, of course, some regions where spinning or weaving became widespread on the land. But as the price scissors went ever more against the rural producers, they had to be tied to agriculture in order to survive.[13] In general, however, increased regional specialization – wine, flax, milk products, timber, etc. – was specialization in agriculture involving an ever more complex network of interregional trade.[14] But the complexity of the market structure to be found in the eighteenth century did not yet exist.

Peter Kriedte has recently summarized the dynamic and blockage of the sixteenth-century economic expansion.[15] The rise in population was accompanied by a revolution in prices, with agricultural products, led by grain, at the forefront. More land was brought into cultivation at the cost of reduced marginal returns, leading to rising production but falling productivity. The expansion eventually led to a destruction of the ecological balance – soil exhaustion, harvest failures, depleted resources. As one result, the share in the agrarian product of the feudal classes was constantly threatened, and one way they reacted was by putting restrictions on the partitioning of viable farms by land-hungry heirs. Where feudal rent had been transformed into money terms, new forms of expropriation and arbitrary exaction were necessary. But in Württemberg, with rents and tithes largely in kind, the lord and state institutions participated in the general economic rise. Württemberg did not change the form of tenure from an inheritable one. What drove it to higher money extraction in the form of taxes was the monetization and higher costs of a military force which developed in the sixteenth century.[16] To characterize the market in the sixteenth century in rough terms is to stress the urban/rural differences: commodity production in the city and agricultural production in the countryside, with the market place as the point of exchange. Also, regional specialization emphasized the market place as the location of exchange relations. By contrast, in the eighteenth century, these kinds of markets were overlaid with an internal market, and the *market place* as the mediator between manufactured commodities and agrarian products did not maintain its exclusivity.

By the 1580s, the population growth came to an end or slowed down considerably. The mechanism of this blockage was a series of harvest failures, coupled with waves of epidemic, notably bubonic plague, which began in the 1580s and recurred at the end of the first decade of the seventeenth century and again in the middle decade of the Thirty Years' War. It is hard to avoid the notion that the great waves of mortality were closely related to the limits of expansion in agriculture.[17] The poorest members of the population were subject to a vast decrease in real wages. Wages need not necessarily have been the primary part of their subsistence in order to be used as an indicator of their status, and all the wage series that we have for Western Europe in the sixteenth century show a large and dramatic fall.[18] This is part of what lay behind the increasing use of the social category of 'poor' in the records of the late sixteenth century.[19] Those with few resources confronted those with property and fought battles over the use of forest land and other common rights. Since agriculture formed the basis of the economy, one would expect the links between people to be tied closely to land ownership, and the reciprocities in a village to be largely mediated through non-monetary links. Illustrating how social relations could be embedded in the daily subsistence activities of agricultural production and exchange, a diary of a pastor from the 1680s shows how much of his day was spent going from meal to meal and collecting rents in kind.[20] This can be contrasted with the eighteenth century, when a large part of pastors' incomes were composed of interest on money lent out to various peasants, salaries, and often expanded and commercialized small tithes.[21]

It is hard to grasp the economic changes associated with the Thirty Years' War. Plague and warfare took their toll so that many Württemberg villages had populations of no more than forty per cent of their pre-war levels.[22] The fall in population and in agricultural prices and the low level of capital savings and available labor led to more extensive farming, but under the burden of heavy taxation. An important consequence of the war seems to have been the stabilization of agricultural production as the dominant basis of social reproduction, but in a way different from that of the sixteenth century.[23] During the subsequent half century, partible inheritance clearly came to dominate the Württemberg villages, and by the end of the period a rural artisan class was firmly established. The artisan class which grew up in the villages may well have been the result of relatively high costs of labor in a depression period, since they could support themselves partly from agriculture. It is also important to see that the conjunction of feudal exactions, in the form of agricultural products, with new heavy taxation helped to support partible inheritance because of the difficulty in maintaining a balance between capital and land. Capital needs of peasants also forced them to accept usurious loans.[24]

It was during this period that the characteristic Württemberg distribution of wealth developed, with no great disjunctions between classes of *Vollbauer* (large peasant proprietors) and cottagers. However, production remained fully oriented to agriculture, and the practices of state domination centered on ground rents or on forms of extraction based on property ownership.[25] Despite economic decline in the second half of the seventeenth century, activity on the part of the state continued to increase. Of course, the presence of the state in the form of competing armies during the Thirty Years' War and the growth of taxation instruments and exactions before, during, and after the war can be seen as fundamental agents of long term economic difficulty. Claims within the structure of the reorganized feudal state based on the needs of a permanent military force brought permanent heavy taxation. It was not the shock of the Thirty Years' War[26] so much as the heavy, continuing taxation exactions that led to the slow recovery of and reinforced difficulties in peasant reproduction.[27]

The issues of taxation and other forms of transfer stamped relations between state and village ever more clearly. The instruments of the state were local officials in village and town, and the sources give the impression that the post-war period for them was one of corruption and booty. Parallel to growing exacting bureaucracy with control from the center – as any investigation into witchcraft can show – were usurious activities, rake-offs, and conflicts over the spoils of office on the part of officials. In this period, villagers were making room for immigrants, confronting enormous problems of capital formation – borrowing money from officials at high rates of interest – and dealing with the inexorability of taxation.[28] Inside villages, public support of the poor became central issues, and families were less likely to recognize responsibilities to distant relatives.[29] The after effects of the war cut many people loose from their original homes and left them deposited around villages with no effective ties, creating disputes over who belonged where and to whom.[30] Village and town consciousness developed over disputes with state officials about residence rights and public responsibilities to support individuals. Villages and towns also increased their own internal self-regulation with regards to quartering troops and collecting tithes and taxes. As the dialectic between village and state increased its tempo, issues of legitimate authority became more acute. Pastors, for example, devised new forms of discourse against rapacious officials, and the theme of spiritual and temporal power came to be a focal point for many conflicts.[31] While the Thirty Years' War left many clergymen impoverished, they entered the second half of the century with new instruments of power in their hands: institutionally, the village church consistory, and ideologically, a theory of repentance.[32]

To characterize the eighteenth century briefly is not simple either. Looking at the period 1720–50 when the pre-Thirty Years' War population levels were again attained, we can see that the situation had altered significantly. More regular employment in the army for young men took a small but certain percentage of people from the villages for a time. Above all, depending on the size of villages, a more-or-less extensive corps of village artisans had been established, which grew in number with the sharp rise in population after mid century. At the beginning of the eighteenth century, artisans could be found among the wealthiest members of a village, but by the end this was very seldom the case except for the bakers, butchers, innkeepers, and millers.[33] While at the beginning of the century, artisans had a secure place among the village magistrates, increasingly all such positions came into the hands of landed peasants. The rise of a village artisan class must be distinguished from the growth of proto-industrial producers, such as the spinners and weavers to be found in the Black Forest region around Calw or on the Swabian Alp around Urach and Laichingen. By contrast with the sixteenth century, town and country differences were not so marked, since small commodity production of a complex set of handicrafts had become so well established in the countryside. Although this was a general German phenomenon, nowhere was the class of artisans so large as in Württemberg. There it reached a density and complexity equal to that of an East Elbian city.[34] Around 1730, that class made up about a quarter of the working population, and by the end of the century about a third.

Artisans were clearly among the land poor and were dependent on their handicrafts for survival. Their existence and growth attests to an increasing division of labor and penetration of market relationships,[35] which had two correlative aspects. The growth of the artisan class was closely associated with agricultural intensification and specialization – the production of fruit, wine, and industrial crops, all of which entered the market. At the same time the development of village and small town people dependent on wage labor also provided a market for artisanal commodities.[36] Although this group remained a stable percentage (about fifty per cent) of the population, with the demographic rise its absolute numbers grew considerably.[37] Schultz characterizes the period in terms of a social differentiation taking place inside a homogeneous peasant/small peasant society.[38] According to Kaschuba and Lipp, the process involved a progressive dependence of village producers on market relations and the purchase of commodities, such that commodities subject to long distance trade entered the local economy. This implied a step-by-step substitution of subsistence economy by commodity consumption and production.[39]

A dominant trend was the growth of market relationships and specialization. In central Europe, there was even the appearance of such characters as the one who gathered from hedges wool left by passing sheep – or the other who gathered horsehair.[40] Their products were sold for cash. But it was not just people who specialized; whole villages also came to specialize in various ways. There was, for example, a village with many varieties of cherries, all with special marketing possibilities – one was sold to wine merchants to darken wine.[41] One village might specialize in growing and selling raw flax, another in preparing flax, and yet another in spinning linen thread.[42] Although any one village would to some degree combine such activities, each gave a special emphasis to its activities. In any event, the trend towards specialization and monetization was perhaps only there to a small degree at the beginning of the century but by the end was in full flower. It coincided with the growing specialization in agriculture, with capitalization, and with marketing. Property holding in villages underwent a series of significant changes, bringing new forms of relations among people.

Agricultural holdings were increasingly subject to fissioning, through inheritance but also through intra-village land sales – considerably more land by the end of the century was sold in ever smaller plots.[43] The slow shift from extensive agricultural methods to intensive ones can be seen in cropping as well as in techniques. By the end of the century, villages were poised to abolish the herd of horses and increase considerably that of cattle, implying new forms of cooperation – one can plow with one horse but two cows or oxen are needed.[44] The capital market also changed its character. Through the fruits of office and inheritance, many state officials and pastors came to expect a considerable portion of their incomes from rents. Widows were also important for the capital market. Interest was officially regulated at five per cent. With time, peasant producers became dependent on this capital market for their loans of 100–300 fl., and depending on the economic situation were more or less burdened with debt. Bankruptcy did not lead to a change of ownership from peasant to bourgeois; rather the peasant's land would be sold at auction to other villagers and the creditors paid off at a loss. Increasingly, money was lent by people no longer in direct contact with each other – the widow of a notary in Stuttgart, for example, to a small farmer thirty or forty kilometers away in a village tucked under the Swabian Alp.[45]

The social forces in the eighteenth century were quite different from those in the sixteenth century. Increasing social differentiation in the later period meant more of a continuum of property holding and income, rather than a disjunction between large property holders and the landless.[46] Specialization made each person more or less describable in unique terms; more people were on the margin and tied together in more complex ways – few people carried on the same kind of work during the whole year. It was more necessary to piece together different kinds of income sources. The honor of a person became more of an issue, and competition for place in the society was organized increasingly around such a symbol. This was also true for a village as a whole, for its reputation and honor were perceived as central for the competitive position of its members.[47] Horizontal links involving inter-cooperation among equals became increasingly well established; con-nubium became more fractionalized and subject to closer calculation. Vertical links were more subject to interflows of patronage and direct exercise of power. Although blood relations remained important as a mapping exercise – to stress legitimacy (honor) or to attach oneself to more successful relatives – the group of blood kin ceased to function as a cooperative one. Fictive kinship – god-parentage – was more apt to be used to forge new vertical relationships.[48]

Inside this structure, the pastor, always an outsider, was part of an increasingly self-confident, well-to-do class. Within the village, he confronted a likewise increasingly self-confident ruling group of land-owners. Issues such as drinking could symbolize the divergent forms of power – pastor/Schultheiss; and the social basis of response to the pastor's message would always be implicated in the articulation of village social structure.

Insiders and outsiders: Village and regional officials

In the chapters that follow, there are a number of matters touching on the nature of village and state institutions and personnel which ought to be made clear to the reader at the outset. Since the time span is from the sixteenth to the end of the eighteenth century, a good deal of change is involved which I will describe where relevant, but in order to keep the discussion reasonably short, I will give a rather static picture.

To start at the bottom, most of the villages that appear in these chapters were in areas of Württemberg characterized by large nucleated settlements of 400 to 1000 people.[49] A village of this size might well form a parish of its own, with church, pastor, schoolhouse, and schoolmaster. At times there would be a smaller settlement, a hamlet or isolated farmhouse, with its own institutions and land but included as part of a larger parish. In areas closer to the Swabian Alp or the Black Forest, settlements were often smaller and sometimes combined together in more encompassing administrative units which functioned like villages. In amongst a set of villages would be found a central administrative town, perhaps containing no more than 2000–4000 people. Together the town and villages made up one of the Württemberg administrative units, the *Stadt und Amt*.[50]

Every person born in a village to a *Bürger* had *Bürgerrecht* in a village, that is, the right to live there and participate in the privileges extended to its members.[51] Upon adulthood, an individual might be forced from economic necessity to go elsewhere, but unless he or she forfeited Bürgerrecht or took it up elsewhere, the right to return was maintained. Otherwise Bürgerrecht could only be attained by permission granted by the village magistrates – often on marrying into the community. Movement from village to village was not very great but could take place. Occasionally, a person took up residence without formally becoming a Bürger. He could then be accorded *Beisitzrecht*, the right to live there but not necessarily to share in village common rights. 'Bürger' had another meaning as well, and referred to the adult, married males, all those who had a right to use the commons, to be employed in village work, and to vote for village officials. Every man upon becoming a Bürger was required to take an oath to the duke, promising obedience. Together, the collectivity of Bürger made up the village corporation, or *Gemeinde*.

One way of assessing the strength and quality of the village corporation is through the tax structure. From early in the fifteenth century, Württemberg had a tax system which extended over the whole duchy and was supposed to fall as an equal burden on all inhabitants.[52] Basically, taxes were assessed on wealth, land and buildings, and only in the eighteenth century were assessments on professions included. The amount of the tax was apportioned from the center on each *Amt* (district). Each Amt in turn apportioned the tax to be collected from the town and from each village. Inside each village, the magistrates assessed property, apportioning the tax share accordingly. Part of the political processes at the regional level and between regions and center was played out around the question of how taxes were to be apportioned. In the sixteenth century, the inhabitants of the duchy won the right to be consulted about taxes and established a parliamentary institution called the *Landschaft* or *Landtag*. At the beginning, the Vögte in the cities – the chief regional officials – represented the Ämter, but by 1629, they were excluded from the Landtag. Agitation, started in the sixteenth century, finally made it possible in the period after the Thirty Years' War for village representatives to take part in consultative proceedings, at which representatives of an Amt were sent to the Landtag. Similarly, at the

Amt assembly where the apportionment of taxes for the various villages took place, villages slowly drove back the influence of the city magistracy.

Given these facts, a few conclusions about the overall political position of villages can be drawn. During the sixteenth century when a clear difference between town and village was apparent, with villages relegated largely to agriculture, the towns through the Vogt and magistrates maintained political leadership in the Amt. Even then the collectivity of villages seldom paid more than a third of the Amt's taxes.[53] After the Thirty Years' War, when the strong differences in economic and social structure between town and village largely disappeared, paradoxically not only did the weight of taxes fall more on the villages, but also their political position inside the regional union increased. At the same time lines of state authority were clarified. The fact of communal self-administration did not mean fewer taxes but more, just as stronger communal organization did not mean less domination but more.

Given the peculiar situation in Württemberg whereby feudal rent, in all its forms, in one way or other went primarily to the duke, his central officials, or ducal institutions, and the fact that an important part of the surplus was paid in kind, there had to be a large number of officials and paid workers to handle the annual movement of produce and money from villages to the center. Since so much of the movement involved grain and to some degree wine, problems of collecting, measuring, storing, processing, marketing, and accounting had to be dealt with. To a large extent, the basic collection took place at the village level under the administration of village officials or deputized villagers, who in turn worked under the administration of town officials. Each kind of exaction, whether ground rents, tithes, or taxes, had its own system of collection and set of administrators. Close connections between village and town officials were necessary, and the tenor of their relations was to a large degree tied up with this process of extraction of feudal dues.

The administrative constitution at the lowest level, the village, can be described as one of self-administration with strong external controls. The chief official was the Schultheiss. In the fifteenth century, he was most likely to be appointed by the duke, but in the course of time many villages negotiated the right of election. According to the *Communordnung* of 1758, he was to be elected in all villages, a right that was confirmed in 1770 after some attempts at abrogation.[54] He was elected by all the adult males (Bürger) in the village as they filed one-by-one before the election official (usually the chief administrator of the Amt). Once elected, the Schultheiss more or less had life tenure. The other chief official in a village was the *Bürgermeister*, who was usually a member of the *Gericht* (court) or *Rat* (council). He was the financial officer, responsible for collecting taxes, paying bills, and keeping financial records. There was often another Bürgermeister, who administered village common lands and buildings, stock piles of grain, and corvées. In addition to the Bürgermeister, there could be other financial officers in a village, such as the poor relief officer (*Heiligenpfleger*), and sometimes the same person held both offices. In a town, the administrator of poor relief could be a very important official, and in both town and village the responsibilities could be quite significant, especially since poor relief was constituted as a capital fund and lent out to Bürger at interest. There were also several posts with mixed administrative and financial duties, such as the *Waldmeister* or *Pförchmeister*. The former administered the village woodlands, which in some places were extensive enough to make them the largest source of village income. Naturally, the position had great possibilities for favouritism and corruption. The Pförchmeister allocated the right to fold the village flock on arable strips, and kept the quite considerable accounts. Often the village Schultheiss held one or both offices.

The other officials of the village composed the Gericht and Rat. A town could have as many as twelve members in the Gericht, while smaller settlements had accordingly fewer *Richter* (or *Gerichtsverwandten*). They were also elected by village Bürger and held life tenure. They met together once a year to select all the village posts that were appointed periodically (mostly for one year), such as field, vineyard, forest, and village police, night watchmen, horseherder, cowherd, gooseherd, shepherd, bullkeeper, and mouse catcher, and once or twice a year for a *Ruggericht*, where all the conflicts and delicts over the year would be dealt with. For the rest, they gathered on an *ad hoc* basis, often after church on Sundays, to deal immediately with some serious offense or pending issue. Another group, usually smaller, of village officials was the Rat, or council. It seems that they did not meet separately but joined the Gericht to form a larger council for certain kinds of business. They appear to have been younger villagers who later assumed places on the Gericht. All the village officials who exercised higher administrative tasks – forest administrator, sheep-fold administrator, markstone supervisor, field supervisor, fire inspector, property evaluator, orphan court juror, inventory taker, bread inspector, meat inspector, excise official, wine excise official, poor law treasurer, sub-customs inspector, horse and cattle inspector, church consistory elder – were chosen by the Schultheiss and Gericht and Rat from among themselves. The minutes of all meetings were kept by a village clerk (*Gerichtsschreiber*), a position usually held by the Schultheiss if he could write. Otherwise it fell to the schoolmaster or to a clerk from the town administration.

Together, the Schultheiss and Gericht and Rat made up the village *Obrigkeit* or magistracy, and they formed a corporation in opposition to the village Gemeinde. Although elected by Bürger, their tenure was not subject to the will of the Gemeinde, and they could only be removed by higher authority when convicted of crimes – chiefly those against the duke and his officials. The Schultheiss stood in relation to the rest of the magistracy and the village Gemeinde much as an abbot to a monastery or a master of a Cambridge college to the college: although elected, upon election exercising the independent authority of his office. However, carrying out the prerogatives of invested administrative power did not mean that he was not dependent on a certain amount of consensus. After all, he was usually a native of the village where he lived, a farmer, and a family member. His position was tied up with all of the relationships which bound people together as neighbors and kin and was part of the conflicts both real and potential dividing the village. For the success of his office, he was often dependent on his ability to get people to follow his lead. Although villages were always faction-ridden, the denial to any powerful enough group of what they con-sidered to be their just demands could make a village essentially ungovernable, or subject a Schultheiss to an attack on his own or his family's interests. An important part of his income was made up of fees and, of course, bribes, and the everyday exercise of his authority at least skirted along the edge of corruption and self-aggrandizement.

Also in a village were two officials who usually came from outside. The schoolmaster, who was often the son of a schoolmaster or occasionally the son of a pastor or even a villager from somewhere else, usually acquired his job in competition with several other applicants.[55] He was tested in the church in organ playing, singing, and doctrine, and in the *Rathaus* in spelling, reading, and writing and the like, and then elected by the village. He taught school, of course, and often had cus-todial duties in the church. He played the organ and occasionally took over clerking duties in the village. Although an outsider, through a local marriage and acquisition of some land and enough longevity, he could become more or less integrated and even at times an important village official. Pastors, who usually came from pastoral families and had been trained at the university, were also elected by the village from among those waiting for a position.[56] But in contrast to schoolmasters, they remained outsiders, in that their children seldom married villagers and their own wives came from outside the village from among their own class. They also never became landowners in a village. They depended for their incomes on a salary from the state, small tithes in the village (on garden produce, flax, and hay) fees, and perhaps some garden land, an arable strip, and some pasture. They also received interest on loans given out to agricultural producers.

The position of the pastor was based on several different elements. Every week he was able to speak from the authority of scripture and to offer an interpretation of events, social conditions, the activities of officials, and village affairs. Once a month, he administered communion. Before partaking of the sacrament, a villager was required to attend confession, which was composed of a public service – in which the meaning of communion was explained and parishioners were called upon to confess their sins – and a registration of intent to take communion with the pastor. This latter was called 'appearing before the chair of confession' (*Beichtstuhl*). In this private confrontation, the pastor was not supposed to be taking oral confession in the Catholic fashion but was to call upon the parishioner to confess his sins to God and to show penance. The manner of contrition and preparation was supposed to be left to the individual. But the occasion was one where the pastor could deal with the known activities of the person before him and could point out the differences between real and sham repentance. Real repentance could not be private in that authentic religious experience was supposed to lead to a changed life. At times, pastors were able to deny people access to the sacrament. However, in many villages and at certain periods, the registration for communion was a mere formality. Its potentiality depended very much on the personal inclination of the particular pastor.

After 1644, a new element was added to the pastor's power, namely the village church consistory, which was composed of several elders (usually from the magistracy), the Schultheiss, and the pastor. This was a kind of morals court, which had the power to summon and punish those who swore, got drunk, and quarreled in their families. It dealt with adultery, fornication, witchcraft, magic, profanation of the sabbath, church and school attendance, and the like.

Village officials were controlled periodically from the outside. By the seventeenth century, at least every two years the chief administrative official of the Amt held a *Vogtruggericht*. Every Bürger was called upon to state whether he knew of any delict against the interests of the state. The official examined the records and protocols of the Schultheiss and Gericht and Rat, making sure that the proper fines had been administered, serious cases had been reported, and all orders from the duke and his officials had been recorded and communicated to the village. This was only the most formal control, for the Schultheiss carried on business with the officials of the Amt practically every week. Every year the highest church official (*Superintendent*) of the Amt visited the village, checking on the conduct of the pastor and the schoolmaster and dealing with notorious problems. As for the Bürgermeister, he was required to send in a quarterly report of his accounts and a final accounting at the end of the fiscal year. The accounts were checked minutely, and he was called in to defend them.

The administrative towns had a slightly more complicated constitution, and some of their officials were officials of the Amt at the same time.[57] At the top was the *Stabsbeamte*, usually called a Vogt, later *Oberamtmann*. He was an official of the duke, not elected by the Bürger, and was at the same time the chief administrator of the town and Amt. He was head of the criminal court, which also had appellate jurisdiction over village courts. All reports from the village level to the duke had to go through him, including complaints about the conduct of a Schultheiss or indeed of himself, and in turn he relayed all communications from central officials to village officials. Every two years, he held a Vogtruggericht in each village. As its chief elected official, a town had a Bürgermeister, who was the financial officer but also represented the town's interests, sometimes against the Vogt. The town also had an elected Gericht and Rat. A *Stadt- und Amtspfleger*, elected by an assembly of the Amt, was responsible for the financial records of the Amt. Finally, a very important official was the *Stadt- und Amtsschreiber*, elected by the assembled Schultheissen and confirmed in his office by the ducal council. The office carried on all the clerical duties in the Amt and was therefore closely involved in village life. While the village Gerichtsschreiber kept the protocols from the Gericht and those over taxes and mortgages, the Amtsschreiber carried on all the clerical duties to do with village finances, marriage contracts, civil contracts, testaments, and marriage and *post mortem* inventories. The office of *Schreiber* always had one or two apprentices (*Incipienten*), who were supposed to be kept on as *Scribenten* for a few years after their apprenticeship. After serving long enough, the Schreiber at his discretion reported to the central authorities in Stuttgart to arrange for a Scribent's examination and promotion to the rank of *Substitut*, which allowed him to carry out the duties of clerk independently. He could also begin to think about getting married. As a group the officials of the *Schreiberei* made up part of the literate town culture – one prerequisite for training being a thorough grounding in Latin. There was always a large enough group available for the considerable work coming from the villages, and they were called in from time to time to take up longer periods of residence. In the phase before marriage, they were a rowdy element, judging from the injunctions against their drinking and carousing.

It would not be proper here to give a detailed accounting of all the relations between village officials and state officials. Only one kind of control system will be outlined in order to provide an example of the articulation of village officials with state administrative machinery. The example is provided by the village Bürgermeister, whose job it was to keep the village financial records and make an annual accounting.[58] All money belonging to the community, payment to officials, costs of quartering troops, income from common land, the sheep herd, and forest use, costs of corvées and repairs to communal property, communal taxes, taxes from the Amt, and taxes collected for the central government came into the village account books. The Bürgermeister was required to keep a notebook with daily transactions (*Rapiat*), an account book with all entries under particular headings, an account book for wood and use of forest, a list of corvées, a list of military exactions, and a list of all fines. He was also expected to keep all receipts, and no entries were allowed without written documentation. At the end of the financial year, the Bürgermeister was required to present all his documents to an accountant of the Amt (either the Amtspfleger or his Substitut) whose job was to examine each entry. Then the whole account book, including the wood and sheep-fold registers, was to be read to the assembled village community word by word in the absence of the Bürgermeister. Any objections were to be reported in writing and investigated. When this process was completed, the entire accounts were then subject to examination by the Vogt or his official, who was to compare each entry with the original receipt or document and examine all notes, registers of tithes, threshing accounts, and the like. He was especially to compare each rubric with the previous year's accounts for changes and unusual aspects. He was to examine costs of trips of local officials, their daily expenses, the details of tax evaluations, the collection of state taxes, and the accounts of quartering of troops. He was to check back with the state treasury officials to see whether all amounts outstanding had been received. An important part of his job was to note any problem in the margin of the accounts, so that the accounting office would correct their mistakes or take a note of an issue the next year. At the end of his report, the examiner was to note all defects and to communicate them in writing to the Bürgermeister and the Amt accountant, who in turn were expected to answer all queries in writing. Finally, the Vogt carried out an official hearing of the accounts in the presence of the village Bürgermeister, the Stadt- und Amtsschreiber (or his Substitut), and the examiner of the accounts. The village also sent the Schultheiss and four deputies of the Gericht and Rat.

This is only one example of the close intermeshing of state feudal interests and those of the village. With village account books containing both the internal financial organization of the village and records of dues paid to the state, self-administration at the local level was coupled with detailed control from the center. This kind of structure must be seen in the context of a state form in which competing groups such as nobility were missing, and in which local officials were at the same time embedded in the interests of the village and functioned as crucial links in the chain of feudal exaction.

The concept of 'Herrschaft'

There are three notions which continually recur and intertwine in the chapters which make up this book: 'person', 'community', and 'Herrschaft'. We will not attempt to offer here a history of the construction of the person, or the changing dynamics of communal life, or the development of institutions of state domination. There is such a history, and each case which we will discuss is to be located somewhere specific in time and with relation to the fundamental alternatives suggested by changes in perception and the web of social relations. As we take up each case, we will suggest some of the specifics of place and time and examine, in so far as the material allows, the range of alternatives for construction of the self, patterning social relations, and resistance. We will also be concerned with refining the conceptions which we discuss for the analysis of change. In the conclusion, we will offer an interpretation of the development of state institutions and the implications of that development for the practice of Herrschaft at the village level, and alternative constructions of the person, using the material from Württemberg as illustration.

Herrschaft is a term which expresses relationships of power, although in a way that is not covered exactly by any of the competing terms in English.[59] It is over-laid by historical specificity on the one hand and by ideological dispute on the other, to the extent that it is helpful to explain the choice of the term here and the use that it might have in clarifying certain processes in the exercise of state power in the period under consideration.

Since any abstract, analytical use of the term is tied in some way to its concrete, institutional position inside feudal relations, we must begin by asking what the common elements of its various meanings are.[60] Herrschaft expresses institutional relationships of authority, such as *Gerichtsherrschaft*, *Leibherrschaft*, and *Grundherrschaft*. Each such term denotes a domain of authority of a specific lord, whether that lord be a single person, such as a duke or a king, or a corporation, such as a monastery, a hospital, or a city council. The term Gerichtsherrschaft referred to the domain of rights and jurisdiction adhering to the exercise of judicial authority. Leibherrschaft defined the relationship of a lord to his collectivity of personal bondsmen (*Leibeigene*). And Grundherrschaft was a matter of ownership and control of land, with various rents and obligations paid by the tenants to the lord. This is far too schematic to catch the complexity of arrangements, the overlapping and conflicting forms of Herrschaft, but it nonetheless suggests several essential points. The relationship was seen as a personal one, above all because an individual could in theory and often in practice be under the domination of one lord as bondsman, of another as tenant, and of yet another as judicial subject. At the close of the Middle Ages, there were some Herrschaft relations which were defined territorially, but most often territoriality was broken up into a kaleidoscope of personal relationships. One of the trends from the sixteenth century onwards was the territorialization of some forms of Herrschaft, with the unification of overlapping rights into fewer and fewer hands. In Württemberg, for example, the duke or ducal institutions by and large held the land, exercised justice, collected the tithe, and included the subjects in a more-or-less territorially defined Leibherrschaft, although the specific rights and obligations varied from place to place. Some writers on Herrschaft confuse the 'personal' relation of subject and lord with a set of face-to-face relationships, and suggest that the nineteenth century saw a depersonalization of Herrschaft.[61] In this argument, the personal presence of the lord is contrasted with abstract, anonymous structures, productive relations, and the like: on the one hand the violence of direct confrontation, on the other the force of circumstance. It is true that there were many forms of Herrschaft in the early modern period where personal relations were part of the apparatus of authority, for instance on the large peasant farm or small junker estate. But there was nothing face-to-face about relations between Württemberg subjects and the duke and his officials in Stuttgart. In chapter 2, the mistake of a peasant who thought he could deal directly with the duke is examined. Although such an argument would take us too far afield, it would also be possible to question whether Herrschaft can be abstracted from the direct personal confrontation of citizens with the apparatus of violence of the modern state.[62] Personal versus abstract Herrschaft does not really seem to be the issue, for in the modern world as well power is experienced in practice in the context of a background of direct violence.

In many of the chapters of this book, we will investigate the problem of Herrschaft and violence. Although we are accustomed to thinking abstractly about the fact that power is masked through various forms of ideology or institutionalization, perhaps it is not so easy to visualize how much open violence is masked by the practice of including it as only one alternative in a situation. Indirect or 'gentle' forms of violence can be exercised alternatively with other forms of Herrschaft.[63] One recurring example (particularly in chapters 1, 5 and 6) has to do with the oath. To take an oath was putting one's eternal salvation at stake, and the state was very careful to stage-manage the situations where such an act would be required. The various possibilities of threat, physical and mental, which surrounded oath-taking ('spiritual torture') provide a useful lesson in the exercise of violence.

As much as Herrschaft has to do with force and violence, there are two essential foundations to that force. On the one hand, each of the forms of Herrschaft we have mentioned more or less clearly expressed a form of surplus extraction. The *Leibherr* had a specific right to death duties – clothes, cattle, or a proportion of the total inventory – a chicken every year, and perhaps a dozen eggs. One of the factors explaining the superb series of *post mortem* inventories in every village of Württemberg was the interest of the duke in collecting the death duties owed to him. *Zehntherrschaft* recognized the right to collect a tithe on grain production. Grundherrschaft involved rents and duties from land holding. Sometimes, in fact, the early formulations of Herrschaft put the relationship into the categories of property, maintaining that the relationship was one of ownership over things or persons.[64] The lord was only taking what he owned with all due regard for the reproduction of the human material necessary to continue the possibility. Various writers asked whether the subject or servant (*Knecht*) was a person and an end in himself, or a thing, an instrument for the fulfillment of the needs of the dominant, but this was just an extreme statement of the fact that one inner kernel of all Herrschaft relationships was a process of extraction of a surplus.

But the other half of Herrschaft was just as central to the institution, namely the offering of protection (*Schutz und Schirm*), whether in the form of clientage, justice, general tranquility, or military protection. Some forms of Herrschaft may have appeared very unbalanced. It might be asked what services were offered by the Leibherr in exchange for death duties and an annual chicken.[65] To raise the question is to suggest three alternative ways that the practice of Herrschaft could be viewed: (1) subjects sometimes put one or other form of Herrschaft into question precisely because it did not offer any correlative service. (2) The sum total of all forms of Herrschaft could be seen together as offering protection, making it unnecessary to question any one form. (3) Herrschaft as a whole or in its particular forms could be seen as always in part arbitrary, not balanced by an adequate return, too costly, and maintained by some degree of violence.

If the correlative terms lord/servant covered reciprocity in the form of liens on the subject's surplus and services rendered to the subject, the imbalance of power and the everyday practices of force necessitated a continuing process of legitimization. After all, the costs of surplus extraction would have been much too high if regularity of compliance was not forthcoming. Some scholars have suggested that 'legitimacy' of Herrschaft first became a problem with the period of the French Revolution.[66] When one examines the daily practice of Herrschaft, however, it becomes clear that 'legitimization' is integral to it. The problem is raised, for example, in chapter 1, within the structure of several services offered by the state and the state church. The sacrament of communion was provided as a central institution and symbol of religious celebration, but was expressly interpreted by officials in terms of offering obedience to authorities. Villagers demanded a just treatment from magistrates and a fair judicial process as the price of their accepting the service and sharing communion. In chapter 2, a situation is discussed where state taxation was put into question because the activities of rulers had called down the judgment of God.

Our examination of Herrschaft in its concrete historical form has suggested some of the elements of any satisfactory abstract, analytical use of the concept, and at the same time an inner connection between the feudal forms of Herrschaft as concrete institutions and modern Herrschaft in industrial nation states. Words such as 'power' are too amorphous to be of much analytical value for investigating the relationships under consideration here. 'Domination' in turn expresses only the carrying through of one's will. What Weber has offered as the central defining element of 'Herrschaft' at once gives the concept its analytical value and provides a program of research running through Western history – namely Herrschaft as the evocation of obedience.[67] This takes the burden of analysis away from the philosophical enquiry into legitimacy, and concentrates it on practice. It combines the problems of force and the process of legitimization. But the definition of the concept remains historically flat if it does not include in its formulation the fact that Herrschaft is about the distribution of resources, the satisfaction of interests, and the fulfillment of needs. Central to the exercise of Herrschaft is always a process of extraction and a correlative set of services. In that context, legitimization is not a rigid relationship but a continuing process with historical specificity.

We have left the definition of the elements of Herrschaft fairly abstract. That the lord or state has services to 'offer' does not exactly define which services nor how they shall be performed. In the dialectic of relations between lord and subject, the process of legitimization does not just function as a mask to hide the practice of skimming off a surplus. It also covers the nature and extent of services offered, which, after all, are no more within the power of a subject to accept or reject than are obligations of military service or taxes, for example. In part, the exercise of Herrschaft takes place through its power of definition, its ability to say who the subject is and what his needs are. In order to legitimize its activities, it has to ensure that the need structure of the subject is in accord with the services to be offered. Furthermore, whether dominating powers are extracting value or 'offering' a service, coercion is always explicitly or implicitly part of the power. Take the example of communion again. It was not enough to provide the 'service', but the Herrschaft had to define at the same time the nature of the community which would share it, and at an even deeper level the nature of the person who would partake. If ultimate recourse was had to the argument that good order necessitated a unified religious institution, thus harking back to the fundamental service of protection (Luther made much of this), the details in its establishment brought the authorities into a never-ending cycle of legitimizing the specifics of that institution. In the end, force could be used to see that villagers conformed to the rituals of the religious cult, as examples in chapter 1 adequately show. In this way, we can see how community was subject to a massive inter-penetration of Herrschaft at many different levels, and that the dynamic in *Herr/Knecht* relationships was not only on the side of surplus extrac-tion but also on the side of rendering services and legitimizing *both* rents and peace-keeping.

'Legitimizing' accepts at the outset that the exercise of power is to some extent arbitrary and that its arbitrariness has either to be justified or masked. This is necessary in part because the needs of the 'lord' do not remain stable, nor does his ability to remain with the forms of extraction. It is also necessary because the forms of extraction have been 'legitimized' in the past, becoming thereby part of the historical con-sciousness of subjects. At the root of 'protection' is the problematic of protection from the protector. In the dialectic between arbitrariness and legitimizing lies one of the central mechanisms for the continual forming and reforming of historical consciousness. Also tied up in the dynamic of legitimizing is the service-rendering of the lord. Within the lord/subject relationship, new 'needs' are continually being generated and old 'needs' denied. Needs as defined by the lord are at conflict with needs felt by subjects, so that the costs of Herrschaft are not just to be found in the payment schedule of rents but also in the continual round of redefinition of needs and their suppression.

Much of the discussion dealing with the lord/subject relation works with a simple two-part model of the system.[68] 'Those up there' (*die da oben*) confront the rest of the population. Recent work on resistance in early modern society has concentrated attention on the village com-munity as a solidary organization confronting demands from the outside in the form of new or excessive taxes or attacks on village privileges and rights. By narrowly defining resistance, by selecting a specific set of documents, and by neglecting to look at the everyday practice of Herrschaft, the new studies fail to examine how people at different levels of society are implicated in the apparatus of domination. The position of anyone in the hierarchy of the exercise of power is not simple, and there are satisfactions and deprivations at all levels. It is impossible, for example, to examine the practice of Herrschaft in Württemberg without a detailed investigation of the office of Schultheiss. As we shall see in most of the chapters, there were important advantages in the everyday exercise of power. But it would not do to look only at personal advantage, for the exercise of office could bring satisfactions of duty, honor, self-sacrifice, or support for values. On the other hand, the exercise of power could also have its costs of isolation, risk, fear, dishonor, and ridicule.

Our chief task seems to be to investigate benefits which accrue to those who participate in the apparatus of power. Considering Herrschaft institutionally, abstractly, as a kind of entity, rather than as a practice, tends to lead away from central elements of its reality. As practice, it is delivered daily in the form of coercion and constraint and yet is subject to its own constraints, since eliciting obedience is always part of the goal. As soon as attention is turned to the systematic practice of everyday constraints, it becomes clear at how many levels Herrschaft is exercised and how many levels are available for resistance. We shall see in chapter 5, for example, how the notion of 'householder' sorted out inhabitants of one village as subjects and objects respectively of village Herrschaft. There we shall see how weak a two-part model of state domination can be, and how no discussion of Herrschaft can be adequate without a thorough understanding of how Herrschaft implicates its objects in its practice and indeed often turns them into its subjects.

Recent discussions of rebellion and resistance have confined themselves largely to what fits into the simple model we have been criticizing.[69] Opposition to taxation counts as resistance, but anger with a corrupt village magistrate does not. But just as the exercise of domination must be sought at many levels, so too must one look for resistance. It can lie at the level of a chosen metaphor, as we shall see in chapter 3, or in the reception of biblical knowledge as in chapter 5, just as much as it can in a highly oblique rhetorical attack on state financial practices, as in chapter 2.

The focus on moments of dramatic rebellion tends to shift the viewer's glance away from the inherent dialectic in domination or Herrschaft itself. A consideration of resistance makes clear that whatever negotiations take place, they are not solely or even primarily through 'representatives' of the two sides. The political process is not responsible in that sense, nor is it easily open to inspection to the outside observer. However the process of negotiation takes place – and a consideration of that complex matter cannot be dealt with at any great length here – it is useful to enquire into the manner in which the dominated express their desires. One such way lies in the reaction to a local event – the momentary popularity of a local hero, the notoriety of some particular occasion. It is hard to stop people from rushing to have a look at whatever is going on. They threaten established authority by posing or suspending belief, by throwing normal categories into question.[70] The issues are dramatized not only by whatever event takes place, but also by the kind of reception it gets. In direct day-to-day confrontations, authorities can take more-or-less clear action, with the balance of power often being on their side. And any popular figure, superstition, or list of demands lies open to the authorities to discredit through the rationality of bureaucratic procedures. The chief weapon on the part of the dominated sometimes lies in the simple activity of gawking, the rush to join the crowd, the excitement of new belief and sudden hope which quickly dissipates, the momentary suspension of assent. A vision or dramatic action can mediate a complex set of values or provide a transitory grasp of an alternative reality. It may vanish quickly as a whole or, even if its memory remains, the internal message may change even as everyday reality changes. Examples of such momentary articulations of social values will be dealt with in chapters 2 and 6.

The concept of community

The following chapters are to a large extent about communities, most of them large, nucleated villages, a few of them collections of hamlets, and several of them small towns. Because these communities are situated in what has been variously designated as 'pre-modern', 'early modern', 'feudal', or 'traditional' Europe, the concept of 'community' or *Gemeinschaft* suggests itself as an organizing element for study.[71] Gemeinschaft as an analytical category has been criticized for its ideological flavor, but nevertheless has become part of the intellectual equipment of most social scientists in one form or another. Whether seen historically as a social form preceding a modern 'Gesellschaft', or as what one finds in the dynamics of small group, face-to-face relationships, Gemeinschaft seems unavoidable. Sometimes, the English word 'community' is given a meaning akin to Gemeinschaft, but it often has been tied more simply to a certain kind of social science practice, namely the concentration on small groups, bounded in one way or another, as units of research. The problem here is that the investigator, by choosing a 'bounded' unit – a community in the second sense

– tends to assume community in the first sense, a group of people with shared goals, purposes, or ends.

It is neither possible nor desirable here to go into the complex literature on community, but it might be helpful to suggest a few distinctions which are central for the analysis in this book. There is an outsider and an insider view of communal processes, and much of what follows is an attempt to analyze the notions from the inside. But we must not expect villagers to provide us with sociological concepts. Even whether villagers think in terms of villages is an open question, for that seems to change with time. It appears to be the case, for example, that in the sixteenth century a sharp dichotomy was drawn between country and city as such, and one does not find many references to a strong identification with a specific village as having a specific character. Such references multiply in the late seventeenth and eighteenth centuries, as examples from chapters 4 and 6 show. Inside a village, the way in which relations are perceived and constructed are close to practice, and certain key terms are constantly reiterated. These concepts and terms are what we are looking for. We also want to use villagers' conceptions to refine our own and to subject them to criticism.

There are two guiding principles in my notion of 'community', and here I mean the small town or village community – the Gemeinde. Community is a matter of mediations and reciprocities and it cannot be analyzed apart from Herrschaft. What makes community possible is the fact that it involves a series of mediated relationships. One central form of mediation, of course, is provided by property – the access to resources, the apportionment of rights and claims, and the acceptance of obligations and duties. Other forms of mediation can be found within the spheres of production and exchange or in the sphere of social value – the way, for example, honor is allocated within the constant reflection of villagers upon each other. By emphasizing relationships, it can be seen that community includes both negative and positive elements, both sharing and conflict. From the theologian's or psychologist's point of view, then, community exists where not just love but also frustration and anger exist.[72] In several chapters, we will find that villagers grasped community most centrally under the terms 'envy' and 'hate'.

In some respects there are as many communities as there are mediated relations. This fact is recognized, for example, in such terms as 'marital community'. It suggests the use of the concept for those relationships which contain multiple links and are structured over time. The issue in most of the examples in this book is to what degree a community is a community; in what way a collectivity such as a village or a neighborhood is bound together through mediated relationships involving aid, conflict, aggression, and sharing. In the way that we confront the reality of village life, we see that community was not something 'pre-modern', unchanging, structural, but was constructed, changed with time, and can only be grasped as historical process because those elements through which relations were constructed, whether 'real' or symbolic resources, were constantly in movement.

Notions such as Gemeinschaft and Gesellschaft when ordered temporally often cloud important issues in so far as history can only enter when a break in forms of society takes place. It is common with such dichotomous concepts to introduce process only in the transformation from one structure to the other.[73] It is forgotten to begin with that reproduction is also a process and as much subject to historical effort as any other process. But more than that, concepts of this kind have to be useful for grasping both real changes and, where relevant, forces for structural stasis. Since we know that villages were constantly altering their structural relations as the nature of state institutions changed, then concepts are necessary for dealing with this matter. But even here Herrschaft appears to be dynamic while 'community' tends to be historically flat. Perhaps we can avoid historical flatness by stressing changes in the way relations between people were mediated. If, for example, a peasant can get along with one horse for plowing, then relations between households are in part determined by access to this important instrument of production. Horseless peasants will be caught up in daily relationships of dependence in order to ensure adequate plowing at the right time. But if, as was common in Württemberg, many villagers in the late eighteenth century shifted over to cattle, relations would have undergone structural alterations. Two cows or oxen were necessary for plowing, and practically no one could make up a plow team on their own. As a result, interdependence in production had to take quite different forms.

What is common in community is not shared values or common understanding so much as the fact that members of a community are engaged in the same argument, the same *raisonnement*, the same *Rede*, the same discourse, in which alternative strategies, misunderstandings, conflicting goals and values are threshed out. In so far as the individuals in a community may all be caught up in different webs of connection to the outside, no one is bounded in his relations by the community, and boundedness is not helpful in describing what community is.[74] What makes community is the discourse. In so far as part or much of what people do does not enter in any way into the discourse, to that extent they simply pass each other by. Yet, the problem of inside and outside is complex. What one does outside of community may have enormous implications for one's position inside, and vice versa.

Although it is crucial to introduce mediation into the analysis of community processes, that should not imply that the village community was in any way autonomous. This point was grasped clearly by the peasant prophet in chapter 2. It was no use, he suggested, for the community to do penance as long as dominant outsiders remained unreconstructed. He was making an essential argument, namely that the Gemeinde was constituted within Herrschaft. That does not mean that authorities or magistrates had access to the 'secrets' of the village and intentionally penetrated into its every corner, as discussions in chapters 5 and 6 show. Rather the inescapable fact of appropriation, for example, had implications for the structuring of the web of village relations. This can be seen in the way the good *Hausvater* was evaluated in the context of seventeenth- and eighteenth-century state policy as the essential link in the apparatus. How this was translated into extra-economic power inside the village is the subject of chapter 5.

The implications of Herrschaft for community can even be seen in the metaphorical structure of communal thought. One central idiom, for example, in the period under consideration was witchcraft. It was the vehicle, so to speak, for emotions of envy which were so central for communal life. And in a more general way it also offered a category for mapping the lines of force between male and female, old and young, rich and poor, powerful and weak, kin and non-kin. Yet witchcraft as a dynamic inside village life was not able to withstand the defining power of church and state authorities. The process of constructing social metaphor and the dialectic between community and Herrschaft are examined in chapters 3, 4 and 5.

The concept of person

The concept of 'person' suggests to us the psychodynamics of the individual. It holds out the possibility of studying the emotional experiences and subjective lives of those to whom we give our attention. Yet there are serious objections to the notion that we can reconstruct the emotional life of individuals as they experienced it, a discussion of which would take us too far from our object.[75] Instead of dealing with individual psychology, the point here is to examine how the person is constituted by his position within a matrix of relations. Our intention is to examine the field in which the self is situated – the social forces and the apparatus of perception of these forces. A further issue has to do with how the different elements of the social map impinge on the individual and his destiny.[76] It makes a difference to the construction of the self, for example, whether an individual finds explanation for his destiny in his own moral capacities, in the ill-will of his neighbors, in the magic practices of kin, in the arbitrary will of God, or in the ineluctable forces of the economy. The positioning of the individual between spirit and flesh, God and the devil, friend and enemy, kin and neighbor is central to the way the person, his cognitive and motivational structures are grasped.

Enmity (*Feindschaft*) is one 'native' category which recurs throughout this book. In the first chapter, we encounter the person inside a field of enemies (*Feinde*) and supporters (*Gutherzigen*), in which envy and hate are central motivations ascribed to certain relationships. In the instances discussed there, it does not appear that hate and envy are emotions ascribed to the evil in people, but they arise from ambiguities or injustices in the apportionment of rights. Enmity was positional and was not understood as embedded in a consistent personality structure or as subject to will.

In the several chapters dealing with situations after the Thirty Years' War, issues of envy, aggression, and fear are raised in the context of kinship and community relationships. The discussions there are largely about how the universe of social relationships was imagined and given structure. A basic distinction was made between villagers and kin, and within kin between 'friends' and 'relatives'. Friends (*Freunde*) were those who were related to an individual through marriage, while 'relatives' (*Verwandte*) were blood relations. In chapter 3, which deals with a young girl suspected of being a witch, a distinction was made between the kind of influences or dangers that one could expect from consanguineal relations and those apt to come from neighbors and affines. It can be noted here that while affines define actual kin, neighbors can be categorized into marriageable and non-marriageable, or potential and non-potential kin, and concomitant dangers distributed accordingly. Marriageable neighbors can sometimes act like affines and can be in a wider sense 'friends'. In the imaginary world of the young girl, aggression of the kind labeled 'enmity' was to be found among neighbors and not among blood relatives. For the pastor in chapter 4, enmity was central to social relations and was closely tied up with family networks in struggle with each other. To fail to make 'friends', i.e. to make a marriage alliance, was tantamount for him to creating enemies. In chapter 5, a sharp distinction is made between blood relatives and 'friends', and enmity was now placed among the wider network of blood relations. Affinal kin were expected actively to support each other as friends.

This basic dichotomy between blood relatives and affinal kin is one of the central axes along which various dangers were divided up – unintended and intended, pollution and aggression. Leach has argued that it is possible in many societies to map the various types of dangers consistently on to the kinship structure.[77] Such a mapping exercise for Württemberg rural society would associate blood relatives with unintended influence/pollution without great specificity, and affinal kin, close neighbors, and potential marriage partners with intentional, contractural, aggressive behavior. Reciprocities in this latter realm were more subject to continual negotiation. Exactly where 'enemy' fits into this scheme is not so clear to see, but perhaps we can make several distinctions. In a village with rich and poor, the generalized envy of the poor could bring about a person's illness (discussed in chapter 1). The effects do not seem to have been specific – not the particular envy of the poor or specific poor people against a particular person. Rather the general condition of envy could bring about a random illness and even death. In this case, one might speak of pollution, and the village in this case is conceived of as a moral isolate, a kind of family. 'Enemy' does not seem to have been a relevant term here. Enemy comes into play from those with intended aggression and most clearly from one's equals – close neighbors, people with whom one can be in conflict over property and the like, affines. Affines are the quintessential enemies because they define the group in which one finds marriage partners, one's equals, those people whom it is necessary to cooperate with in order to survive but with whom one is in the greatest competition.[78] Witchcraft is interesting here because it has two aspects, the polluting or seduction aspect – getting others to become witches – and the aggression/envy aspect – attacks on animals, causing sickness of children, etc. I cannot claim to see consistency in the symbolism throughout these cases, but would argue that in each case where kinship is examined, some kind of a consistent mapping exercise takes place, distinguishing between affinal and blood relatives, between pollution and aggression, between friend and enemy.

The way the world surrounding the person was mapped played a central role in the way people explained their destinies to themselves and to each other. Two considerations are important for us here, namely a distinction between intended and unintended danger and the locus of explanation for what happens to the individual.[79] In chapter 1, we encounter direct, aggressive danger in the form of witchcraft and unspecific, generalized danger arising from social divisions in the community. The envy by the poor of the rich could bring about some specific individual's sickness just as the direct magical attack on the part of a neighbor could. In the period after the Thirty Years' War, the distinctions between consanguines and affines, and between kin and neighbors, played an important role in the way a fix on social relationships was taken. Blood relationships gave status to the individual in village society and were a 'given'. One could expect pollution or taint in so far as negative danger was to be expected – say in the way alcoholism might be inherited from an uncle or witchcraft run in families. One of the issues in the post-war period was just how far blood relations extended and what responsibilities one had for kin. Attack and conscious aggression, however, were to be found among step-relatives, affinal kin, and neighbors. Neighbor women tested bread borrowed from neighbors for witchcraft, and they made sure they took communion with a dying neighbor to prove they had not caused the death.[80] A husband might be under attack from his wife or a wife from her husband through bewitched meals.[81] By the eighteenth century, in the context of negotiable affinal relations, epithets such as 'witch' were flung about with abandon in case of conflict, but relations between blood relatives, whether close or distant, even when structured by enmity did not have the notion of magical attack.[82]

These distinctions are useful in emphasizing the fact that the person is grasped under different kinds of powers, which in turn are embedded in different kinds of social relationships. If the deep rift between poor and wealthy was an essential aspect of the community in the sixteenth century, so the notion of person and destiny was related to that fact. The sorting out of family obligations and the meaning of family in the social reorganization after the Thirty Years' War was likewise crucial for remapping the position of the person. The split between modest landowners and handicraftsmen and the growing disciplining of the village population within new hierarchical forms of state authority provide the context in which the person was understood in the eighteenth century.

From the cases offered in this book it is not possible to construct a history of the person, yet a few suggestions will be put forward here. In the instances discussed in chapter 1, the person was understood within the categories of community and Herrschaft, both of which posed issues of justice. Envy and hate were emotions determined by external conditions – by injustice, oppression, or legal ambiguity. In this situation, guilt was not so much a feeling as a condition, less a part of consciousness as one of position. Above all emotion was a reflection of external condition and not part of an integrated motivational structure. The role memory plays in integrating such a structure was missing. In this kind of situation, if disaster befell an individual, he knew where to seek for an explanation, namely within the fissures of the community or among those in competition with him over land, inheritance, and the like. He could make himself ritually dangerous by making his own enmity public.

In the aftermath of the Thirty Years' War, Herrschaft and community were again central, but with rather different emphases and slightly different logic. In chapter 2, we encounter a vision where sin was grasped as individual but retribution as collective. But this was not just a matter of sin/retribution inside the community, for the village was grasped in its essential insertion into the wider network of Herrschaft. Retribution for the sins of the lord was visited on the subjects. In this situation guilt was not tied to an inner feeling of remorse and a personal search for salvation – nor was it the external problem of one's position vis-à-vis others in a conflict over rights. Rather guilt was subsumed under the radical, arbitrary power of God to punish. Disaster to the individual was interpreted at once as collective and irrational.

In the fourth chapter all the turning points in the life of the pastor studied were sought by him outside himself and his own moral capacities. Explanation for what happened to him was grasped within the web of kinship relations and the world of partisanship. By offering a radical vision of everyday life as a partisan struggle, he offers an alternative vision to that of the prophet from 1648 discussed in chapter 2. There was no link between the everyday life in the village and the more inclusive political and social structures. The fortunes of the person were not tied to social and economic conditions nor to the dynamics of Herrschaft – a loss from the vision of the prophet. Instead, the pastor reemphasized the Lutheran division between the flesh and the spirit and offered a totally negative view of the former. No longer were social splits capable of general effect, nor was the person tied up in retribution visited on the community – rather there was no justice at all in the realm of the flesh, and society was a never-ending struggle of will against will, and person against person, inside protective webs of kinship. Every occasion for good or evil had an explanation, and all fortune was the outcome of personal forces. In this situation conscience played little part.

By the mid eighteenth century, we can see that 'conscience' had come to mean different things according to one's position in the social structure. There was as yet no notion of the person as a single, integrated center of awareness. Indeed, one observer noted that villagers 'did not know how to remember'. Thus conscience, in the terms discussed at the time in elite culture – as a steering mechanism of behavior, linked to consciousness as a consistent unity – could have no meaning. Action was not cued by integrated sets of principles. Conscience for everyone was retroactive rather than proactive, just as it had been conceived of in the Reformation.[83] It now became an active device in a set of social relations understood under the rubric of 'fear'.

From this sketch and from the material discussed in the book, it should be clear that the 'person' is an historical construct.[84] The elements we have discussed here – the sense of guilt, conscience, the nature of human power, enmity and friendship, individuality and collectivity – were reorganized continually as shifts in the structure of Herrschaft and changes in the social order took place. It should also be underlined that even inside the small society of the village there were alternative conceptions of the person. It is possible for some to have held the view that the sin of an individual would bring collective punishment from God while others interpreted the signs as evidence of their own personal guilt.

A central issue that emerges from the material is the extent to which the notion of the person entails a bounded and integrated motivational structure. Not only is the problem of the conjunction of belief and action a central problem in this respect, but it also has implications for the way the historian views popular culture or the anthropologist views social structure.[85] We handle the issues in some detail in chapter 6, where there is a confrontation between a commissioner sent from the central authorities in Stuttgart and the villagers under investigation. He expected to find a more-or-less clear set of ideas consistently held, from which the terrible act of burying a live bull emerged. While on the one hand he denied rationality to the villagers – they were not 'used to thinking about cause and effect' – on the other hand he had no other model of motivation than that rooted in consistent opinion, however false. But the motivational universe of the villagers does not seem to be understandable in terms of a set of ideas but rather in terms of that discourse which takes account of the set of relations and changing positions in village social life. It does not seem that the relation of belief to action is one of principles and action which follows from those principles. Rather action emerges out of the tension between necessity and desire to act and the fluctuating set of relations caught up in argument. The analysis of this problem will take us into the nature of village 'gossip', 'rumor', and 'knowledge' and will show that motivation was at once as plastic and as bounded as the ever changing set of village social relations.

1

••

Communion and community: The refusal to attend the Lord's Supper in the sixteenth century

Whoever, therefore, eats the bread or drinks the cup of the Lord in an unworthy manner, will be guilty of profaning the body and blood of the Lord. Let a man examine himself, and so eat of the bread and drink of the cup. For anyone who eats and drinks without discerning the body eats and drinks judgment upon himself. That is why many of you are weak and ill, and some have died.

I Cor. 11.27–30

There I met an old man
Who would not say his prayers.
I took him by the left leg
And threw him down the stairs.

English nursery rhyme

The sources for this chapter are the church visitation records for the duchy of Württemberg from the 1580s, available in the Protestant Church Archives in Stuttgart.[1] Records from church visitations were kept from the 1520s to the 1820s, although their character changed radically with time, and there are many gaps. For the sixteenth century, only the decade after 1580 is complete. In general, the records are reports made by the superintendent of each diocese upon the occasion of his annual or semi-annual inspection of his parishes.[2] Each parish received a page or two of attention, with most space taken up with details about the pastor and schoolmaster. Occasionally a particular dispute between pastor and parishioners or a notorious case of unchristian behavior came in for more-or-less extended comment. In the 1580s one such recurrent case involved the refusal to attend communion on the part of some individual or individuals in a village or small town. In each instance, the bare outline of a story was given, and there are no additional documents to be consulted to add more information. As we proceed through the material, we will retell most of the cases in their entirety, which will allow the documents to speak for themselves and provide an opportunity for us to look closely at the logic of each narrative and the terms of social interaction.

In 1587, the chief civil magistrate (Vogt) of the town of Göppingen together with the church superintendent summoned the seventy-year-old Lienhart Seitz from the village of Holzheim to appear before them.[3] The pastor had reported that the old man could not learn to pray and that he had never attended communion. Concerned for his soul, the two officials warned that if he did not learn to pray, they would have him put in chains and let him die and be buried like an animal. Despite this rather crude approach to the problem, they thought that he might just be too old, perhaps senile, and that in any event the primary responsibility lay with those who took care of him. Accordingly, Seitz's cousin was reminded of his duty, but he complained that Seitz had been so impatient with the servant he had sent to see him that the matter seemed hopeless. Everytime Seitz was sent to the pastor, he indeed started out but never arrived at the parsonage. Nonetheless, there was no question but that the old man was mentally awake and alert; after all he was still able to make a sharp deal on a horse. It was just that he could not keep the Lord's Prayer in his head. Summoned again and threatened with the jailhouse, Seitz promised to go along to the pastor and give the whole thing another try even though he did not expect much success: no matter how many times he repeated the Lord's Prayer, he always got stuck at the passage where he was supposed to forgive his enemies.

It is clear from the story that there was nothing wrong with old Seitz's memory. After all, one of the remarkable facts about the Lord's Prayer is its brevity, and he had always been able to make it almost to the end. Praying as such also did not seem to be the issue; certainly, this was not a problem of private devotion and inner spirituality. The only way anyone could have known that he could not repeat the prayer was if he had failed to do so at some public occasion. He did not try to get by with indistinct mumblings, but stopped and refused to say the words that would suggest to the Lord that his enemies were worthy of forgiveness. Furthermore, it can be inferred that he attended church, for otherwise his failure would have had other dimensions. In addition to his problems with praying, he never went to the monthly celebration of the Lord's Supper, which was also tied up with problems of enmity, as we shall see from the rest of the texts studied in this chapter. Taking the

various elements together, the story was about public ritual and enmity
– and that conjunction provided the central tension in most of the cases
of refusal to attend communion.

The way that the two officials dealt with Seitz provides us with the
basics of church discipline as it was practiced at the village level during
the second half of the sixteenth century. In the early years of the Reformation in Württemberg, two related issues were debated. The first
question was whether church discipline was better carried out by means
of local morals courts or by centralized juridical institutions.[4] It was
finally decided in the 1550s not to adopt the community solution but to
provide for a series of ever more centralized steps. Deviant behavior
was first dealt with by warnings from the pastor. He reported to the
regional (*Spezial*) superintendent in difficult cases, who in turn could go
to the higher (*General*) superintendent or to the central church council
(*Kirchenrat*).[5] The most important institution for enforcing discipline
was the church visitation by the regional superintendent, which provided the occasion for reports from pastors. By contrast, after 1644,
when the village church consistory was established in Württemberg,
church discipline became rooted in local institutions.

Parallel to the question of institutionalized discipline was that of
whether issues of morality belonged under church or state control. In
the sixteenth century, moral discipline remained officially a matter for
the state.[6] In addition, civil punishments for religious infractions also
belonged to secular authorities. This explains why both the chief
regional civil and church officials were concerned in Seitz's refusal to
join in fundamental religious rituals. There was always ambiguity over
the meaning of communion, since the pastor was empowered to warn
the impenitent not to take the sacrament, and with the exercise of great
caution could exclude such a person. In this way, issues of ecclesiastical
and moral discipline centered on the sacrament. As in this case, both
church and state combined to enforce ritual compliance, yet made participation in communion rest on behavior and attitude. It is hard to
know whether the crude threats of the officials were serious or not, or
whether in fact an abstainer from ritual would have been chained up in
prison. I suspect that on that issue alone, few people would have ended
up in jail. Yet the nature of the threat symbolizes part of the issue. They
said he would be buried like an animal – which from another case can
be interpreted as without burial sermon and ringing of the church bell.[7]
This implies that what makes an animal an animal is the absence of
ritual, and the fact that Seitz had withdrawn himself from ritual put him

symbolically outside the range of human society. In concrete terms, the officials were concerned with the fact that communion made Württemberg subjects members of what one might call a sacral community. It was one of the institutions which defined people as belonging to a lord under the Lord. Since the community was understood as being constituted within ritual, the problem for analysis is how that relationship – community/ ritual – was understood in different ways and subject to different practices on the part of authorities and community members.

> Hans Weiss from the village of Neckartailfingen had had his right hand cut off for violating his oath several times. He was subsequently confined to the village territory. Since then he had not attended communion. At the visitation, the superintendent asked him the reason for his failure to go to the Lord's Supper. He could not go because he had envy (*Neid*) and hate (*Hass*) against the village authorities, who had unfairly reported him to the Vogt. They would hound him to his death, if they could. The following year he was again reported for leaving the village during church services. He said he could not attend the Lord's Supper because the Schultheiss acted so unjustly. The latter countered that he only did his duty by punishing Weiss when he left the village during church services. His defiance was reported to the Vogt. Weiss had then landed up in jail and only escaped severe corporal punishment by the court's mercy (*Gnade*). The superintendent warned him to forgive the authorities and to stop slandering them. If he did not forgive, he would not receive God's mercy (*kein gnedigen Gott haben*).
>
> Weiss did not believe that God would let him live much longer anyway, so why didn't the authorities just chop off his head and make an end of him?
>
> The superintendent suggested that the evil spirit had taken Weiss' heart. Weiss answered that he had never seen a devil so how could one sit in his heart? He was then asked if he believed in the devil and hell. He did not know, it could well be. This prompted the superintendent to prove their existence from scripture, which was then countered by Weiss: he had never seen the devil take anyone and when he died he did not wish to go to him, rather the latter would have to drag him to hell. 'Does he not want to be saved?' 'Yes.' But that could not happen unless he recognized his sins, pardoned his neighbor, attended church, and went along to communion. Stubbornly, Weiss went out the door.
>
> The only thing to be done with such a defiant, envious, stubborn person, the superintendent reflected, was to put him in jail until he saw the error of his ways.[8]

The issues in this confrontation turn around alternative conceptions of physical and spiritual danger, the relationship of the physical to the spiritual, and the connection of the individual to the collectivity. Hans Weiss chose to interpret the superintendent's warning about the devil in a physical sense. His answer and the dialogue between the two men were not really about the existence of God nor about that of the devil: in the end, he too was concerned about his salvation. Underlying his dispute with the superintendent was a difference in the logic of the operation of the heart, which the superintendent conceived of as a battle-place between God and the devil – much in the way Luther did.[9] This cosmic struggle or drama was reenacted in the heart of each individual and had to do with personal salvation. What dangers and possibilities existed had only to do with the individual. As the superintendent saw it, the issue resided in the individual putting his heart at God's disposal by forgiving his enemies. Weiss also made the heart central by reference to envy and hate, but he did not conceive of his heart as a battleground, a stage for cosmic drama between God and the devil. The real danger, as he made clear, would have been to partake of the sacrament in a ritual state of envy. In his behavior, he maintained a public, openly declared enmity with village authorities. He challenged them to kill him but refused to place himself in the greater spiritual danger that they tried to force him into. From Weiss' point of view, the envy and hate he had in his heart arose from injustice within the village and from his relationship with the Schultheiss. While on the one hand civil authorities had been the cause of his hatred, on the other church authorities were putting him in spiritual danger through the ordeal of communion.

In the debate between the superintendent and Weiss, a central disagreement over interpreting the meaning of the sacrament emerged. As far as the superintendent was concerned, the issue was one of personal, individual salvation. But Weiss was suggesting that the church administrator was either being naive or was guilty of duplicity – for him the matter was clearly one of social control, and a close look at the institution shows that Weiss was right. Periodically, every member of the community was subjected to the ordeal of examining his heart for resentment. One either had to reconcile oneself to the authorities – to forgive – or face spiritual danger in taking the sacrament. The biblical text, hammered out time and again from the pulpit, was clear – anyone who ate and drank 'unworthily', ate and drank 'judgment upon himself'. There was also a suggestion in the text that people could get seriously ill or die from eating when the heart was in an improper state. For Weiss, it seemed that there were two alternatives, either to accept the authority of the state or to take poison.

In the Reformation, considerable debate took place over the issue of force. Luther in the early 1520s in his discussion on civil authority argued against the use of force in matters of belief.[10] According to him, faith was a concern of the individual heart, of conscience, and the use of force was not only wrong, but it could also not have the desired effect. Most of the Reformers made Luther's principle of conscience more-or-less central to their discussions, especially when it came to the question of state power. In this regard, Johannes Brenz is instructive because of his importance in the Württemberg Reformation. In 1530, while in Schwäbisch Hall, he composed a memorandum on the subject of whether magistrates had power over conscience.[11] Brenz derived new conclusions by redefining conscience, arguing first that law is necessary to define right and wrong and secondly that conscience is missing where the Holy Spirit does not enlighten.[12] 'It is clear that there is no conscience where there is no sign of the Holy Ghost, for without Him every sign is deceitful, illusory, and false and not to be taken for conscience.'[13] Wherever the devil's work is apparent, there is no actual conscience, no more than counterfeit coin is real money or a painting of a man a real person. Brenz concludes quite remarkably that when one acts against those people who do not believe, one is not acting against their conscience, since by definition they cannot have any. 'Where there is no faith there is no conscience but only the mark of the beast.'[14] Then there is a passage full of import for the violence which church officials thought necessary to enforce religious uniformity in Württemberg villages: 'where, however, there is no faith but only stubborn error in a person, such that he is quarrelsome and will not obey the truth, one need have no hesitation'.[15] As far as Brenz was concerned, magistrates should exercise their office to support those with conscience, whether weak or strong, and to punish those filled with falsehood.[16]

Key phrases in Brenz's discussion are 'stubborn', 'quarrelsome', 'obedience'. Such terms are only understandable under assumptions of the exercise of Herrschaft. They are terms by which officials defined the objects of their disciplinary measures and are central for understanding the way the exercise of Herrschaft took place. In the context of Brenz's text, the issue seems to have been deviant belief and religious practice – heresy and anabaptism. But the terms could easily be extended to superstition and to refusal to participate in ecclesiastical ritual. The distillation of Brenz's thinking appeared in instructions to the officials concerned with the periodic visitation of each parish. In the Visitation Ordinance of 1547, the inquisitors were to find out generally about 'idolatry, false teaching, superstition, blasphemy, [and] scorn for God's word', and specifically about people who did not attend church services or take the sacrament.[17] By the end of the century, they were simply to watch out for people 'contemptuous of the Word and sacraments, sectarians, and magic healers'.[18] What Brenz defined as consciencelessness and as the object of disciplinary correction was made concrete in church law as sectarianism, superstitious magic, and failure to attend recurrent church rituals. By putting the failure to take the sacrament in the context of heresy and superstition, it was thereby interpreted as an aggressive challenge to orthodox religious practice. In the example of Hans Weiss, the conjunction of failure to join communion and stubbornness defined the situation in which state authority was exercised.

It is important in reflecting on this case to understand that the establishment of religion on a territorial basis was not just a question of uniformity and good order. Nor is it helpful here to refer to religious settlement abstractly in terms of state building. Here is an example where the state attempted to elicit obedience directly through religious institutions. Taking the sacrament was not just a matter of belief or of practice but was understood as an ordeal. The authorities made the issue one of forgiveness/enmity, just as Weiss himself did. In the story, Weiss defied the magistrates in several ways, culminating in his refusal to attend communion. Both sides agreed that sharing the sacrament was a meal of reconciliation, but they disagreed on whether reconciliation was possible while the objective conditions remained unchanged. It was perhaps this splitting of subjective experience from objective life which lay at the heart of Luther's teaching and continued to inform the perspective of the churchmen–administrators later on in the century. It was a notion far from Weiss' mind.

Another central term for Luther's doctrine of communion was 'grace' or 'mercy' (*Gnade*). His substitution of faith for works turned on the notion of unmerited grace. In the Weiss story, the term 'mercy' is also encountered but in a secular context. But because it appeared in a discussion about attending communion, it seems entirely in place. Weiss had received unmerited grace from the secular courts. The conjuncture of themes and the fluid overlap between spiritual and temporal orders exemplified in the story suggests that Luther's doctrine of grace would have been received in the context of the practice of Herrschaft of the sixteenth century.[19] As Luther made clear, the exercise of mercy does not flow from compassion but is a free exercise of will. Its goal is to elicit faith, which without too much distortion we can gloss as 'obedience'. Certainly in the secular realm, mercy and obedience were correlative terms. And that was just the point that the superintendent was making. He could not understand Weiss' disobedience seeing that he had once received mercy. Thus in the Weiss case the alternating moments of the practice of Herrschaft appear clearly – the use of the oath for control, severe punishment not for the deed itself but for violating the oath (partly spiritual), the use of other spiritual instruments (communion) to enforce quiet behavior, and finally the extension of unmerited mercy.

In this alternating round, two of the elements, oath and sacrament, deserve special comment. The oath was a means of putting a person's eternal life at stake in order to control external behavior. But the sacrament demanded more, an attitudinal change, not just a promise; reconciliation rather than mere external obedience. Here it seems that churchmen–administrators were taking a step away from grace as unmerited to grace as conditional, conditional on reconciliation with magisterial authority – grace as mediated through the state. Not to forgive the authorities, not to be reconciled with the exercise of Herrschaft, put one outside the means of grace.[20]

An important part of the text from I Corinthians on communion is chapter 11 verse 27, which argues that anyone taking the sacrament *unworthily* is guilty of impiety or blasphemy and subjects himself to judgment. It was suggested that self-examination take place beforehand. The problem here is how 'unworthiness' was to be understood. Luther interpreted the passage in a way which drew its sting. He said that Paul was just speaking against people who fall on to the sacrament like pigs and make a carnal meal (*leibliches Gefresse*) out of it – who treat it simply as daily wine and bread.[21] For those who know that the sacrament is more than pig slops, who know that it is the true body and blood of Christ and want to receive God's grace, for them there should be no fear of attending.[22] It was not a question of feeling worthy or unworthy but only of needing grace; that is, the accent was put on faith. Anyone who felt the need to go could not be unworthy – after all God did not provide the sacrament as poison.

In general, Luther's teaching on communion was taken over in Württemberg, with, however, some displacement of emphasis. The reformer Vannius preached against the medieval form of preparation for communion – *contritio, confessio, satisfactio* – but argued for searching the conscience and confession, the latter act taking place in assembly with the whole congregation – not an oral confession but self-examination.[23] The accent here seems to be shifted from pure receptivity to preparation – it is the difference (to stay within the metaphor) between coming to a meal hungry (Luther) and setting the table first (Vannius). Johannes Brenz put the accent of 'unworthy' on belief and unbelief.[24] Whoever takes the sacrament without faith is unworthy and faces not just bodily punishment but eternal damnation.[25] Every day, many unbelievers partake of the sacrament.[26] With the Lutheran belief that the unbelievers were in the vast majority, it seems a bit unreasonable to have required everyone to share in communion.

In the Church Ordinance of 1559 in Württemberg, the purpose of communion as a consolation was stressed in completely Lutheran terms. It was meant to strengthen conscience.[27] The pastor was to warn his parishioners on the evening before communion that anyone who joined must show remorse and repentance for his sins, must wish for absolution and forgiveness, and resolve to keep from sin and show himself to live in Christian obedience. That way, no one would receive communion to his damnation. The pastor was to preach a sermon on repentance and afterwards question each person individually. If there were any there who lived scandalously or in wickedness and did not show repentance and a readiness to improve their lives, then the pastor should advise them against attending until they improved.[28] In this passage, worthiness was shifted from faith to behavior and the fearsomeness of the sacrament underlined by the pastor's advice not to attend when deep in sin. Two curious resolutions of the assembly of superintendents late in the century throw further light on the state of unworthiness. On 2 January 1795, they resolved that while anyone was the subject of a paternity suit, he should be excluded from communion. In another resolution about the same time, a wife living in conflict with her husband, even though innocent, was not to be allowed to take communion privately if she had resentment in her heart – demonstrated by *her* unwillingness to offer reconciliation.[29]

> In the villages of the 1580s, worthiness was a central issue, and much discussion turned around the state of the heart – whether or not it was composed or at rest. Three men in Oppelsbohm would not go to communion because of their unworthiness arising from quarrels

among them.[30] Wolf Seytz in Gemmrigheim would not take the sacrament because he was unable to forgive and thus could not fulfill the
'conditions' set by the pastor.[31] In Pfullingen, two men had
quarreled, and one, despite the fact that he was very sick, would not
go to communion.[32] A former Schultheiss in Hohenhaslach said that
because someone had impeached his honor, his heart was agitated
(*unruhig*) and not in a fit condition to go to communion.[33] The next
year, the same man was in dispute (*Unwillen*) with his son over
inheritance problems arising from his remarriage.[34] He could not
attend because of an agitated heart. Michael Verich in Heimerdingen
did not even go to church because he was unworthy to hear God's
Word.[35] The pastor said he was a quarrelsome person. In Cannstatt,
five men and their wives had not gone to communion for five years
because they lived with each other in envy and hate.[36]

A common theme emerges from all these cases. One could not go to
communion with an agitated heart (or as in a case cited later, a bad
conscience).[37] In such a state one was unworthy and liable to bring
down judgment on oneself. In almost every case, the agitated heart was
the outcome of a quarrel, a running dispute, or a libel action. There are
many hints that the same connections were made by most of the pastors
– certainly the superintendents' conferences worked with a similar
logic. The 'conditions' spoken of by one person were probably to
forgive the other party. Inside village daily life, the sacrament was
interpreted as a meal of reconciliation. It was used by pastors as a key
institution for settling conflicts (when not for controlling behavior).
But villagers put another interpretation on it. Conflict was a civil matter
to be settled in courts, and during the time that a matter was pending, no
meal of reconciliation was possible. The sacrament could not bring a
peaceful heart; rather, a peaceful heart was a precondition for taking
the sacrament.

Part of the situation here stems from the way the Württemberg tradition of the elements of the sacrament was derived from Luther. Loofs
argued that in Lutheran territories in the early years, the church service
was more or less a revised form of the mass, with the notable innovation that communicants received both elements, the wine as well as
the bread. Within a few years, Luther's doctrine of consubstantiation,
that Christ was really present in the elements, which at the same time
remained real bread and wine, was largely forgotten; certainly,
Melanchthon dropped the notion after 1531. Only around 1555 with
Brenz's formulation of doctrine for the Württemberg church did

Luther's doctrine become standard for questions of communion.[38] It was central for the Lutheran notion that the wicked received the body and blood of Christ in partaking the sacrament, giving special force to the idea that the unworthy ate and drank judgment to themselves. In the Church Ordinance of 1559, it was even suggested that partaking of the sacrament in an unworthy state was a form of madness.[39] If a man or woman took the sacrament and on that same day drank alcohol or danced or acted in some other scandalous fashion, they were to be put in the village madhouse (*Narrenhäuslin*) on bread and water for a suitable period.

The theme of quarrel as establishing a condition within which attendance at communion would be unthinkable recurs in many of the visitation reports. A typical case came from the village of Feuerbach where Hans Alber had not gone to communion for some time.[40] His excuse was a quarrel with his brother over the inheritance to a farm. He was waiting for the court to settle the matter, after which he would forgive his brother from his heart and attend the Lord's Supper. In some ways, the elements found here are similar to those in the story about Hans Weiss – the action turns around the conjunction of heart, forgiveness, and communion. Alber was not at all prepared to place himself in danger by taking the sacrament while his heart was in an improper state. However, the solution he suggested to the problem throws sharper light on the issues. The internal condition of the heart arose from a situation that was external to the individual and could be set aside by formal steps taken by an institution, in this case the court. The state of quarrel arose from a conflict over property, an ambiguity in the apportionment of rights. It was a formal condition that could be put aside once a judgment had been offered. Until then a public state of conflict prevailed. Once the ambiguity had been dealt with, the conditions no longer pertained, and forgiveness was automatically to follow. The 'hatred and envy' appear not to have been subject to the individual's control, but defined a ritual state deriving from the legal ambiguity of property rights. As long as a conflict was under jurisdiction, it was assumed that the heart would be agitated. In such a condition one was unfit to share in communion, unworthy to take the sacrament, ritually in a state of tension with the community. Alber saw no contradiction in forgiving his brother once the rights had been clarified in court: the *memory* of injustice was not enough to maintain enmity with his brother. As in the case of Hans Weiss, non-participation in the sacrament was the formal, public recognition of a quarrel. Hatred or a heart in an improper state to receive communion existed coincidentally with the fissure in social relations. Alber recognized a formal procedure for setting the heart right, but Weiss could see no solution except in his own death, since for him the matter lay in the hands of the authorities who had demonstrated no good-will towards him. Forgiveness, setting aside hatred, and putting the heart in order do not seem to have been subject to one-sided, individual action.

It would be useful to take a close look at the problem of memory here, since from the villager point of view forgiveness seems to derive from formal, settled, legal situations, not from psychological states. Despite the fact that a situation may have generated a great deal of passion, there was no expectation that the emotions from that state would remain. This suggests that a notion of the person as a center of awareness integrated by memory was missing for these people. When the Schultheiss from Hohenhaslach was called in for failing to attend communion, he said that as soon as the court settled his affair of honor, his heart would be composed (*ruhig*) again so that he would be fit to attend.[41] In a case cited later in this chapter, Bartle Ganser said he would be able to forgive his enemies after his court suit was settled.[42] Thomas Rapp in Enzweihingen was beaten up badly by two fellow villagers.[43] As soon as the court dealt with the matter, he would forgive them. From this data, it is a rather bold leap to argue that the role memory plays in post-Enlightenment personality structure is missing. Yet there is evidence to show that the bounded, integrated center of awareness which is part of the later, Western definition of the person had not yet developed. We can contrast here, for example, Luther's understanding of *Gedächtnis* (remembrance), which derives from his discussion of the phrase from the sacrament text, 'This do in remembrance of me.'[44]

'Remembrance' has to be distinguished in this case from 'memory' on the one hand and from 'devotion' (*Andacht*) on the other. *Gedächtnis* seems to be used by Luther to extend to consciousness, but that moment of consciousness which is in a state of stimulation or liveliness.[45] Such a state occurs when one attends communion and takes the sacrament. The accent lies in remembrance as an exercise, one which leads as a result of its power to integrate the person to a unity in faith and good works. The use of the sacrament can be seen as a reminder, a marker, a stimulant.[46] Remembrance, however, is not quite the same thing as memory despite certain overlapping aspects. The notion of the self as a consistent center of awareness presupposes memory as the instrument for organizing that sense of personal unity. It is part of the exercises which post-

Enlightenment individuals are schooled in, whereby the self unfolds in a
series of internal dialogues with its past. Breakdowns of the self are
interpreted in terms of repressions of aspects of consciousness as
memory. In Luther, however, there is no sense of the individual as an
integrated center of consciousness. Remembrance or *Gedächtnis* is an
exercise which can unify consciousness. What distinguishes it from
memory is, first, it is not an internal examination but mediated
experience. It relies for its unifying effects on consciousness arising
coincidentally with communion, which mediates the real elements of
Christ's flesh and blood. Second, this consciousness cannot be kept alive
except by repeated partaking of the sacrament.[47] Thirdly, while people
receiving grace are able to integrate their actions in the form of good
works and neighborly love, those who fail to receive the sacrament,
those not touched by grace, are not the same kind of persons, and their
actions are not predictable even to themselves. They have no consistency in behavior or personality structure. As Luther put it, if one fails to
attend the sacrament, faith becomes daily weaker and cold. Love of
one's neighbors decays. One becomes tired of doing good works and
unwilling to resist evil.[48]

This contrast between two radically different kinds of persons is
caught in Luther's distinction between *Gedächtnis* and *Andacht* (devotion), which etymologically are closely related words. He views
'devotion' as a self-appointed task, an attempt to offer God a service, a
good work. Like all good works, it violates the condition of man as a
receiver of grace. It introduces anxiety and doubt. Luther suggests that
'devotion', in contradistinction to 'remembrance', by falsifying the
condition of receiver, of gift taker, leads to radically individualizing
attempts to appease God and in consequence breaks community.[49] It is
important to see that Luther interprets individualism not as the outcome
of integrated consciousness but as its opposite. Further, his understanding of the issues is put within the context of community and exchange.
He works essentially with two images of community. On the one hand
are people radically individualized, seeking to earn their own salvation.
They relate to each other according to the rules of the market place
(*Jahrmarkt*), implying here a model of exchange mediated through
money.[50] On the other hand are those in the relation of gift takers, who
although standing unmediated before God, can do so only in community. In this comparison between Lutheran and villager represen-
tations, elements of 'person', 'exchange', and 'community' are seen to
conjoin in different ways worth further exploration.

Another way to examine the nature of the person is with the notion of guilt. What was at issue for the church authorities was not just the notion of individual responsibility before God, but the idea of an emotion of guilt which could prompt the individual to seek God's forgiveness. But an alternative notion of the relation of the external to the internal, or the collectivity to the individual, is often revealed in these confrontations. The case of the widow Theinlin from Warmbronn near Leonberg demonstrates how guilt could be seen as arising from a condition external to the individual – as rooted in the public opinion of the collectivity.[51] The widow was called in by the superintendent because she had not attended the Lord's Supper for twelve years. She related this to the fact that during the entire period she was involved in a libel action (*Schmachhandel*). Many people had accused her of being a witch. After a warning, she declared herself ready to communicate, but she failed to appear because, in the meantime, someone had slandered her son, calling him a demon (*Unhold*). She then took the matter to the court in Leonberg. If she were to win her case, she would then come to communion as innocent (*unschuldig* – literally not guilty). The widow Theinlin appears to have been using here a notion of guilt that was formal and legal. It was in some way external to her will and proceeded from her notion of the public. The question of her guilt could be settled one way or the other in the courts, but until judgment was passed her status would remain ambiguous and her guilt not disproven. Because her innocence was not yet established, she could not attend communion. The external conditions not being right, her heart could not be said to have been in a 'worthy' condition. The logic of the conflict here suggests that it would have been possible to be a witch – someone who could give off evil influence – without either wanting to or knowing about it. The church's notion of guilt as conscious and following from wrongdoing was not the issue for the woman. The court could establish whether she was a witch; whether without willing it she could have had an evil influence in the community.

If this villager notion of guilt suggests the lack of what we might call a 'superego', it is useful to point out that Luther's concept of conscience (*Gewissen*) is not dissimilar in this respect. Guilt remained an external fact for the villagers. For the widow Theinlin, the issue was the uncertainty of her position, and this is exactly what was so important in the Lutheran notion of *Gewissen*. For her, the uncertainty derived from the fact that the court case was not yet settled, and, as we have seen, this is a theme running through many of the cases in the visitation records. We have here a set of elements which are combined together – guilt, uncertainty, judgment, communion. For the villagers, uncertainty derived from pending legal situations, which would eventually be settled in secular courts. Once settled, communion was a seal on reconciliation. For Luther, conscience and certainty (*Gewissen* and *Gewissheit*) were closely tied together. In arguing against the Catholic mass as an offering, he maintained that making an offering is tantamount to trying to reconcile oneself with God,[52] and whoever tries to do that sees God as angry and unmerciful, has a heavy conscience, and ultimately can never be certain of having the offering accepted.[53] Certainty and a good conscience derive from belief, from the sheer acceptance of God's unmediated grace. In another place, he argued that going to communion with good works instead of faith means that conscience can never have any rest.[54] It seems clear from this that conscience was not conceived of as a steering mechanism of behavior, not as an internalized mechanism of control. It is subsequent to sin and cannot be used to correct behavior – just as for villagers no reconciliation could be expected from an agitated heart.[55] From this basis, it follows that the relation of the conscience-stricken to God can only be that of gift-receiver, the object of grace. In his doctrine of communion, Luther precisely refused, by stressing the real presence, to make the means of grace purely spiritual and subjective, for, if the matter were on a purely subjective plane, it would put the certainty of salvation in danger.[56] In both cases, guilt and conscience were not made totally subjective – which suggests similarities in the way the person was understood. By contrast, the churchmen–administrators of the 1580s were suggesting a split between subjective experience and objective position, the possibility of reconciliation based purely on attitude. In this way, the conflicts between them and the villagers demonstrate a clearly different notion of the person. As we shall see, such a subjective notion of the self was a radical attack on the way the villagers constructed and perceived reality.

> In the village of Neckarhausen, Mathias Dettinger had not gone to communion for six years. Both the Schultheiss and the pastor had talked with him but to no avail. He told one village member that many people went to the Lord's Supper every four weeks to swill the wine but remained exactly as they were before. They gnawed on God's leg and chewed (*fressen*) him right up. The pastor said that Dettinger was generally selfish and quarrelsome and that no one could come near him. The superintendent asked why this was so. He said he had many enemies who would not let him prosper. He asked

God all the time for the Holy Spirit so that he could forgive his enemies. At home above the table, he had a picture of the Last Supper. This was a reminder to him of the bitter suffering and death of Christ and was as good as receiving the sacrament. Many hypocrites went to the Lord's Supper and wanted to bite off the feet of God and the saints. For such blasphemy, Dettinger would not be punished with the jailhouse alone.[57]

In the town of Kirchheim unter Teck, Bartle Ganser had not taken the sacrament for twenty-eight years. His explanation to the pastor for his godless life was that he could not forgive his enemies. Even if God appeared that day or the next, he would not be able to forgive them. To the superintendent, he said that as soon as his court case was taken care of, he would show himself a Christian. The superintendent said that he expected Ganser would always start new proceedings, would not forgive, and would not go to communion.[58]

Also in the same town, Jacob Heer had not gone to communion for four years. He gave as his excuse the great enmity (*Feindschaft*) he had against the Bürgermeister and other officials. How could he go to the Lord's Supper and see in front of him his enemies, who had treated him so unjustly? He found it strange that they could go in good conscience (*Gewissen*). He acted so angry that the superintendent and pastor were afraid of him.[59]

In the village of Bottnang, there was an old woman, crippled on her hands and feet. Despite her misery she had remained from the Lord's Supper for several years. She was warned that in her great poverty she would want to receive the blessedness (*Seligkeit*) of the holy sacrament. She said simply that she would never go and no one could talk her into it no matter what was done with her. Her attitude stemmed from the accusation that the old Schützin was a demon (*Unhold*) (many people suspected this woman), who rode her at night and thus brought her to poverty. The woman also said that she had outstanding proceedings in the courts against the old Schützin. The superintendent told her to let her envy drop, otherwise she would get buried like an animal without a sermon or bell ringing.[60]

The notion of 'enemy' (*Feind*) and 'quarrel' (*Span*) are fundamental in analyzing the villagers' notion of the person. In these cases, it appears that enemies were mostly people to be found in the village or town where the particular person being interviewed lived. In so far as one defines a village as a group of 'neighbors', it appears here that neighbors

and enemies are intimately related terms. Whatever dangers villagers
faced from outside, much of what happened to them was interpreted in
terms of the dynamics of internal village life. In the matrix of relations
composed of outsider/insider, friend/enemy, occasional/permanent,
villagers were able to determine the nature of person. Enemies were
people one knew, who were inextricably tied up with day-to-day relations. In the last case, the old woman tied her destiny to personal relations of ill-will. She did not find her poverty embedded in price
changes, economic trends, inheritance institutions, or state expropriation. Rather, the way she viewed reality was in terms of the fissures
between neighbors and the play of personal forces.

Besides examining the field in which the person was framed, the
nature of influence or threat that could go along with the villagers' concept of the person is also important. There was the threat of everyday
conflict, the damage to reputation, the attack and defense that centered
on juridical institutions. There was also the sphere of magic, the threat
posed by witchcraft. In the last case, both forms of aggression were
combined, for the old woman considered herself to be under attack
through witchcraft and was at the same time engaged in court proceedings with her adversary. In this case, witchcraft can be seen to involve
direct, malevolent, intended aggression. And the old woman being
interviewed by the superintendent was by no means the only villager
who considered her opponent to be a witch. If the latter was able to
exercise intended power, specifically singling out individuals for attack,
the question arises whether there could be unintended, unspecific
forms of magical, or perhaps we can say mystical, power. And further,
what forms of power were available to a person under attack? How
could one counter either the intended, magical attack of a witch or the
unintended, mystical power of someone dangerous because of some
marginal or ritual state?[61] The unintended, unspecific danger will be
taken up below. Here I want to point out that the village view of the
person was grasped as constituted within ritual, as existing in a matrix of
relations (friend/enemy), and as consisting of certain powers. In all
three ways the central mediating institution was communion. It was the
ritual that constituted the social order and defined its tensions. There
were times when it was dangerous to join the symbolic meal. Under
attack by one's enemies, the heart would become agitated, and in such a
state there were severe consequences for those who participated.
However, there are further hints in the refusal to attend the sacrament. I
suggest that by not attending, a person publicly announced the exist-

ence of a quarrel. He announced the exceptional status of being outside ritual and publicized the agitation of his heart. In such a state, two things were possible. In the first place, the individual probably increased his power to resist attacks from his enemies. And secondly, being in a 'ritually' dangerous state, he was without specificity dangerous to his fellow villagers. If, in the last case, the old woman was subject to the envy of her enemy, she in turn was interpreted as being envious. In many of the cases, envy and hate were precisely the issue, and enmity was interpreted in such a context of ill-will. That envy and hate could lead to magical attack was apparent to every villager. Thus in a state of non-participation in ritual, an individual could appear to fellow villagers as dangerous. It was then in the interests of the community to ensure justice and thus reconciliation for its members. The suggestion here that a fission in the community could be seen as having unspecified mystical consequences is at best hinted at in the sources we have examined. More credibility to the notion is provided in two further texts.

Such conceptions as we have studied show that the relationship of the individual to the community was central to an understanding of communion. One moment where the alternative conceptions were articulated was in the administration of the sacrament to the sick. In the 1580s, many pastors refused to carry out certain customary practices any longer. Two examples can be examined here.

> In Kleinsachsenheim, it had been an old custom to ring a bell when a sick person was to receive communion at his home. This would be a warning to all good hearted (*guthertzigen*) people to come along and partake with him. The pastor had done away with the custom in the recent plague. The villagers (*armen leüt*) requested that the superintendent command the pastor to continue the usage as he had found it.[62]

> In Gerlingen at the recent visitation, the Schultheiss and village Gericht complained about the change of customary practices. Since the time that the gospel had been preached in the village (i.e. since the Reformation), it had been a Christian practice, without any hint of superstition (*Aberglaube*), to send the sacristan through the streets with a bell whenever a sick person was to receive communion. Since the village had gotten so large and populous, not everyone knew who was sick. By ringing the bell, a signal was given whereby many people came along to aid in calling on God to help the weak and at the same time to offer instruction and consolation. In particular, however, at

that moment the well-off sent a little wine and something to eat to the needy and poor. Now that the bell was no longer rung, these activities had largely ceased. The old custom came to an end the last time the plague raged so violently in the village. The petitioners requested that the pastor reinstate the custom. A marginal note by the superintendent said that this custom existed in many villages. It caused the well to remember that they could easily fall sick and die. Even if one did not share communion in the house with the sick, out of sympathy one could say the Lord's Prayer.[63]

In the first village, the custom had been done away with by the pastor. In the second, it had been stopped during the last plague, probably also by the pastor. Since the village magistrates brought the complaint and stressed that no superstition was involved, it is clear that whatever role the pastor had played in bringing the custom to an end, he had no desire to revive it. From the actions of the pastors, then, it is clear that superstition was quite precisely the issue.

Although the officials in Gerlingen suggested that ringing the bell when a sick person was about to take communion was a practice which began with the Reformation, that does not seem to have been the case. The Württemberg reformer Vannius in the 1530s noted that in the pre-Reformation period, whenever communion was taken to a sick person at home, the church bell was rung.[64] The issue seems to have been over whether it was legitimate for anyone to take communion privately. For the Protestant Reformation, the sacrament could only be administered publicly because it was subsumed under the category of the word. For Luther, there were two parts to the sacrament, word and symbol, but there was much more to the word than to the symbol.[65] He even referred to the sacrament as a 'visible word'.[66] The word was understood as something that could only be mediated publicly, which presented a problem with communion for the sick, since the community was not present.[67] This was also the case with ringing the bell. In a series of ordinances issued in Württemberg, it was made clear that the only reason to ring the church bell was to assemble the community. It was a 'great superstition to ring the bell for the dead and not hold a sermon', for example.[68] Despite the various reservations, the Württemberg Church Ordinance of 1559 recommended communion for the sick.[69] It noted that communion was normally to take place in the assembly of the church, but that the church was there even when only two people were gathered. Thus sacrament and community were seen as indissoluble from the point of view of Protestant church thought. The ritual was coupled with a sermon to the assembled community and with penance offered by each individual gathered in the collectivity.

The rural population appropriated the sacrament and remodeled it along lines which altered the way the individual/community nexus was conceived. In the end the church administrators, despite their emphasis on communitarian aspects of the sacrament, saw only spiritual danger and that only for the individual if taken improperly. In the short text from Kleinsachsenheim, a crucial phrase occurs: namely, the 'good hearted' (*Gutherzigen*), who were expected to join the sick person at the sound of the bell.[70] The term seems to suggest that a good heart would be the opposite of one with envy or hate, one which was not agitated. By implication, anyone with secret resentment against the sick person would be forced to make the state of his heart public. It was possible that malevolent, magic attack was responsible for the sick person's illness. Naturally, it would not have been expected for the whole village to crowd into a small room to prove themselves. It would have been more a matter for close relatives and neighbors to gather to show that they did not bear any ill-will. Anyone who unexpectedly failed to show up would have been suspect. Given this interpretation, one could suggest that intended, malevolent witchcraft was to be expected from those who were closest to a person, from close neighbors, friends, and relatives. These were the same people who were also expected to offer the greatest aid and support. They were also the people one was most likely to be in dispute and carry on court proceedings with. The importance of such relationships was underlined precisely by the fears attached to them.

Such an interpretation is strengthened by the example from Gerlingen. Just as in Kleinsachsenheim, people were to come along and share in communion and to pray with the sick person. But an important element was added: the more prosperous members of the village were expected to send food and drink to the poor. This suggests that the danger to the sick person was generalized to the village level. Envy and hate in the village at large could be the cause of an individual's illness, not just malice directed specifically at him. Some activity was necessary to re-establish a moral unity in case the danger arose from this point. Thus the rectification of the social rift was centered in two meals – the mystical communion where the individual was surrounded by his friends and neighbors – those withstanding the moral test – and the redistributive gift of sharing along the axis rich/poor. Thus the social division between prosperous and needy was considered by the villagers as one important direction from which danger through hate and envy could arise. The moral unity/disunity of the village was captured in the notion that sickness could arise from it. The individual was not free morally, spiritually, or physically from the state of the collectivity of which he was a part. And an important aspect of social structure, as they perceived it, was difference in wealth.

One can see here why superstition was precisely the issue, for the pastors were ambivalent about the possibility of physical danger to the individual arising from the moral disunity in the community. God might justly visit sickness on the individual in retribution for his sins or to test his faith. He might even go after a community or whole society to call them back to Himself. But His actions arise from His will and are not subject to human logical connections. In any event, display of His power was directed towards awakening the sense of personal guilt. The alternative conception saw one possible danger point in the generalized envy of the poor against the rich. The pastors tried to stop the custom of ringing the bell precisely so as not to let everyone know that the event was taking place. The superintendent, on the other hand, was willing to let the practice continue, but offered a reinterpretation. When the bell rang, it was to serve as a reminder to the well that they too would someday fall ill and die. They should prepare themselves spiritually. This put emphasis on the individual's relationship with God and at once established the matter on a subjective plane. It cut out any sense of dangerous mystical influence from person to person. Nonetheless, there was a communal element in the superintendent's remarks. One could go along and share in the sacrament. If not, one should pray (recite the Lord's Prayer) for the sick person out of sympathy. The sense of the individual here was subjective, a person who shared in another's sorrows and who was concerned in this way for his own salvation. Ultimately, though, he was alone, unmediated before God. For a villager, there was danger from his fellows, from his neighbors, from his family. He was not divorced nor divorceable from the others. His unity was part of the unity of other things – the family, the neighborhood, the village. He could be threatened physically by the disunity found there (in the form of envy or hatred) – and he could threaten.

The mystical power that threatened a person arose from relations within the family, neighborhood, or village. It did not come from 'outside': not the envy of the poor in general but of the poor in 'this village' gave rise to the conditions from which evil consequence flowed. The village did not totally bound the population from which danger could proceed, as sometimes individuals from outside *were* identified as posing a threat. But the multiple strands of relationships within the village or parish were the set of relations from which primary danger flowed. It was, of course, in the context of the village that the practice of ringing the bells stopped, and in both cases the incident which prompted the action was the visitation of the plague. During the 1580s, it was quite usual for upwards of a hundred people to die in the space of a month or so in a village of 600 or 700 people.[71] It was characteristic of the plague that it would rage in one village one year and leave the neighboring villages untouched, perhaps visiting them a few years later. In such a context, the village as a moral isolate would have been more than ever emphasized. With the notion that sickness could result from the ill-will of others, the frequent deaths resulting from the plague might well have pitted groups against each other in frantic efforts to overcome the evil will of others, not by a policy of reconciliation but of mutual defense and aggression. The alternative interpretations of custom by pastor and villagers would have been starkly revealed. In any event, we can assume that the plague was not the occasion of religious revival and moral regeneration.

There are two aspects to Herrschaft discussed in this chapter. The first is the more direct one of the use of religious institutions for buttressing the lines of political authority. Pressure to participate in communion was massive and many-sided. It involved not only the continual intervention of the local pastor but also irritating restrictions on the part of the magistrates, such as that experienced by Hans Weiss from Neckartailfingen, who was not permitted to leave the village during the celebration of the ritual. In a more subtle way, anyone not participating became labeled as stubborn, blasphemous, asocial; important frames within which people with power were able to view situations. Periodically the heavy hand of the state could be brought in and recalcitrants subjected to hearings, threats, and occasionally jail. But the refusal to attend was usually coupled with other transgressions, with punishment made more intense because it was the result of multiple failings.

Not taking the sacrament was put on the same plane as anabaptism and magic, suggesting an association with heresy or superstition, both directly subversive of the public cult. In the end, one final sanction was possible, for the scorners of the sacrament were not given a burial sermon, and no bell was rung for them. In fact no bell was to be rung for separatists, scorners of the Word and sacrament, stillborn children, and children who had not yet learned the catechism and taken the sacrament.[72] The 'superstition' of ringing the bell for these people lies clearly in the fact that all of them are outside the political community as such – the separatists had taken themselves out (one of the issues for them being the sacraments of baptism and communion), and children who had not shared in communion had not yet officially joined. For the officials, the sacrament was in this way the central symbol defining the social and moral community – in terms of entrance, exit, and boundaries.[73] The ideology of the sacrament developed by the churchmen–administrators had two aspects to it. By placing abstainers on the margins of society, it became ambiguous in what way normal rules of justice applied to them and gave magistrates a freer hand to invent suitable methods for dealing with them. Secondly, the official theology was designed to split the subjective and objective elements in the Herrschaft/obedience nexus. Under pressure to attend the ritual, a villager had to learn to keep a quiet heart, reconcile himself to domination, and not view the relationship between 'lord and servant' under the aspect of fair exchange lest he became agitated. The ordeal demanded more than just external compliance, and the question remains to what degree peasants were able to resist such massive inroads into their consciousness.

But the lessons about Herrschaft in this discussion of the sacrament do not stop with analysis of everyday practice. There is the question of the larger framework in which dominating powers seek to define the terms and institutions in which Herrschaft is exercised. Massive resistance can seldom take place here, partly because numerous people are implicated in complex ways in the institutions and partly because the terms of resistance are not clear either to the dominating or to the dominated themselves. There was, of course, resistance to the sacrament of communion as defined by the state church on the part of 'separatists' or 'anabaptists', but these people were soon cut out of the body politic. But far more usual was the acceptance of the ritual and an uneasy tension maintained as the population restyled it to fit their needs. It was through the sacrament that various state officials attempted to mediate their conceptions of the person, guilt, conscience, and justice, and through the same ritual that villagers fought over just the same matters. Refusal to attend did not place the ritual itself at issue; rather, the peasants appropriated it for their own purposes. In the material offered here, we have only been able to gain a glimpse into the process by which the structuring of the symbolic world of peasants took place. The issues joined in the 1580s remained central ones for the ensuing centuries, often shifted on to other institutions. It will be our task to examine some of the ways the complex interaction of different levels of discourse took place.

2

A prophet in the Thirty Years'
War: Penance as a social metaphor

Oh Christ-believing soul, take this to your heart.
Do penance, show remorse, that God His goodness part
To turn in mercy in Christ's name
Well-earned judgment He has had proclaimed,
And through His Spirit all our hearts direct
To lead by His support a Christian life erect.

> From a chapbook about the prophet, Hans Keil, 1648[1]

Return, faithless Israel, says the Lord.
I will not look upon you in anger,
for I am merciful, says the Lord;
I will not be angry for ever.
Only acknowledge your guilt,
That you rebelled against your God.

> Jeremiah 3.12–13
> (quoted in the chapbook about Keil)

Oh, Almighty God, Heavenly Father, evil, evil have we done. Our sins dolefully call out. Our sins are more than the stars in the heaven, more than the sand on the sea, more than the dust on the earth. Because we have sinned excessively, the punishment has overwhelmed us. We have dishonored You, our Lord, and therefore You have left us to ruin. We have provoked You, Father, to anger and You have turned away Your fatherly heart . . .

> 'A Prayer of Penance'[2]

This is the story of a visionary, a vintner named Hans Keil, from the Württemberg village of Gerlingen in the district of Leonberg, just to the west of the capital city of Stuttgart. He was not what one normally thinks of as a rebel, although his message and how villagers received it afford a view of the way popular values enter into the general process of

61

negotiation with authority. On the morning of 4 February 1648, he met
an angel up on the hill, in the vineyard above his village. As might be
expected under such circumstances, the angel had a message for Keil –
this time of penance and punishment – which for those of us who view
the matter with historical distance contains a good deal of irony. Keil's
angel appeared in the thirtieth year of a long-lasting and destructive
war. Soldiers had frequently run amok; plague had killed hundreds of
people in most villages in short, furious bursts of thirty to forty days;
some villages lay completely in ashes, but everywhere houses and barns
had been abandoned and fields were left uncultivated. We can,
perhaps, compare the results of war in seventeenth-century
Württemberg with similar horrors in our century. Yet the angel took
the trouble to threaten the population with collective punishment. The
banality of the message given the circumstances of its production should
not stop us from giving it close attention. It provides an insight into the
symbolism of hierarchy, class conflict, and domination. Hans Keil's
vision had hints of political meaning deeper than the prophetic topoi of
repentance and remorse implied. But the story itself has elements of
tragedy and farce, and it will be our purpose in part simply to relate
what the documents present to us.

> On the day that Hans Keil had his vision he wrote down what had
> happened 'in his own hand'.[3] Early in the morning he went to the
> vineyard to care for his vines, taking with him a small book from
> which he read the morning benediction. He repeated the Lord's
> Prayer and called upon the Almighty to desire to save the people
> from their distress (*Trübsal*). Thereupon a man dressed in white
> appeared and addressed him: 'The Lord give you a good day.' Startled,
> Keil could give no answer. The man said, 'Be comforted, your prayer
> has been heard by the Lord. Be comforted, for I am the angel who
> stands before the Lord. What I tell you, you must report to your
> prince in Württemberg. God will punish the land and its people
> because of their sin if they do not repent (*Buss tun*). For the Lord has
> visited all of Christianity for the last thirty years with war and
> bloodshed, hunger, pestilence, and all kinds of punishment, but no
> one pays any attention, and every day brings new provocation
> (*Ärger*). Therefore He cries, "Oh woe, oh woe Württemberg, oh
> woe, oh woe Germany, oh woe, oh woe all Christianity, oh woe, oh
> woe the great sinfulness." You shall have fire from heaven, the
> Turkish sword, and plenty of hunger.' He took the knife from Keil's
> hand and cut six vines, which began to bleed. This was a sign that the
> Lord would give a respite of six months: 'First, for the Lord does not

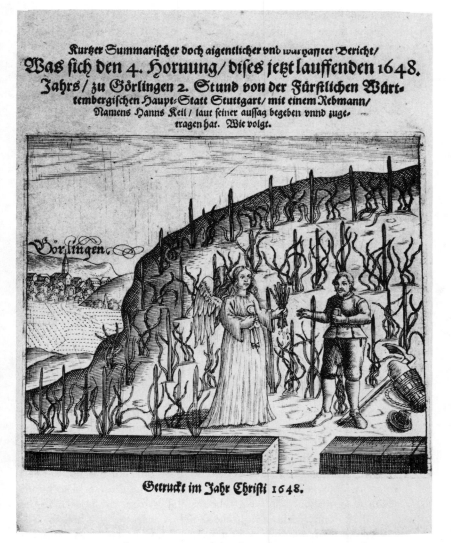

Kurtzer Summarischer doch aigentlicher vnd warhaffter Bericht/ **Was sich den 4. Hornung/ dises jetzt lauffenden 1648.** Jahrs/ zu Görlingen 2. Stund von der Fürstlichen Württembergischen Haupt-Statt Stuttgart/ mit einem Rebmann/ Namens Hanns Keil/ laut seiner außsag begeben vnnd zugetragen hat. Wie volgt.

Gedruckt im Jahr Christi 1648.

1. Hans Keil meets an angel (*Württemberg Hauptstaatsarchiv Stuttgart, A209 Bü 1462a*).

want people to die in their sins but wants all men to be saved (*selig*). However, the Lord laments (*klagt*) and is very angry, and His anger breaks out into a flame. Secondly, the Lord laments over cursing (*Fluch*), which is common among all people (*Menschen[s]kinder*), so that in one hour often over a thousand cursings occur. Whoever curses the smallest curse drives a nail into the limbs of my Lord Jesus. Whoever curses three times in one day cannot be saved. Oh woe, oh woe, oh woe to those people who often curse thirty times in one hour. For them the abyss of hell stands wide open. Oh woe, to the blind world. Why do you not consider God's suffering and his five wounds? The Lord will give power over these people to accursed Satan and to a thousand wicked spirits, who will fly in the air and drag the accursed (*die Fluchen*) in their misery away, tear at them in anger, and with body and soul take them to hell. Third, my Lord Jesus laments over the scandalous adultery which is so common among all people, among the lords, among the servants, among men and women, and among all people. No one controls it anymore. One commits it almost everywhere publicly. Indeed the whole of Christianity lies in fornication. It will soon receive more vexation (*Ärger*) than the dumb animals. It will certainly come to pass that the Turk with his power will be given authority over the whole of Christianity. Fourth, my Lord Jesus complains over the shameful vanity in which the female gender is almost completely lost, so that the noble gift of God, the precious grain which the Lord lets grow in the ground for the nourishment of mankind's bodies, is misused so shamefully in vanity. The woman (*Weibsbild*) is damned (*verflucht*) who wears lace on her hood. Such a woman stabs the Holy Trinity in the soles of His feet and carries the crown of the chief hellish king of the arch devil. Woe, woe to the one who misuses the gift of God. Such a one will be paid with hellish coin. Fifth, my Lord Jesus and Master complains about the great extortion (*Schinderei*), when the high potentates, kings, princes, and chief lords who carry on the government inflict a *Weisspfennig* on the common subjects of the land. The rate that that tax travels from one official to the other makes twice the amount necessary to satisfy the government. All right is forgotten and everyone has regard only for money. Oh you extortion (*Schinders*) money, why do you make the world so blind? Oh woe, oh woe, oh woe, whoever takes from the poor man the smallest penny without right, he shall be covered with a hellish coat. Sixth, the Lord complains about usury. Whoever lends his neighbor a groschen expects two before the sun sets three times. Seventh, the Lord complains about games that are played on Holy Sunday, putting obstacles thereby in the way of the name of God and blaspheming Him. Sunday is the day of the Lord, which one should keep holy with celebration and praying but which has been shamefully made into a day of cursing. That shall certainly mean that from the day of celebration will come a day of mourning. Eighth, the Lord complains about the office of priest, for almost all priests pursue avarice, when they should be explaining God's Holy Gospel and preaching the Word of the Lord. They are at the pulpit with their mouths but with their hearts on the fields, in the vineyards and wine cellars, at the grain salesrooms, and with their money bags. That shall certainly mean that the Word will also become dark, and that will be the inheritance of the priests.' Up to here is the version that one person copied from Keil. Then follows the ending from another. 'Ninth, the Lord Jesus complains that the Holy Son and the all-Holy Name of God which one should praise, honor, and glorify are profaned by godless hunters (*Waidknechte*). They blaspheme with god-blaspheming swearing and cursing, over which the Lord Jesus is mightily angered and offended.

'This you should report to your prince and warn him to bring the sword against all of this wickedness. For the Lord will send such a terrible weather that people will run together and cry, "oh woe, oh woe". In this storm seven cities will fall and three will fall through fire. And in the storm many people and animals will perish. The storm will consume the whole land so that the people will hunger and die. Then a fierce people will descend and will plunder the remaining places. The people will completely languish, for the Lord will call together all of the heathen and shall make an end to Christendom. Alas, it is upon the world, the sun has sunk and the evening bell has rung. Alas, where are the ten wise virgins who meet the bridegroom with burning lamps? Alas, they are all asleep. Oh woe, oh woe, the doors to hell stand wide open and the devils make ready their ropes and bonds. All this you should tell your prince so that everyone turns quickly from sin. The punishment is for everyone.

'Further, that you should have a consolation, if people give up sin and earnestly do penance and avoid the vices which I have described, then instead of the punishment which has been pronounced, it will be for you as snow melts from the heat and rough weather is driven away by the wind and the fully developed fetus separates from the mother's body – in this manner misfortune will depart from you, war will leave you, and all extortion (*Schinderei*) shall be broken. In short, you shall have joyful sunshine for the little while until the great day of the Lord. This is a warning for all potentates in the whole of Christianity, if they do not do penance.' At this point the text breaks off.

This document was apparently a compilation by two different individuals who copied down what Keil had written, while at the same time discussing the matter with him. Another version agrees substantially with this one, with small differences in wording.[4] In that, points six and seven of the original were conflated into one point (seven), and point six complained about the blasphemy of hunting on holy Sunday. A point nine was added about conversion and penance. Another version followed the first we have outlined up to point six and then jumped to the new point nine.[5] It ended as did the first. A final version[6] retells the whole story in the third person, giving the following points: (1) the story of the bleeding vines and a six-month period of warning; (2) about cursing; (3) about adultery; (4) about pride; (5) about extortion; (6) about usury; (7) about gaming on Sunday; (8) about the office of priest; (9) about profanation of Sunday and feast days with hunting – a critique of the *Waidknechten*. This document ends as the first one does.

Keil invented his vision for shock value, so in part he overstressed his case. Just how far he was willing to take any one of his ideas, and which ones he wanted to stress, changed a bit from account to account and depending on whom he was talking to. His central theme was sin and retribution, and he usually saw the connection in terms of the political community – the duchy of Württemberg. He flipped back and forth between Christendom, Germany, and Württemberg with a rather unsure hand. But punishment and retribution were always regarded as encompassing the larger community. In part his wavering arose from the equation of his own state with the truths of Christianity. If Protestant Württemberg was surrounded with enemies and unbelievers, that gave focus to his perception of boundaries. On the other hand, Christendom as such had received the message from God, suggesting that punishment had to take place within its boundaries. The margin was set just where the Turks began, those people on the edge waiting to descend. In any event the sins of the collectivity were at issue. What defined the moral community for Keil was that group of people disobeying a specific injunction not to sin in a certain way. At least that was one way to grasp the collectivity. Another way to grasp it was in the central dynamics of Herrschaft – Lord and servant, magistrate and subject. In part his vision was an essay on that relationship.

In Keil's vision there are eight issues: cursing, adultery and fornication, vanity, extortion, usury, profanation of the sabbath by gaming, clergy, *Waidknechten* (hunters) and hunting on Sunday. The sins go in general from those pertinent to the village to those perpetrated on the village. Only the first two were sins upon which he could have had any direct influence. With cursing, Keil was dealing with his everyday experiences and considered it at greater length than the others. He said that simply everyone commits this sin – all *Menschenskinder*. He kept turning the thought around to get at it in an extreme way but always relating it to retribution. Cursing drives a nail into Christ's limbs. If that image wouldn't do the trick, he arbitrarily denied salvation to those who swear more than three times in one day – and yet there were people who swore thirty times in an hour. Then he described the retribution in detail. With the second sin, Keil himself changed the meaning of 'everyone' by universalizing the classes – it happens among all *kinds* of people, the two social divisions being lords and servants and men and women. While Keil made little of the male/female dichotomy, the lord/servant image was central to his thinking. Having introduced the categories in the second sin, he proceeded from then on largely to take up the sins of the dominant classes: the lace-wearing lady, the tax-collecting magistrate, the money-lending *rentier*, the luxury-loving, gradgrinding pastor, and the Sunday-profaning hunters. Only the practice of gaming on Sunday may have reached down into the popular classes, but it could well be that aristocratic or military sport was at issue here – horse racing, rather than cock-fighting. Reference to the *Waidknechte* or hunters also seems a bit veiled. The chief sportsman, was, of course, the duke, together with his closest associates. A direct attack being too dangerous, Keil chose to center the criticism on the accompanying personnel. In fact, he may have been referring to a recent incident when villagers had been called out on Sunday to take part in a wolf hunt.[7] The local pastor appears to have preached a sermon on that occasion on profaning the sabbath. Neither the pastor nor Keil dared attack the prince directly but made the point by appealing to values shared widely in the society. Thus while Keil's message was a general call to repentance, the thrust of his criticism was directed against dominating groups within the society. As he enumerated the sins, the retribution was sometimes specific to the sinners – the gates of hell opened for those who curse, the vain paid by damnation, the extorter covered by a hellish coat – but most of the sins implied consequences for the collectivity. Adultery and fornication would result in a reign of terror brought by the Turks – implying an end to ducal authority. Sunday would become a day of mourning. The Word of God would become dark, suggesting the loss of truth, of a chance to do penance altogether.

Keil took up the issue of peasant surplus in several ways. He directly criticized ostentatious display by arguing that wealth is rooted in the production of food. A part can go for necessary functions but not for display and not for unnecessary signs of domination – and certainly not for the use of women who have no governmental function. He was later taken to task by theologians who pointed out that vanity was a matter of both sexes, but Keil was getting at a deeper notion of the marks of power and function. His point about extortion was related to taxation and the charge that each official got his rake-off at every level. Although taxation itself was not directly made an issue, emphasis was put on sticky official fingers, which caused the burden to fall excessively on direct producers. He was also well aware that enriched officials could dominate him more effectively. Usury was put in the context of neighbor to neighbor, but was more apt to be a matter of urban/village money-lending or of loans from officials to peasant producers. While the criticism of ministers was expressed in general form, it was related to tithes, usury, and business practices, all of which were attacks on peasant production. An associated point was his reference to the imminent take over by the Turks. Villagers had been subject to a tax called the *Türkensteuer*, whose purpose was to protect Christendom against attack.[8] But if the tax did not get past the tax collector, then there was danger the Turk would descend.

The consequences of retribution were not at all specific to the sinners, but involved collectivities – cities, the land, Germany, Christendom. Furthermore, the kinds of punishment Keil was interested in were symbolized by things which were not specific in their effects – storms, fire, the descent of the heathen. In all of this there are two basic implications in Keil's message. First, the consequences of sin are not only, and perhaps not primarily, individual. A sin such as cursing or adultery is coupled with consequences for the moral/social community. Adultery would lead to a complete loss of public authority and self-determination – and because the instruments of punishment were heathen, to a loss of the proclamation of the Word. Cursing was linked with blindness, and extortion coupled with a blind world. Gaming 'hindered' the name of the Lord. The conduct of priests led to darkness. Secondly, the 'community' was grasped in its basic hierarchical nature. Community is what Herrschaft is. There is no culture of good underneath a covering of corrupt officials. Herrschaft and collectivity are grasped dialectically. If the preachers fail to preach, there is no Word. Vanity among wealthy women leads to hunger for all. Extortion of officials leads to the monetization of all relations, even those between neighbors (who fall into usury). Hunting on Sunday by the duke and his officials leads to corruption of the accompanying personnel and to gaming at all levels of society. The social community is rent asunder by the

exercise of Herrschaft. Yet the answer to all of this was the discipline of
the sword, recognizing a hierarchical solution to a hierarchical problem –
at least this was the way the vision first puts the issue; this was the
message he was to take to the duke. His other message put the answer to
the problem on another level, namely penance. And here, it was the
penance of everyone which was necessary – yet there are two ways in
which this could be taken. 'Everyone' could mean all people in the
collectivity, *or* people of all stations. The first meaning would follow
out the notion that the sin of one person had implications for the community. The second implies that it is no good for one part of the collectivity to be cast into remorse and to do penance unless the other part
does penance as well. In a sense, both meanings are part of Keil's
message but are drawn from different parts of his experience. As a
member of the village community, the person was grasped under the
category of the whole. Ill-will, magic, or envy could lead to consequences
for other members of the community. The other part of his experience
was taken from Herrschaft, and that recognized the futility of
autonomous action.

The core of Keil's message related penance directly to punishment.
He was giving a warning to convert and stressing that the punishment is
a this-worldly one. In the context of the medieval teaching on penance
and remorse, which distinguished between *contritio* and *attritio* – between remorse based on love of God and love of God's justice and that
based on the fear of God or punishment – this was a clear message of
attritio.[9] There is no element of faith and love. The demand for a special
day of penitence was put in a context of warding off the collective consequences of sin, and was not seen as the collective expression of a community of joy. Penance was not derived from a personal sense of guilt
but was understood as a kind of collective rite of exorcism, a way of
appeasing God for the drastic consequences to the group for an
individual's sin.

On the day that Hans Keil had his encounter with the angel, the
superintendent and Vogt of the central administrative town of Leonberg
sent a report to the duke on what had happened.[10] Essentially, they
repeated the account related by Keil himself, adding that the blood
which flowed from the grapevines continued to do so when Keil
brought them into the village. Blood was all over his stairs and courtyard. The pastor, the Schultheiss, and others had touched the vines and
got blood on their hands. Both of the officials filing the report noted
that the vines appeared to be drenched in blood. Although Keil was

determined to go to Stuttgart with his vines to bring his message to the duke, he maintained that the angel told him to wait twenty-four hours. The officials cautioned him to stay at home until they heard from the duke about what to do. They reported that Keil was about thirty, a vintner with little property. He had three children, the oldest of whom was dumb. Keil led a Christian, honorable, unreproachable life, went to church regularly, and was always obedient to authority. No one had ever heard such visions and fantasies from him before.

On the following day (5 February), the two officials reported that they had received an order from the duke that under no circumstances was Keil to be allowed to go to Stuttgart.[11] They questioned him again and obtained some vines to forward to Stuttgart. Keil stood by his testimony of the previous day and gave the officials a text, which he had written down so as not to forget. Since it was so hard to read, the schoolmaster had made a clear copy. The vines sweated blood again the previous night, and more blood flowed on to the bench on which they had rested. Keil was a little taken aback when asked if he would be willing to take a physical oath, but although he was prepared to do so, he hoped that it would not come to that. While the officials were able to convince Keil to stay home, his wife made a great scene, howling and yelling that no one should hinder him in the accomplishment of his task. The officials examined the six vines again and looked at the spot on the bench, but were not able to see that it was blood. Keil's servant had allegedly cleaned it up with sand. It was noted that the pastor in Gerlingen used the same phrases from the pulpit that were to be found in Keil's writing. Two broadsheets were also found hung on Keil's bedroom door, one containing a story not unlike his own – although it was not about bleeding vines but about bleeding ears of grain. From inside and outside the village, Keil was pulling in the crowds, and many of the people said that he should not be held back from what he had been commanded to do.

As was usual in cases of this sort, standard bureaucratic procedures were brought into play. All of the reports and materials gathered from Keil were sent on for the church consistory to examine and furnish an opinion, which in its final form was composed of two parts, the first an examination of the authenticity of the vision and the second an internal examination of its content.[12] In the first part, it was agreed that since there were many mistakes and errors in the style of the vision as reported by Keil, there was no great likelihood that it was a godly vision; it certainly did not square with God's word. There was of course the possibility that it was a satanic illusion because the vines appeared unnatural or supernatural. However, it was more likely that Keil had fallen into depression and melancholy. In fact, he appeared to have taken up sermons or police ordinances into his imagination. Either deliberately or unconsciously, he had made the vines bloody himself. In general his vision was a gloss on the troubles of the times. No one could deny the terrible blasphemy which offends God so greatly. Because of mockery against the bloody expiatory sacrifice of Jesus Christ, a bloody sword had been prepared. Notwithstanding the many ducal ordinances, fornication and adultery were common. The inequality and excess of the taxes (*Contribution*) together with their passing from hand to hand had called forth a universal lamentation and complaint and was likely to lead to a desertion of the country. In addition, Jewish usury was a plague, and there were too many grain and cattle traders. Profanation of the sabbath was common, with hunting, traveling, and working. All this had often been explained from the pulpit, but there had been no change. Frequent gaming, unnecessary amusements, all too expensive banquets, vain and deformed clothing, all these could be observed, while the ministers of the gospel were going hungry. In order to restore discipline and education, there had to be a change, but no instruction from a black or white angel or from a new prophet was necessary. It was enough to listen to Moses, the prophets of the Old Testament, Christ, and the apostles. The threatened war together with the ruination of the land and one's own guilt-laden conscience should lead to remorse and improvement to escape the burning anger and judgment of God. What was needed was a revival of the practice of penance and prayer, which had fallen everywhere into disuse, and a renewal of church control (*Kirchencensur*) and general discipline.

> There then follows a detailed criticism of the contents of Keil's vision. He thinks that the Thirty Years' War has been a punishment for all Christians, but the simple man knows no other Christians than those in Germany. One cannot suppose that the angel told him that as a command from God. As for no one converting, if that were true there would be no Christianity any more, and God's Word on earth would have completely disappeared. With reference to the Lord crying over cursing, Christ is no longer in the condition of abasement and does not cry anymore. He is at the right hand of God. As for the notion that anyone who swears three times a day cannot be saved, no matter how many times a man sins he can be saved, if only he does penance. Where sin is great, grace is abounding. The passage that

says that whoever does even the smallest sin drives a nail into Christ's limbs on the cross is the kind of thing that is said in sermons but has no basis in scripture. The passage that says that damnation will rule those who curse would simply mean that Christ gives the blasphemers to Satan and their penance would have no meaning. As for all of Christianity being adulterers and fornicators, that implies that there are no chaste people, which goes rather too far. One doubts whether the Turk could take over all of Christendom or that if he did that that would end adultery. To assert that through vanity all women are lost is much too hard. It is the excess, not the simple wearing of lace that is the problem. As a simple peasant, Keil speaks of vanity as a purely female thing, but it is also male. One cannot speak of the Trinity as a human with feet. The reference to the chief hellish king of the arch devil is wrong, for he is the hellish king himself. Keil forgets the justice of the authorities and overstates the case about usury. Surely it is impossible that all people could or would do penance. In any case, that is never required in the Word. The part about the ten wise virgins shows the ineptitude of the vision – not all ten were wise, only five. How was he supposed to tell his vision to the prince word for word – a simple man could not be expected to retain so much? It is no consolation if everyone has to do penance, for one cannot prevent all mankind from sinning.

The consistory members were in agreement with some of Keil's basic notions. After all they composed the stuff of many sermons. Apparently, his chief problem was taking the language all too literally, not seeing the warnings as part of a long term program of discipline but as realizable here and now. A revolutionized collectivity was not possible nor even to be wished for. Nonetheless, the lack of discipline in the mass of the people had led to bloody judgment. Cursing and swearing were literally seen as causes behind the judgment of God. The difference in interpretation lay in the way punishment was grasped. Keil imagined a deed/retribution nexus, but the consistory, while holding formally to a notion of retribution, saw punishment as part of a plan of correction. It led to remorse and improvement and was summed up in a program of formal disciplinary measures – general discipline, a day of penance and prayer, the village church consistory. When they considered the details of the vision, they immediately took the large view, the broad geographical scope, the historical depth. Nonetheless, one can see how deeply rooted their notion of penance was. It differed from Keil's primarily in the central notion: the person/community nexus. For Keil, one bad apple made the whole sack rotten. For the consistory, to change the image, the problem was to create an institutional method for chastising and correcting people – for hedging the individual in. Where Keil centered his interest on the sins of the dominating groups and read the signs of war and epidemic as punishment for such sins, the consistory centered its criticism on the trespasses of the broad strata of population – amusements, celebrations, dress, matters which were dealt with in the many consumption ordinances – and pointed to the dangers to the soul. Although they pointed to unjust taxation, they moved customs and morals to the center of the stage, where Keil had insisted on expropriation.

One of the three members of the Württemberg church consistory who reviewed the documents was Johann Valentin Andreae, the Württemberg churchman who had written a Protestant Utopia (*Christianopolis*), a reform pedagogical work (*Theophilus*), and several works dealing with the Rosicrucians. He was a severe critic of the state church settlement established by the orthodox Lutheran, Johannes Brenz.[13] Therefore he could share with Keil a negative view of officials, criticizing strongly the immorality of the Vögte, for example. He was above all concerned with church discipline and was the central figure behind the establishment of the village church consistory in Württemberg in 1644.[14] Although he found the Lutheran solution to church discipline, namely public confession and communion, inadequate and although he stressed education and control of morality, he was far from modifying Luther's doctrine of justification by emphasizing penance.[15] Churchmen like Andreae were in the end concerned with a detailed control of popular life. In *Theophilus* he argued for two or three 'streetwise' men of unblemished reputation who would watch out for dicing and card playing, swearing and cursing, immoral singing, idleness, family quarrels, disorderly servants and disobedient children.[16] In other words, he was mostly concerned with control of popular culture and disciplining the population in terms of hard-working, well-ordered family groups. His view of the meaning of penance was closely tied to the contemporary ideology of statecraft, with its stress on the disciplined house as the basis for public power. Ironically Andreae, the churchman–administrator, looked to reform of the broad population as a key to solving problems, while Keil, the peasant, could see no solution that did not start with a reform of dominant groups. For Andreae, the accent was on systematic discipline at the local level but through an institution of external control. There was no attempt to develop the self-reflecting individual on the basis of a program of edifying reading.[17] The notion of the village

church consistory meant in the end strengthening the Herrschaft function of village magistrates.

Three days after Keil had his first vision, he was again visited by the
angel in the vineyard. The Vogt and superintendent reported that this
time far more vines were covered with blood, in all about 200.[18] The
two officials examined the uncut vines themselves and found them
flowing with blood. When they arrived, the vineyard was filled with
people from the village, all of whom saw the blood and touched the
stalks. The schoolmaster was delegated to cut off some of the vines to
send them to Stuttgart. Although in fact most of the vines were dry
when the two officials arrived, some of them were still sweating.
Several people wrote with the blood. The news had spread, and a
pilgrimage had started. Not waiting to talk to anyone, Keil went off to
Stuttgart straight away. This time the angel had not talked so long with
him. He took Keil by the hand and said, 'God give you a good day.
Have you delivered the vines that I gave you?' Keil explained that he
had been hindered by the magistrates, whom the angel then called the
servants of Pharaoh. If they refused to believe the second sign and the
angel had to come again, then he would come with fire, albeit to com-
fort the poor believers but to terrify the unbelievers.

On the next day, after they had been given an order to see if there
had been anything suspicious about the encounter with the angel, the
officials reported again.[19] The pastor from Höfingen related how he
had been with the pastor from Gerlingen when Keil came in to
announce the second visitation. Both of them went to the vineyard with
the whole community. The Höfingen pastor was not able to determine
whether the blood came from the top or bottom of the vines, but in any
event he was suspicious. After a short search, he found a grassy plot just
outside the vineyard which was full of blood. There was also a quill
there, which he thinks was used to paint the vines. He sent along a piece
of the quill to the officials, who concurred in his opinion.

According to the report, much of what Keil wrote was in the words
of the pastor from Gerlingen. Keil was often in the pastor's house (the
pastor was godfather to Keil's children), and during the period of flight
(after the battle of Nördlingen, 1634) lived there. The pastor defended
all of Keil's vision with extraordinary vehemence, had taken on new
prayer services, and kneeled before the altar. It seemed quite possible
that there was fraud in the matter, judging from the fact that the pastor
was so anxious to show a wonder. He was an old, pious man but a great
melancholic, strangely morose, and thoroughly stubborn. When he got

2. Hans Keil spreads the message (*Württemberg Hauptstaatsarchiv Stuttgart, A209 Bü 1462a*).

an idea, he believed that no one could oppose it. From the moment that the incident took place, people had been crowding into the village. At a recent prayer service, there were several hundred strangers, and in Keil's house there were so many people that the officials could not get in. Although people had begun to offer Keil gifts, he had shown no inclination to accept them. Most serious was the fact that because the officials had refused to let Keil go to Stuttgart, the people in the village, the city, and the surrounding countryside treated them as adversaries. Evil gossip and rumor were circulating. The common people (*Pöbel*), supported by the pastor, considered the officials to be Pharaoh's servants, and they were now in serious danger of life and limb.

In his second vision, Keil began to hedge his message a little. God's judgment would distinguish between the believers and unbelievers – that is those who believed or who did not believe in Keil's sign. (The unbelievers became here the authorities, while the believers were the populace running in to see the show.) Keil's insistence began to take on an anti-authoritarian tone, likening the local magistrates to the servants of Pharaoh. If they were the servants, who then was Pharaoh? The image of Pharaoh strengthened the image of repression and, as we shall see, brought the taxation issue to the center of discussion. The notion of 'Pharaoh' spread, and various people started to take reports to the surrounding market towns. The commission of enquiry later decided that the tax issue was what the whole matter was all about, but their cynical reduction of the issues to one of a confused, ill-conceived tax protest does not capture the significant power in the image of 'Pharaoh' – the prince who made unreasonable demands and reduced his subjects to below the level necessary for their survival. If one regards Pharaoh as a heathen prince, then Keil's original vision was already fulfilled: the heathen had already established their rule.

From this point on, most of the story involves the attempts of the central authorities to get the truth from Keil, while in the background fresh rumors developed, broadsheets were circulated in the markets and inns, popular folksingers sang about his deeds, and the village began to interpret the vision in a way threatening to the authorities – the undertones of a tax revolt grew louder.

The pastor from Keil's village, Philipp Christoph Schertlin, received an order from Stuttgart to come and testify.[20] He tried to get out of going, pleading catarrh, coughing spells, toothache, and miscellaneous pains in the body and gall-bladder. He summoned the Schultheiss to make out a document denying that he had ever had anything to do with

Keil (except as godfather and as daily recipient of meals in his house).[21] Having serious reservations, the Schultheiss told the other village magistrates not to sign, but after the pastor threatened to report the matter publicly in church, some of them signed. The Schultheiss still refused, which effected a break between the two men. Still the Schultheiss reflected that the pastor would forget about his anger the next time he needed a large sum of money fetched from Stuttgart. After delaying a bit more, the pastor finally went to Stuttgart where he was questioned by the High Council.[22] The chief point had to do with the degree of responsibility the pastor had for Keil's message – much of the phrasing appeared to come from Schertlin. He maintained that he preached simply and not very well. Most of his sermons were about penance and were structured around the Ten Commandments. Although he was godfather to Keil's children, the latter had not been in his house for a long time, and he did not have enough contact with him to be able to furnish information. He was unable to remember whether he had said in his sermons that the appearance of the angel was a work of God – thereby strengthening the opinions of the common people (*Pöbel*). However, he did certainly say that the devil cannot preach penance. He also said at the first appearance of the angel that if people refused to listen to the angel of the church, then God would send another messenger. Willing to let matters drift and wait for the outcome, he refused to condemn or justify the vision. He admitted that many of the passages of the message seemed suspicious, and he could not imagine how the angel was able to speak in written language. Denying any active role in the encounter with the angel, Schertlin said that he never gave Keil a quill or paper. As for the vines, he thought that blood came from the leaf scars but not from the insides of the vines – they looked dipped in blood. He made excuses for praying in the vineyard and for holding extra prayer meetings in the church. All of the people in the vineyard expected a prayer, and he had in fact not held extra meetings in the church but kept by the regular services. He used an old prayer, which was commonly recited by children in the school, but he did not think of the passages that refer to prophetic signs when he used it. Ordered not to use it again, he was told to remain by the ordinary prayers. The High Council concluded that the pastor was morose and a melancholic. He was zealous and careful to bring the people to penance. The officials wanted a general proclamation to call all of the people to penance, rule (*censur*), discipline, and moderation.

Among the documents found in the Keil dossier is a prayer entitled,

'Ein Schön Gebet führ das gemeine Anligen der Christenheit' (A beautiful prayer for the common concerns of Christendom),[23] which is apparently the one referred to in the testimony. Schertlin's prayer was in many respects orthodox Lutheran. It suggested that people are sinners who are in need of God's mercy, and fitted nicely into the Reformation tradition of not mediating the relation between God and men through good works. There is nothing that the sinner can do except convert. Still there were a number of things missing in the prayer. God appears totally under the constructs of anger, justice, and punishment. True, the point of the prayer is to plead for mercy, but none of God's actions are to be interpreted in terms of love. He is feared as revengeful, arbitrary, and unpredictable. Schertlin even prayed that God would have the good judgment not to discipline without due measure those he had justified, implying that God does not know his own strength.

> 'Lord God, Heavenly Father, Holy Trinity, Eternal Unity, Almighty Majesty, we see and acknowledge Your anger against our many sins, impenitence and self-certainty (*Sicherheit*), and we are deeply sorrowful (*ist unns hertzlich laid*) that we have ever awakened Your anger . . . We acknowledge our guilt and humbly come before Your fatherly face with weeping hearts and eyes and are terrified of Your anger . . . We call on You and turn from Your anger to Your grace, from Your stern seat of judgment to Your throne of mercy . . . Oh Lord God be merciful and not terrible to us, discipline us with measure and not in Your scorn (*Grein*), do not destroy us . . .'

The center to Schertlin's thinking was also not the individual and the individual's conscience, but rather collective sin, guilt, and punishment, just as with Keil. He understood evil in the world only under the rubric of God's punishment and punishment only as collective: 'Protect us from foreign bondage (*fremden Joch*) and especially from the burden of war, rebellion, and other horrible punishments, bad harvests, hail and storm, inflation, plague and other terrible epidemics.' Further he seems to see it in God's nature to be angry, such that there has to be an object of that anger: if not us, then someone else, and that someone else should be the enemy. 'Hear the prayer of Your children and pour Your scorn not over Your people and over the sheep of Your pasture, but pour out Your anger over the enemy who do not know You and do not hold Your word high, and over that people who do not call on Your name . . .' Thus in Schertlin we find the same framework as in Keil's vision. The times were grasped as punishment and punishment as collective.

Included always in the collective were the magistrates and political authorities. Right after the call on the Lord to turn from his anger to his mercy and an appeal to Christ's shedding of blood, Schertlin's prayer continued: 'We hope, dear Lord, that You will not leave us in disgrace (*Schande*). Protect our churches and schools from false teaching, give us true teachers, support, bless, and protect those You have given to us. Protect those who rule, and defend our beloved high and lawful magistrates, together with their associates, including councillors and officials, and protect us from foreign bondage . . .' The inside/outside was grasped in terms of the political community of Württemberg – with its institutions of teaching – and the foreign enemy, the potential despot. In his metaphor, the community in all its respective parts is in God's fatherly hands. The image is one of encapsulation, boundedness, inclusivity: 'We commend into Your hands our souls, bodies, lives, husbands (*Mann*), wives (*Weib*), children, servants, magistrates, subjects, houses, farms (*Hoff*), fields, churches, schools, family (*Blut*), property, and honor.'

Given the pastor's perception of the calamities as punishment, special force can be seen to lie in his statement that most of his sermons were based on penance. And it must have meant essentially the penance of the collectivity, since the punishments he outlined were collective, and in his imagery he conveyed a sense of the person embedded in families, Herrschaft institutions, and village community. In the end, his prayer was a kind of exorcism, a marking out of territory in which God's wrath should be tempered. The 'prophetic signs' which disturbed the consistory members so much could have only been the passages suggesting harvest failures, epidemics, war, and storms as punishments. Their perception of the relation of the individual to God was radically opposed to Schertlin's. In Andreae's notion of discipline and piety, such apocalyptic visions had little room.

On 9 February, the Schultheiss reported that Keil and two other villagers, including the doctor, had taken or sent written reports of the events to the city of Calw.[24] On 14 March, it was reported that a colporteur called Buchhänslein had made a copper etching of the incident, composed a song, and was distributing a broadside from inn to inn.[25] He had been in Tübingen but was now reported to be in Strassburg. An etcher in Ulm, Mathias Stembold, had several pieces in the press, and a bookseller from Augsburg had brought a pile of them to Tübingen. In Stuttgart, the bookbinder, Joachim Funckh, had ten copies. Another colporteur in Esslingen had forty copies he had

Als Ich Hans Keyl / Burger vnd Innwohner zu Gairlingen / den vierten Tag Frebruarij Anno 1648. für ein Gesicht gesehen / vnd was mir von demselbigen offenbart worden.

Erstlich / wie ich in meinen Weinberg kommen bin / habe Ich den Morgenseegen gelesen / auch das Vatter Vnser. / vnnd daß vns GOtt einmahl auß diesem Jammerthal erlösen wölle / gebetten: Gleich darüber sahe Ich einen Mann vor mir stehen / in einem langen weissen Kleyd / der sprach zu mir: Der HErr gebe dir ein guten Tag. Aber vor Schröcken vnnd Angst gab Ich jhme kein Antwort. Da sprach Er: Sey getrost / dein Gebett ist von dem HErren erhöret worden. Ich bin ein Engel von GOtt zu dir gesandt / daß du sollest deinem Lands-Fürsten in Würtenberg anzeigen / GOtt werde Land vnd Leuth straffen von wegen der grossen Sünden / wann man nicht werde Buß thun / daß der Herr hat die gantze Christenheit in dreyssig Jahren heimbgesuchet mit Krieg vnd Bluovergieffen / Hunger / Thewrung vnd Pestilentz / Vndergang / vnd mit allerley Straffen / aber kein Mensch kehret sich daran / sondern werden alle Tag nur ärger. Darüber fanget er an zu schreyen / Wehe / Wehe / Würtenberg / O wehe Teutschland / O wehe der gantzen Christenheit / O wehe der groben Sünden / Fewr vom Himmel / das Türckische Schwert / auch Hunger genug jhr haben werdet. Vber das nam Er mir die Häppen auß der Hand / vnnd schnitt damit sechs Reben ab / vnd gab sie mir in die Hand / die verwandelten sich in Blut / das hab zum Zeichen daß euch noch sechs Monat frist gegeben wird. Allein folget / dann der HErr will nicht haben / daß der Mensch in seinen Sünden verderbe / sondern Er will daß sie sich bekehren vnd seelig werden.

Zum Ersten klagt Er / vnd ist darüber hoch erzürnet vnnd sein Zorn entbrandt in jhme / vber das vielfältige Fluchen vnnd Schweren

3. Hans Keil's prophecy in print (*Württemberg Hauptstaastsarchiv Stuttgart, A209 Bü 1462a*).

received from his brother-in-law in Heilbronn. These had apparently been printed in Strassburg. The reports make it clear that by 14 March, a little over a month after Keil's first vision, copies of several broadsides and chapbooks were circulating in all of southern Germany. In fact, within a few days of the incident, Keil himself and several of his close associates ensured that publicity would take place by taking several written reports to contacts outside the village. Reports continued to come in about the spread of the broadsides in the region between Ulm and Strassburg. None made their way to Frankfurt. By mid to late April, most of the colporteurs had been located, and all of the copies that the authorities could find were destroyed.[26]

> During the second week in February, two members of the High Council went personally to Gerlingen to take evidence for themselves.[27] As they arrived, they found a large crowd from all of the neighboring villages and districts (*Ämter*). Rumor had it that the angel would appear that day and hold a sermon of warning and perform a fresh wonder. The officials first questioned the village Schultheiss, who was in fact the next door neighbor of Keil. He affirmed that Keil no longer had any special connection to the pastor. Keil had a great pleasure in broadsides and songs about all kinds of wonders, signs, and apparitions. He bought them at the surrounding markets and often related the contents to the Schultheiss, the pastor, and anyone who would listen. In fact Keil had offered a few to the Schultheiss who had had no real desire to read them. In Keil's house several examples of the broadsides were found. On his bedroom door there were two, one about a sign of blood in Bohemia and another about a bleeding loaf of bread in Kempten. In his Bible they found two more which had similarities to his vision. One was about the appearance of an angel to a poor gardener who sighed deeply from his heart over the wretchedness and hardship of this life and over the misery of the times. The angel greeted him and spoke about the godless life in Germany, characterized by lechery, cursing, swearing, vanity, and pride. There was another song about war being the consequence for not doing penance. In a third was found the phrase, 'Oh woe, oh woe, you blind world. Oh woe, oh woe Germany.' Asked why he had so many fine broadsheets and songs, Keil responded that he could mirror himself in them and prevent himself from sinning.
>
> The council members were also interested in whether the phrases in Keil's writing were similar to those preached by the pastor in Gerlingen. The Schultheiss said that on Three Kings' he preached against hunting on feast days and Sundays. He said, 'Oh Württemberg,

Oh Württemberg, how evil will it continue to go with you.' The pastor refused to say that he was talking about the prince but rather about the other servants, who had to answer before God. The Schultheiss also said that the pastor had expressed his opinion about the recent taxation (*Contribution*). His listeners were not to give what was unreasonable without first letting themselves be put into stocks or rot in the tower. He had another commandment from God and told them not to pay the taxes. But the pastor said that the Schultheiss got it all wrong. He had preached that one should render unto Caesar what was Caesar's and so forth. One owed the magistrates honor, fear, obedience, and tribute. Should they order something against the commandment of God, then one is obligated to follow God. That would happen, for example, if the magistrates should hinder the holding of church services or the Lord's Supper. As the pastor talked, the inquisitors noticed that he used the phrase, 'Mein Herr Jesus Christus', which was the same phrasing used by Keil's angel.

The authorities were concerned with the relationship of Keil to Pastor Schertlin. They were most anxious to know whether there was any collusion or if perhaps Keil was in fact just a cover for the pastor. There is more evidence which comes later in the story, but there is enough already to make some essential points. Keil, who was no passive receiver of Schertlin's message, was a pious man who eagerly attended the church services and sermons. What emerges from the story is how the themes of sermons and the events of everyday life were reworked, discussed, and commented on by various inhabitants of the village. Keil was in no way isolated but was thoroughly integrated in his neighborhood and village life. In community discourse, the perception of the extraordinary events of the previous thirty years became indeed understood as signs of God's displeasure. And the pastor by no means left events of the times uncommented upon. If punishment followed from sin and keeping the sabbath holy was an essential commandment, then hunting on Sundays could not be avoided as a sermon theme. There was no way, except by dissimulation, that he could fail to criticize the Württemberg prince once he took up the subject. Everyone would have understood. Likewise, there could be different interpretations about what he was saying about taxation, given the level of implicit meaning in such a message. What was conveyed in his messages was a notion of the political community – Württemberg – collectively confronting God. Keil grasped the message in the way that he saw Herrschaft as both implicated in the conditions which led to punishment and as the only solution to the evils.

The officials questioned all seventy Bürger (adult married males) of the village together with several women and outsiders about whether the vines had really bled.[28] All the people held the matter of the bleeding vines as a true wonder from God – none had the slightest doubt. At the place where it happened they doffed their hats and warned strangers to do likewise. They held the place for holy. The maid of one of the local notables would not go to see the vines without first kneeling and praying. Many witnesses said that they had seen blood on the point of the twigs, which then had flowed onto the stems. There was also blood on the leaf scars. No one was able to say that they had seen blood flowing from out of the stalks or from the scars. Although some had said that they had seen freshly flowing blood, they soon retracted their statements. One man retracted after being asked if he would be willing to take a physical oath. Some testified they had seen blood flow from freshly cut stalks. The pastor from Mönsheim came an hour after the event but was able to write with a stalk. Several people testified that the stalk had sweated blood and called upon the testimony of the pastors. The minister from Höfingen wrote 'Jesus' with a stalk but saw no running blood. The district clerk (*Amtsschreiber*) wrote 'Gott mit uns'. Even though the pastor from Mönsheim came when the blood had practically dried out, he was still able to write 'Jesus Christus'. He borrowed a bit of thick blood from the pastor from Gerlingen. The clerk saw no flowing blood but was able to get his supply from several stalks and filled his quill several times with fairly thick blood. One of the local officials said that the people from Gerlingen supported the story of the freshly flowing blood because they did not want to be made ridiculous if there was nothing to the visions and signs. In fact some people from Waiblingen had tried to make fun of them by alleging they had discovered some new bleeding vines in the vineyard.[29] When they refused to give them up, the Schultheiss rang the bell, and all of the villagers gave chase to retrieve them. Still it was not clear what the motives were, since the Waiblingen people then claimed that blood flowed from a stalk after they had prayed.

The contradictions in this passage are very instructive. No villagers had any doubt but that the vines had bled. Many reported having seen fresh blood flowing from the stalks. On the other hand no one was willing to take an oath on the subject. Keil himself earlier said that many people thought he had dipped the vines in blood.[30] A local official suggested that the whole matter was one of village prestige. People from other places regarded the incident with a mixture of credulity, skepticism, and ridicule. Even the pastors and regional officials tried to get into the act, immediately appropriating the blood for their own purposes. They were either demonstrating their leadership in piety or exorcising the devil by writing protective formulae – perhaps both at once. In any event, it is misleading to analyze the incident in terms of belief and argue that the notoriety of Keil's prophetic encounter with an angel proceeded from some underground current of unenlightened popular culture. For one thing, the political meaning of simply discussing the issues and running to and fro to see what was going on was clearly grasped by the authorities. On 14 April, a mandate about Keil was sent out to be read in every village.[31] 'Among the common people (*gemeinen Mann*) everywhere, hostile and partly very serious, dangerous, irresponsible, unfounded discourse (*Discurs*) and gossip are being carried on.' Everyone was to be told to keep themselves from 'apparitions, signs of wonder, and self-made miracles'. Anyone caught discussing the subject was to be arrested, questioned, and reported to the duke. In this way, the authorities grasped discourse as act. Perhaps they did see the shaping of a more-or-less unified front of dangerous ideas, but the passage suggests that they understood that there were many levels of opinion represented by the people who ran along to Gerlingen. Keil had succeeded in capturing a number of issues in his vision and providing a vehicle for resistance. Whether one believed in his angel or in the bleeding vines is in some ways beside the point. Simply to be caught up in the excitement forced both sides to make articulate their common ground and their divergences. Giving credence to Keil and his visions was one way of negotiating with Herrschaft.

The report of the officials ended on a note which they considered a key to the whole set of events. In Keil's Bible, they had found a document written in his own hand addressed to the duke. He pleaded for the duke to extend his mercy because of the extraordinary burden of taxation, which he put down to the fraudulent practices associated with its collection. He wanted permission to deliver what he owed personally to the duke. From this document, the officials concluded that the whole point of the vision was to get to see the duke and deliver this message to him.

> The issue of taxation had been a central point of the vision and now threatened to become part of very serious unrest. On 13 March, the chief magistrate of Leonberg sent in a report that the central issues of the Weisspfennig and extortion among the officials, which had been taken up by Keil in his vision, threatened to develop into rebellion.[32] He enclosed a report from the Gerlingen Schultheiss who considered

himself in danger of life and limb. If there was another work of wonder, there would be an uprising and rebellion. Hans Keil and a fellow villager, Hans Michel Vogel, related the following story to ten Bürger the day before. 'A while ago in another village, the Schultheiss announced that he would be collecting the taxes (*Contribution*). However, the villagers replied that they were unable to manage them. They could not pay and would not give any more. The Schultheiss said that they simply must do it, or he would have them skinned alive. As he spoke a man of great stature (that was, God preserve us, the accursed devil) knocked on the door and asked for the Schultheiss. He took him into a copse on the pretext of having something important to say to him. After a while the huge man returned with the Schultheiss, whom he had skinned alive. He showed the skin to the villagers and said, "Because your Schultheiss dared to skin you, I have therefore done it to him." Then he disappeared.' The Schultheiss in Gerlingen said that he had to collect the taxes now and that it could only be done with force. He felt himself in great danger.

Towards the end of the month Keil was arrested and taken to the fortress at Hohenneuffen.[33] That brought an outcry from the village. Keil's wife accused the Schultheiss of not taking steps to protect her husband. He had sounded the bell to confront the people from Waiblingen but would not do so to free her husband. At the Day of Judgment she would cry vengeance on those who brought her to misfortune. The women of the village had fetched the men from the vineyards, and they were gathered with Keil's wife at the Bürgermeister's house. The Schultheiss was isolated and apprehensive. On 25 March, Keil's wife petitioned the duke to free her husband.[34] Unable to afford to hire any laborers and with three children to feed, she needed him for the work in the vineyards. She pleaded for his release or at least for the right to go to the fortress to take care of him. Two days later the Bürgermeister, village court, and council offered to go surety for Keil and requested his release.[35]

Meanwhile on 25 March, the High Council ordered that Keil be stretched on the ground for two days, given only bread and water to eat, and then questioned.[36] On the second day, the jailor reported that he had found Keil lying still with his prayer book on his breast.[37] After being revived with vinegar and water, Keil related that while he was reading, a form dressed in white with a red cross on its breast appeared to him. He was told to take certain messages to the magistrates and would only talk with the prince. Within a few days, rumor of this vision had spread throughout Württemberg. A Gerlingen villager heard in

Stuttgart that a terrible storm had threatened the Hohenneuffen fortress with destruction.[38] It was said that there were messengers from the pope and emperor at Stuttgart, who wanted to treat Keil better than he was treated in his own country. The common herd always believed such things. The Schultheiss in Gerlingen reported that the people's belief was strengthened by the pastor's sermons, to which almost everyone went. The pastor was also the kind of man who believed almost anything, and he had promised to go into the fresh news in his sermon on the following day. The whole village hung on him and Keil. The pastor made gross remarks against the Schultheiss in all of his sermons, and the latter had to bear it all with a terrified heart.[39]

> Keil was questioned about his latest vision on 5 April.[40] As he read the hymn, 'O Gott verley mir deine Gnad', the angel appeared and commanded him to tell his prince that God would send horrible punishments if people did not do penance. For a long time, God had given warning through priests and terrible signs of wonder. He would send a sign of fire, and the clouds which hang between heaven and earth would give forth blood. Boundless gorging and drunkenness were common. All kinds of infamy (*Schand*) and vice (*Laster*) were common so that God and His Word were despised, derided, and persecuted. Cursing and swearing were common among great and small, young and old, and many no longer considered them sins. Vanity in dress became more observable every day. Adultery, prostitution, and lechery predominated everywhere, so that many were seduced by accursed Satan. Infamy and vice were becoming greater every day. Although the priests attacked everywhere with the sword of the gospel, little penance was noticed, but everyone went his own way. If people did not do penance, God would send terrible punishment, for discipline and the law were tied together (*Zucht und Strafrecht*). People would see that God is as powerful as he was at the beginning of the world. Having delivered his message, the angel gave his hand and said, 'God preserve you', whereupon Keil fell over. He does not know how long he lay there. On the following day he was unable to eat.

By 10 April, Keil was feeling the effects of his imprisonment, isolation, sparse diet, and the cold.[41] He began to bleed profusely from the nose. After cleaning himself up and eating a little soup, he appeared before the jailor the next day again covered in blood. After eating a little soup again, he then wrote a confession.[42] He also told the head of the garrison that he was ready to tell everything. The commission recommended that he be put back on the ground with water and bread and after two days be sent to the inquisitor who was to pretend to torture him.[43] Meanwhile Keil's writing had been shown around in Gerlingen. Feeling deceived, his wife wrote to the duke to get permission to see her husband.[44] On 25 April, Keil somehow managed to break out of the fortress and get back home to Gerlingen. Recaptured by the Vogt in Leonberg, Keil told him he was willing to tell the truth, to take an oath on it and seal it with the Lord's Supper.[45] The wonder had never taken place. He did it all out of simplicity because people did not improve themselves from the pastor's sermons. He wanted to scare people into stopping their swearing and cursing and to bring them to the fear of God and to penance. The first time, he had fallen and bled and let the blood fall into his hat. He then cleaned his face with his kerchief. The next time he made his nose bleed into his hat and added some spit. He found a quill and painted the stalks and vines. He put his hat on the grass, where it tipped over, and then forgot to retrieve the quill. He cleaned his nose with his kerchief, which he later washed without his wife knowing about it.

> In the subsequent weeks Keil was repeatedly questioned to find out if he had had any accomplices. By 16 May, he was allowed to write his confession which went as follows (as addressed to the duke)[46]: 'I, Hans Keil, subjectly acknowledge my misdeeds in so far as the vision is concerned. I cannot hide it even if I am struck blind. I did it because I feared God my whole life and have often in one month not sworn and was terribly shaken when I heard other people swear. I have often warned them. Thus I meant by all of this that I would bring everyone to avoid sin. In actual fact, cursing and swearing has markedly declined among the common people.' He asked for mercy, admitting that he had sinned badly and gone into darkness. Now he was into the light. He wanted to go back to his wife and children. Not fearing to have his whole wealth confiscated, he would improve his life and become a good example. All he wanted was to remain alive. He did what he had done to bring everyone to penance, thinking that if everyone would do penance, there would be peace. He admitted that he went into error and darkness. He was the only one to have anything to do with it. Pleading to be allowed to go to his wife and children and not to the inquisitor, he agreed to accept a fine and offered to help the forester in Gerlingen who was too old to hunt wolves and chop ice in the winter. He asked for mercy as a child asks from his father. 'I only wanted to bring everyone to penance.'

Questioning and torture went on for the next several weeks. Finally, Keil admitted that he had had help from the pastor in Gerlingen, who when confronted with Keil, vociferously denied it.[47] It appears that the authorities themselves were not willing to trust evidence gained in this manner very far. During the questioning a report from the Vogt of Leonberg concerning Keil was filed.[48] The Schultheiss in Gerlingen said that during the previous winter Keil had often visited the spinning bees (*Spinnstuben, Nachtkärze*) in various villages and each time read aloud from a book about Dr Faustus. The women warned him that they did not have to listen to that. If he wanted to read, he should read something proper. Since then his mother had been suspected of witchcraft, and there was rumor that he was a sorcerer.

In June, the final judgment over Keil was given. He was to be delivered to the executioner, put on the pillory, and whipped.[49] He was then to be exiled forever. After a year, Keil's wife petitioned to have him come home. He was living unhappily among Catholics, unable to earn his living and far from his wife and children.[50] Her request was not granted.

Hans Keil was the village reader, and he surrounded himself with written material. There were broadsides tacked up on his bedroom door and on the walls. In his Bible, he tucked from time to time other broadsides and various things he had written. He carried a devotional reader with him to the vineyard and was used to while away the time with a prayer book. All this kind of reading could be taken as private exercise, and in this way he stood in marked contrast to the Schultheiss who had no interest in looking at the latest newssheets from the market. It could have been, of course, that the latter was opposed to stories of wonders and apparitions but, according to the text, he gave no moral judgment but just expressed lack of interest in *reading* them. Keil was probably unique in the village in his wide ranging interests in the written word. With Keil, we also have an early example of reading as an exercise in the process of self-definition. He read so as to 'mirror' himself in the texts. He also described the practice of reflecting on what he read as a method for strengthening his will – to keep himself from sinning. Exactly how this is to be understood is not clear. We could perhaps see here an early version of the pietist examination of conscience with which we are so familiar from the eighteenth century. But if we look at his message again and take into consideration the fact that his reading was centered on stories of wonders and sudden retribution for sins, we can see that Keil read quite differently from the manner of the later pietists. He read to scare himself, so to speak. That is, he tried to convince himself or to remind himself of the consequences of sinning, so that he would be too frightened to sin. He read the signs of war and pestilence as punishment and was concerned with keeping this present in his own and his fellows' consciousness so as to act as a control. It does not seem that with Keil we have an early popular attempt to examine the internal workings of consciousness in order to discipline behavior. Rather we seem to have a character well within the bounds of post-Reformation piety.

Keil, of course, did not just engage in private reading but regarded what he did as a public exercise. He discussed the broadsides he bought with other people and probably read them out loud. At any rate he did read out loud in the winter evening gatherings called *Nachtkärze* or *Spinnstuben*, where women spun together. However, he did not always choose to read what they wanted to hear.[51] In fact his choice of the Faustus legend suggests that his reputation as a reader skirted along a fine line between piety and magic. It may have been that the Schultheiss was trying to discredit Keil after the fact by suggesting that he and his relatives were tied up with witchcraft, but still it would seem that the willingness to play around with wonders, to search out the latest literature on apparitions, and to read the Faustus material to scare women, themselves all combined to give Keil an ambiguous reputation in the sphere of spiritual power. It is interesting in this regard that when he told the story about a Schultheiss being skinned alive, it was the devil who provided justice for the suppressed population.

The village reader, by participating in an external public and by mediating between that public and village discourse, played a complex role beside the pastor, schoolmaster, and literate village officials. When Keil emerged as prophet, he did not just appear from nowhere. He had found apparitions and signs of wonder good to think with before, and his audience did not find it untoward that he now produced his own. He was already a figure of local reputation and importance before he met the angel.[52] He was also closely allied to the pastor, who had developed into a severe critic of the various forms of state expropriation. The lines between the Schultheiss and Keil/Schertlin had already been drawn before the event. Most of the stories that Keil retailed dealt with an examination of injustice and punishment of sin. Afterwards, when Keil was discredited and Schertlin had angrily written 'Imposter' next to his name in a baptismal entry for his child, there were still aspects of the Keil story which kept appearing. Jerg Keil, a cousin of Hans, in October 1648, got into a dispute over the collection of rents in kind: 'One takes what belongs to the people with violence.'[53] He accused the Schultheiss of being alone responsible for driving out Hans Keil by alleging he was a sorcerer. Apparently, there was still a strong faction for Keil which wanted to turn him into a prophet ('or better, a rebel'). In effect the synthesis that Keil had pulled together between criticism of Herrschaft exactions and repression and the prophetic form continued to be useful well after he had confessed, been exposed, tortured, and exiled.

> After Keil finally admitted his deception, he wrote a confession outlining how he came to put together his vision.[54] It is a good example of the way he pieced together materials out of what he had at hand. In one of the broadsheets he had bought, there was a story about a man cutting vines on Sunday. An angel appeared who told him that that was not right, and he was to tell his magistrates. Keil also read about an angel appearing to Cornelius in the book of Acts. That gave him the beginning to his prophecy. He also had a broadsheet on his bedroom door which told of an angel appearing to some reapers. He cut some ears of corn with a sickle, and they changed to blood. That added another element to the story. As for adultery, there were two men in Gerlingen with wives and families who also had women and children outside the village. He developed his point from that. He had a great deal of experience with swearing and cursing, so he said that anyone who swore three times could not be saved. He had heard about starch turning to blood several times, so he added the passage about starched lace. As far as the Contribution was concerned, he had noticed that all those who collected it or had anything to do with it became increasingly well-off. He also saw that whenever anyone borrowed money to produce grain or wine, he had to pay back half the value again. The pastor had preached on Three Kings', when the villagers had been forced to hunt wolves, that hunting on Sundays and feast days was not right. Keil himself had not gone on the hunt. He also had seen that when people played games on Sunday they swore and cursed. He had a broadside about a baker's daughter who in a state of rapture predicted terrible weather in 1648. Also there was to be a descent of the Turk if peace was not concluded. Keil took his weather forecast from that.

The way that Keil constructed his vision from the bits and pieces he had at hand suggests Levi-Strauss' description of the *bricoleur*:

> 'His first practical step is retrospective. He has to turn back to an already existent set made up of tools and materials, to consider or reconsider what it contains and, finally above all, to engage in a sort of dialogue with it and, before choosing between them, to index the possible answers which the whole set can offer to his problem. He

interrogates all the heterogeneous objects of which his treasury is composed to discover what each of them could "signify" and so contribute to the definition of a set which has yet to materialize but which will ultimately differ from the instrumental set only in the internal disposition of its parts.'[55]

Just like the *bricoleur*, Keil took the bits and pieces with which he had always worked and refashioned them.[56] He took an angelic appearance in a vineyard and another where grain was turned to blood and combined them to create his sign, the significance of which changed in combination with the rearrangement of all the other signs. In his point about adultery, it was not that he abstracted from two cases in the village but that he attached that fact to the common threat of sudden attack by the Turks. If we can take Keil as one example of popular culture, we can see that his method of thinking was not composed of a 'set of ideas' analogous to but perhaps not as interesting as the ideas of 'high' culture. Rather, the bits and pieces were rearranged to make new meaning out of his situation and to provide new significance for his fellows. The composition was part of action, not so much an exercise in formulation as an attempt to give form to events. We will not handle Keil correctly by asking about the structure of his ideas; rather the issue is to understand his ideas as *structuring*. The particular assemblage he put together and the situation for which it was composed have to be understood together.

It would be too easy to look at Keil's notion of penance – a notion that all one has to do is to show remorse in order for God to heap his blessings on the population – mechanically, or as a kind of magic. On the one hand, he assumed that God's retribution keeps pouring out so long as people remain unmoved by His demonstration of power. On the other hand, it was not at all possible to make restitution for sin. Keil never proposed a program of reform or good works or some kind of personal atonement. He centered his message on a change of attitude, making it active ('do penance' – *Buss tun*) and collective (a day of penance and prayer, *Buss- und Bettag*). By coupling penance and prayer and by reading the events of his time as *punishment*, Keil was stressing the arbitrariness of God's power and the central religious notion of grace.

With the recent work of Kittsteiner, we have a restatement of how central *grace* was for the Reformation, and how the contemporary notion of conscience, which differs so substantially from that of our own, was part of a matrix of notions of which grace was a part.[57] To reduce a complex argument to a few points, conscience can be considered as an emotion which is experienced subsequently to illegal, unethical, or immoral action. Or it can be seen as a mechanism of self-control, something which directs action and which makes subsequent feelings of guilt more or less irrelevant. As this latter notion was developed in the eighteenth century, 'virtue' came to replace any notion of 'grace', but in the sixteenth and seventeenth centuries grace and a *post facto* notion of conscience went together. In Reformation terms, the sin having been committed, no amount of atonement on the part of the sinner could remove the stain. Rather, he was subject to the arbitrary power of God in the form of grace. As an illustration of this notion, Protestant thinkers commented on the Parable of the Prodigal Son, where the return of the lost son was accepted quite arbitrarily with joy by the father. The older son, who displayed the prudent virtue so prized by later commentators, was despised and relegated to a minor position, when he was not seen as positively evil.

I would suggest that Keil's theological notion and the way he understood the state – and indeed the way he eventually experienced the state – were structured in the same way. In his message he was trying to show the gulf that separated men from God. He maintained that anyone who swore more than three times a day could not be saved, but he did not really mean that, for he then went on to outline a program of salvation. It was just that he was trying to argue that all was lost unless people called on a mercy they had no reason to expect would be granted. To experience remorse, to 'do penance', was to call on the arbitrary power of God to shed his grace.

In the same way, Keil knew that no amount of hard work, cooperation with his fellows, or obedience to authority would necessarily be 'rewarded'. Certainly that could not have been expected in a situation of taxation extortion. He had experienced the uncontrollable power of marauding soldiers – and had even been one himself – too often to expect life to be in any way predictable. (He had even saved his own life by a throw of the dice.)[58] He knew that the state expected certain behavior from him, which, like sabbath observance, was totally disregarded by those with sufficient power. His answer to the problem was to seek for grace, to go directly to the duke and deliver his taxes personally. His fantasy was a kind of metaphor by which he explained to himself his misfortune. He was not the citizen of a state whose nature depended on his virtue and that of his fellow citizens, and whose fortunes defined his own destiny. Rather he was subject to the arbitrary forces of expropriation and could only call on his lord for mercy – release from extortionate taxes, from excessive appropriation for vulgar display, from usurious lending practices, from highliving clergymen, and from God-tempting magistrates, the retribution for whose sins was visited on everyone. In the end, when Keil's wife petitioned for his return, her advocate suggested to the duke that this was a *purum casum gratiae*.[59] But the duke refused to extend mercy for 'so great and wanton a transgression'. Whatever abundance of grace was to be sought for from God, there was none forthcoming from the state.

3

....

The sacred bond of unity: Community through the eyes of a thirteen-year-old witch (1683)

For the Word of God is living and active, sharper than any two-edged sword, piercing to the division of soul and spirit, of joints and marrow, and discerning the thoughts and intentions of the heart.

Hebrews 4.12

When you sit down to eat with a ruler,
Observe carefully what is before you;
and put a knife to your throat
if you are a man given to appetite.
Do not desire his delicacies,
for they are deceptive food.

Proverbs 23.1–3

One of the useful ways to think about culture is to consider it in terms of process, which offers a radical alternative to treating it in terms of the product, the thing produced rather than the terms of its production, or concentrating on ideas or tools to find shared assumptions and conditions. Culture can be process in at least two ways. On the one hand, individuals continually 'process' the data of everyday life, the repetitive work routines, the relationships with neighbors, the casual encounters with strangers, the real and symbolic moments of violence. People only give half their attention to much of what passes by each day, but they frame it in some way or other just the same. And their ability to respond to reality is the outcome of process in another sense, in the way that everyone continually carries on an active 'argument' with his fellows. Even the trivial conversations of daily existence set the boundaries of relationships and reinstate the rules of exchange.

Since a close community is relatively impenetrable for the outsider, the investigator from his position often views its culture as highly unified. Its closedness and its unity seem to be part of the same thing. On the other hand, historical research has often sought for unifying principles of 'open' societies, where closedness is by definition not part of the problem. In the latter situation, however, it is difficult to see how culture could be any more bounded or unified than, say, class. It is not just that they are both blurred around the edges and present fuzzy targets for the technical instruments of measurement. Rather, it is because culture is a series of arguments among people about the common things of their everyday lives.[1] What they share are the material and symbolic things which connect them, not the attitudes, positions, perceptions, strategies, or goals.

If we consider culture as the 'medium' as it were, in which conflicts are worked out, faulty and partial visions are adjusted, domination is attempted and resistance set into play, then we can use the concept as an instrument for investigating the dynamics of power, the distribution of resources, and the nature of hierarchy. In this very essential way, culture is part of a struggle over things, meanings, and positions. It is precisely because it is an argument, or a set of exchanges, or an attempt to wield or resist power, that we learn more about it by starting with the relations of the people who share a culture, than we do by assuming that culture is about a set of tools or ideas, a unified set of notions which a people share. Culture is generated in the interplay of shared situations, which are often 'replayed' several times with slight variations, allowing the patient researcher repeated lessons on the many possible values and strategies with which people confront each other.

The story related here is just one of the thousands of witchcraft investigations of the sixteenth and seventeenth centuries. Most of the details are repetitions which the keen reader of the witch literature has encountered time and time again. But we would miss what the story has to tell us if we remain at the level of the sediment of the historical process – the mad notions of this particular benighted set of theologians and country bumpkins. Our concern will not be centered on the phenomenon of witchcraft in the seventeenth century as such.[2] We will be mostly concerned with the metaphorical structure of language and how metaphors can be understood to provide a grammar of social relations.

In 1683, a thirteen-year-old servant girl living in the Württemberg town of Leonberg was reported to the pastor for spreading tales of witchcraft among the other children of the neighborhood.[3] Anna Catharina Weissenbühler, originally from the village of Warmbronn, was one of seven children of Elias Weissenbühler, a fifty-year-old mason incapable of carrying on his craft because of a crippled arm.[4] Weissenbühler was a Catholic immigrant from Upper Austria, probably one of those people who had been displaced by the events and aftermath of the Thirty Years' War. In any event he had settled in the small Protestant village with his wife and seven children. After his wife's death, he decided to marry a vagrant Swiss Calvinist woman. But when the local pastor refused to wed them, he gave up his residence (Bürgerrecht) in Warmbronn and abandoned his seven children, only one of whom was married and independent. All of the unmarried children went into service, Anna Catharina becoming a servant for her married brother.[5] Apparently she was not treated very well, and she ran away to the nearby village of Gerlingen to her cousin (*Base* – female cousin), the wife of the shepherd Andreas Kölle (also referred to as her cousin: *Vetter* – male cousin). She was there for half a year before she ended up in Leonberg as a nanny for the wife of Hans Michael Feineysin. Feineysin was also referred to as her cousin at one point in the hearings.

> On 21 June, the superintendent reported the case to the High Council (*Oberrat*) in Stuttgart. He said that the thirteen-year-old girl reported without any hesitations that she had learned witchcraft from Madalena, the wife of Gall Baum, when she was a servant girl in Gerlingen. Madalena had taken her often to the witches' dance by day and by night. Her story had caused a great scandal in the town and its territory. The girl spoke to the superintendent quite freely and without the least sign of fear. She was gifted and had many fine prayers, although she could not pray the morning and evening benedictions or the catechism. However, she was eager to learn. Her master intended to send her to school, and the superintendent expressed the hope that she was still rescuable.

In this manner, the superintendent began his first report on the matter. It is at times confusing and indeed contradictory. He gets some of the characters wrong and confuses relationships – all of which he straightens out in his later reports – here calling Madalena, Gall Baum's wife, for example, a cousin of Anna Catharina. This point could be of some importance because in the actual story the young girl told, none of her direct relatives peopled her fantasy world in a directly threatening way. However much of her life was ruled by an absconding father, impatient brother, a cousin she ran away from and another who eventually kicked her out, blood relatives were not lifted into her fantasy world as malevolent figures.[6]

In his prologue, the superintendent established a few important points. He was concerned above all with Anna Catharina's discourse. He pointed right away to the ease and freedom with which she spoke and kept circling back in one way or another to that fact, for in the spoken word lay her salvation. He jumped immediately from the quality of her narrative to the fact that she knew and could relate many prayers – in a later report she was criticized severely on this point – but she needed more prayers, especially ones related to a temporal progression designed to fill up the day. Sending her to school followed directly from the need to learn more prayers and to 'pray' (*beten*) the catechism, that is to commit it to memory and to repeat it orally. It is this concern with the word, on the one hand, and with the symbols of communication, on the other, which run through the story as related by Anna Catharina and as re-related by the superintendent.

> While Anna Catharina was in service to her cousin, the wife of Andreas Kölle in Gerlingen, Madalena, the wife of Gall Baum (she is) referred to as 'die Gallassin' throughout) asked her in her house if she wanted to learn witchcraft. When Anna Catharina said no, Gallassin responded that she could be forced. She disappeared into the pantry to get a lettuce, but came back with a knife. She pricked Anna Catharina's stomach, from which flowed a bowl full of blood. The latter did not know what Gallassin did with it, but she supposes that she gave it to the ('God preserve us') devil. The superintendent noted that one can no longer see on the skin where the knife penetrated.

Many of the details which the young girl related were common currency in the culture, and a vivid imagination had plenty to draw on. Very important here is the fact that what is presented in the documents is the superintendent's redaction of the extended conversations he had with her. Much of what she said came out in dialogue with him, and of course some aspects interested him more than others. He then wove together a report, emphasizing the points he thought to be most relevant. The story began with a meal which failed to take place. We will note throughout the entire narration that the point often turns on a blocked communication – a meal not delivered or left uneaten, a word not spoken. In fact the symbolic importance of the inner moral community as one which shares meals together is central to the narration.[7] At the opening moment, Gallassin offered esoteric knowledge and a meal – the lettuce – but the dialogue contained in the original offer and in the symbol of shared food was suddenly turned into a brutal seduction. Anna Catharina ended up providing a meal for the devil and, as we shall see, probably the means for preventing her future communication. The superintendent highlighted these points because seduction, as became apparent, was the central issue for the community and because the opening up of communication was central to the drama.

> Gallassin and other wives from Gerlingen took Anna Catharina with them to the gathering on the mountain in the woods. They also took her, her father, and her brother with them from Warmbronn. The wives from Magstetten also came to get her and drove out to get food and drink. There was often a great clamor. Once when she was together with the witches, Gallassin held her arm so that she could not get away. Later when she was nanny in Leonberg for Feineysin, on the sixth day of her service, Gallassin came to her in her chamber and took her down the hill and put her on a small white goat. Gallassin got on a white buck with no horns, and they rode together to Gerlingen, to the forest, and to other places. Now that she sleeps in the same room as her master and mistress, she regrets that no one comes to get her any more. She said that when she was riding around she recognized the mason's wife, the mason, the shoemaker, and the son of Gallassin. Too many people were witches for her to able to recall them all.
>
> Gallassin told her to fall accidently with the child she had in her care, or she would force her to. She told her to place the child on a bench and arrange a knife so that it would fall on it. The superintendent asked if she had had anything to do with the Evil One. This she denied, but did say that she had seen the devil. He had a goat's foot, was completely black, and was not like a human. He never spoke to her. If she were a witch, she would say so.
>
> At her second examination by the superintendent on 2 July, several points of clarification were added. Anna Catharina said that she had showed the knife wound to her cousins (*Vetter* and *Base*) for whom she worked as a servant. She thought they would tell the pastor and the village Schultheiss. Instead, the old woman, the shepherdess Kölle, bought a yellow salve from some man, which Anna Catharina applied three times a day with a white linen patch. When she was at the witches' dance, after eating and drinking, she sat in a ditch and washed the dishes. Gallassin's son played the bagpipe. They had meat, cabbage, bread, and salt to eat. The witches licked the salt away from the bread. They stole wine from her cousin's cellar. Besides Gallassin's son, there were no men there. The devil led the dance. There were not many people from Gerlingen at the dance. One could see from Gallassin's face that she was a witch.

Madalena (Gallassin) was questioned about Anna Catharina's testimony. She denied that she ever had any interest in learning witchcraft. She pointed out that if she had cut the girl with a knife, the latter would have died. She had never in her life been in Warmbronn. She did go to see the girl in the sitting room where she lived – others were present as well – to find out why she had said such thoughtless things about her. Gallassin says that she is not related to the girl. If she did know the alleged arts, she certainly would not communicate them to a little toad (*Kröte* – toad, bitch) like Anna Catharina. She says that when the young girl ran away to the woods, it must have been to where the devil enticed (*verführt*) her. Anna Catharina was questioned again on this last point. She ran away because she feared having to learn witchcraft. When she went to her brother in Warmbronn, he beat her. She spent the night in the forest where Gallassin came to get her and bring her to Gerlingen.

In all the details of the girl's story, there is very little which was not standard, everyday witchcraft stuff. There were the two worlds which she juxtaposed: that of the village or villages in which she had lived and another on the mountain and in the woods where another set of rules applied. The wild was the reverse image of the everyday, yet contained some of the aspects of her own special position, which suggest at once the real in the fantastic and the alienation in the normal. The mediation between the two worlds was effected by an animal, which although domesticated is unrestrained in its habits. The population of the wild world was composed of witches, transposed from the normal world, and in command, led by the devil. They also brought along various other people – notably Anna Catharina's father and brother. There was no suggestion, however, that they posed a threat – of corruption or seduction – to the girl. They were just there. None of her adult female or male relatives were transposed into her fantasy world in a position of danger to her. The threatening figures were non-related women, notably Madalena – 'die Gallassin' – and the devil, characterized by a goat-like physical appearance. The only other male who had any role to play was Madalena's son, who piped the music to the abandoned dance. This suggests the inheritability of malevolence and evil power. Just as Anna Catharina's direct relatives posed no mystical threat to her, however much she might have been mistreated by them, so those who did passed on their powers through blood. The threat to her came from the world of adult women. There were no children present with the witches.

The center of activity in the transposed world was eating and drink-ing. But the feasting violated normal communication as she understood it. There were no rules, and noise dominated the scene. Her description of the witches licking the salt from the bread suggests the violation of normal human customs. The food they ate was at least in part stolen. Taken together, one has in Anna Catharina's description of the scene a set piece of the unstructured sharing of food in which nothing is trans-acted. There is no exchange between the actors. They have produced nothing for each other and gobble things in an unrestrained way.[8] In the sheer abundance of food lay a further statement of the lack of necessity of meeting each other's needs. Assigned the task of washing up, only Anna Catharina appears to have made any contribution to the feast. Her task was the vain one of bringing order in a situation where disorder reigned. On the other hand, there seemed to be no way that she could enter directly into the madness which surrounded her, just as she found no place in the real world.

> On 9 July, Maria Catharina, the wife of Hans Michael Feineysin, for whose child Anna Catharina was nanny, was questioned. She said that the young girl had said to another that she was afraid she would have to fly out again in the night. Maria Catharina Feineysin heard a noise that night in her cupboard and called out to the girl three times, but there was no response. The next morning the girl seemed ner-vous. Upon questioning, she said that she was out on the heath with Gallassin that night. She made a noise while leaving because she took the wrong way. Thereupon called in for questioning, the girl told the story about riding off on a goat with Gallassin. The latter told her she would give her some poison to put into the porridge of the child she took care of. She was also supposed to take some lice off her cousin (Maria Catharina), the child's mother, and put them in the child's porridge to kill it.

Here again, food appeared as a 'relational idiom'.[9] Between the world of adults and herself, relations were continually blocked. Be-tween herself and her charge they were at best ambivalent, and her fan-tasy ran towards terminating them. It seems that there are two parts to the food image. On the one hand, the sharing of food can be a most intimate activity, defining a moral community of direct exchange among its members, however hierarchalized or subject to inequalities. The reverse part of the image is that this most intimate activity is also subject to the greatest dangers. Food can turn out to be poison, and the activity implying trust can be based on deception.[10] There seems to be a contradiction about where the poison to use on the child was supposed to come from, either from Gallassin (with intent) or from the child's mother (without intent). The image of the mother providing the poison for her child works with the notion of unintended danger, something characteristic of consanguineal relations. By contrast, intended aggression was grasped in terms of relations between neighbors. In either case, Anna Catharina would have been the means through which the deed would have been carried out. The indecision in her fantasy perhaps derived from the ambiguities of her position as a growing girl between the world of family and that of adult village culture.

On 10 July, the superintendent reported to the High Council what he had learned from questioning the various witnesses. Madalena, the wife of Gall Baum, was an old, nasty wife with a bad reputation because of what she did to her son Gallus. The latter was thirty years old and a bit crazy (*um etwas verrückter Sinne*). She allowed him to become engaged to her maid and to post the banns three times, then she halted the wedding on the grounds that he was not fit to be married. She was told by the authorities to proceed with the marriage or get a legal separation. She delayed so long and so wearied the fiancée that the latter went back to her home in Breisgau and got married there. The son was also considered to be malicious. Although a little crazy, he was well read and could play the bagpipes. So godless that the parents themselves had to fear him, he swore terribly when angry. When threatened with the magistrates, he let them think that he would kill himself. The father was old and decrepit but had a good reputation. Going on to summarize what he had found out, the superintendent noted that the Feineysins would no longer keep the girl. He said that there was no *corpus delecti* and asked if the whole matter was just one of bad dreams or whether she was subject to melancholy. He recommended that she be sent to the schoolmaster for a time.

On 16 July, there was a further report after Anna Catharina had been sent to the schoolmaster for instruction. On that day, the schoolmaster reported that the Evil One had talked to Anna Catharina in the barn and told her that she must come that evening to the dance. He himself wanted to dance with her. He put a mark way up on her tongue. Maria Catharina Feineysin reported that Anna Catharina's brother also has such a mark on his stomach and noted that Gallassin had a red spot on her head. Anna Catharina had been going through the barn to take a meal to her cousin (*Vetter* – Feineysin). It was then that the devil had stopped her. She called out to her cousin that she would have to go out again that night. She said that the devil had been with her. Feineysin kept a watch that night but nothing happened. When the girl was questioned, she said that the devil said they would be merry (*lustig*). He wanted to take her to the dance and give her food and drink. He took red dye (*Tinte*) from her and put it into the fire and let two drops fall on the ground. He took the drops up, made her stick out her tongue, and let them drop way back in her throat. The tongue and throat hurt so badly that she could not eat rightly. After this testimony, the Vogt ordered a doctor to examine the girl, her brother, and Gallassin. He found a small mark on the stomach of the girl but could not say whether it was of natural or unnatural origin. He also found a spot on Gallassin's head and a spot on the brother's stomach.

Anna Catharina was in the act of taking food to her cousin when she was interrupted by the devil. It was then that the latter promised her another meal, one in which her everyday concerns would be forgotten for a time. On the other hand, he immediately took action to see that she would not be able to eat. It is significant that of all the attacks from the devil that Anna Catharina could have imagined, the one that forced its way to the front of her consciousness was the image of an interrupted meal, the inability to consume the offering. As we shall see, the spot on the tongue was a block to all communication, preventing things going out as well as going in. The means by which this was done was a few drops of red dye, which recalls the opening incident of removing blood from the girl. There is the implication that Anna Catharina was prevented from relating through the idiom of food or through oral discourse by means of her own blood. One could recall here the notion of poisoning the baby with lice taken from its own mother. The link between the girl and her brother – blood relatives – is made by the image of the red spot on the stomach. The similar red spot linking Gallassin with Anna Catharina came about by the aggressive action of the older woman. The images taken as a whole deal with the themes of intentional and unintentional danger, the problem of entry to the wider social group, and the structural ambiguity in kinship relations.

The next report by the superintendent and the Vogt together was made on 18 September. Anna Catharina had been sent to the Leonberg schoolmaster for instruction (*Information*). He had been teaching her the catechism and syllabication. She was on the verge of learning to read. Previously she had only been able to recite the Lord's Prayer and the Creed and then only in a barbarous fashion. Since she had been taking instruction, she had not been taken to the dance nor troubled by the Evil Foe. It must be said that since the news of the children at Calw who were led astray had reached the town, there arose a great antipathy against the girl among the common people (*Bürgerschaft*), indeed also among the 'honorability',[11] They wanted to find another place for her where she could not gossip with the other children. She would no longer be tolerated in the school of the city. But the authorities should not follow the common rabble's opinion to the disadvantage of the girl. The schoolmaster was tired of her and would be very happy to be rid of her. However, the schoolmaster could see for himself that since she had been in his instruction, she did not go out at night. There was no chance of sending her back to her home village of Warmbronn. She had already been neglected by her married brother and had to run away. It would be necessary to wait until she learned more and became better informed in Christianity and prayer.

On 24 September, the superintendent and the Vogt filed another report. The schoolmaster had agreed to keep the girl. Most of the court and council, including some of the Bürgermeister, were displeased and had become hostile to the two officials (superintendent and Vogt). They had publicly discussed how to offer opposition and no longer sent their children to the school. The financial officer of poor relief (*Heckenpfleger*) arrogantly refused to pay the schoolmaster for the girl's board.

On 17 September, the schoolmaster reported that the girl stroked a cat on the back, and now that cat was lame. One of the hens started to cry and died. A lot of foam came out of her beak. The child made excuses for herself and said that she had done nothing. Since then, two more hens had dropped dead. Every night, the schoolmaster locked the doors, but three times they had been unlocked in the morning. Whenever he called to her at night, she answered. She was not allowed to be with other children and had to sit alone at a table. The schoolmaster's wife was afraid to cross the courtyard to get the food cooking on the fire. This fear arose because the child had made excuses for herself.

The struggle between the superintendent and the town dwellers over Anna Catharina was centered on the 'word'. The superintendent argued that the results of instruction were plain to see. The steps in his argument are quite revealing. To begin with, she was learning the catechism and syllabication. Implied here is that the schoolmaster was teaching her the meaning of the passages in the catechism and the rudiments of reading. She had come so far that she could almost read. And *then* comes the conclusion: previously she could only recite the Lord's Prayer and the catechism barbarously. The thrust of this argument is that understanding the meaning and the technical capacity to read were geared to the end product: formal recitation. Reading was a kind of *Hilfswissenschaft* to oral discourse. The superintendent placed great hope on formal instruction: the end to 'barbarous' discourse would put fetters on the devil's power. While the superintendent's hope lay in restricting her communication, the town dwellers considered the efforts to be too late. They were afraid of her spontaneous discussion with the other children and saw her unfettered communication as posing a threat of seduction. She was made to sit alone in the classroom, and all communication with other children was blocked. Nonetheless, the fear was so great that parents stopped sending their children to school.

> On 26 September, the Bürgermeister and the Richter filed a petition in which they went over the entire case. They had not been able to see the reports filed by the Vogt and superintendent but had noticed that the girl had been sent to the schoolmaster for instruction. They had hoped she would be sent back to the village of Warmbronn, but she had been kept in Leonberg for over ten weeks. She had learned a little praying, but not much more could be expected. While at the schoolmaster's, she stroked the cat, which then became lame. His hens were dying, and the locks on the parlor door opened by themselves. The girl had a bad (*schlimmes*) face. The magistrates recalled what had recently happened at Calw, where many children had been seduced to witchcraft. It could be that the Wicked Enemy was using his tool for the same purpose here. The parents had heavy hearts and anxious souls. They were in fear for the eternal destruction of their children and wanted Anna Catharina sent away. They were afraid that she would run up to some of the other children in the school. A wicked seduction could take place suddenly (*gleich*). The girl told the schoolmaster that the devil sits on her tongue so that she can hardly swallow. When she should have recited something from the sermon, she was unable to speak for a while.

> On 8 October, the schoolmaster filed a report. He said that his original hope had been dashed. The girl had twice again been to the witches' coven. She had been fetched by the women from Gerlingen. In church or when she wanted to read or learn, the wicked spirit was on her tongue. The schoolmaster and his wife had requested twice

that she be taken away but were threatened with a fine or jail. People were afraid to send their children to the school lest they be contaminated (infected – *anstecken*). Five hens on which she had spit had dropped dead. The cat she stroked became lame.

Anna Catharina had come up with exactly the correct response to the situation. She too testified to the power of the word by blocking up that channel. She was refusing to fulfill the expectations of the superintendent and the schoolmaster. In so far as her communication remained spontaneous, unfettered by the substitution of formalized speech, she remained dangerous. None of the communities wanted to keep her. The image under which she was subsumed were those of contagion and seduction. And the expectation was that such a thing could occur with rapidity. All that was necessary was for the girl to speak with the other children. Her word was like her spit which could cause the sudden death of chickens.

On 9 October, the superintendent and the Vogt sent in their final report. The child had been taken by Gallassin and her son to the witches' dance twice by force and beaten up. She was made to take wine from the cellar of the Schultheiss in Gerlingen. The schoolmaster's horrible (*grundböses*) wife had taken the girl's bed from the parlor and put it into the hospital where she had to sleep alone. When the wife threatened to leave, the two officials gave her a reprimand, but she remonstrated with fury and wicked words. She did not cease even with the threat of jail. She screamed and ran out, slamming the door. Later she returned and threatened to find people in Stuttgart who could help get rid of the girl. The officials checked the girl's story and found that the Schultheiss in Gerlingen had neither wine nor barrel. He never had a barrel of the size she described, nor did the cellar have a door such as she described in her story. Any wine that was missing would have been noticed. The night she spoke of, everything froze, and she could hardly have gone out in her nightdress. Her story did not seem to be the result of dreams or of *illusiones diabolice*. She also gave a number of people as present at the dance who had been dead for some time. The officials wanted to give the child to an elderly, honorable, and pious couple who were without children. They could read and write.

On 4 November, the Untervogt reported that Anna Catharina's father, Elias Weissenbühler, had reappeared in Warmbronn. He had previously given up his Bürgerrecht (citizenship) there and run off with a vagrant Swiss woman, leaving the children behind. He was

Catholic, originally from Austria; she a Calvinist. He came back to see if he could sell his house (which was not worth more than 30 fl.) but was thrown in jail. He said he wanted to leave to join his wife and take his daughter along. He had no movables and was badly clothed. He was to be let go but not allowed to take any of the children.

On 13 November, it was reported that the village of Warmbronn refused to take the girl. They submitted a protocol containing a complete list of households in the village, proving that there was no room for her.

The discussions between Anna Catharina Weissenbühler, the superintendent, and the various inhabitants of Warmbronn, Gerlingen, and Leonberg centered around one of the crucial problems of the sixteenth and seventeenth centuries, namely the nature, power, and extent of the 'word'. Essentially, the word was grasped as a paradigm of unmediated communication, an issue that had been central in the Reformation. In various ways, it was crucial to any understanding of power and went to the heart of the nature of domination. As in any metaphorical structure whose shape is determined to some considerable degree by hegemonic powers, resistance took place largely within its limits. Space for self-determination lay in providing alternative models of reality or in turning the existing models to one's purpose. In this case, the engagement was frontal, through the word, and oblique in the manner in which a mediated understanding of communication was modeled in other ways by the girl.

It would not be very useful to try to place too much weight on the notions of one thirteen-year-old girl undergoing all of the troubles of a normal child in puberty and desperately trying to find her place in that particularly difficult adult world. The situation was made more complicated by her having lost her mother, been abandoned by her father, and been left to assorted relatives to be supported/exploited. In the context of the time, however, she had the very powerful weapon of witchcraft, in this case starting with her perhaps childish boast to her comrades that she had been running around with witches. The metaphors of magic/witchcraft, food/eating, and word/tongue intertwine in the discourse, providing a shifting 'reading' of the communication process. Each metaphorical structure here can be considered as an idiom in that the structure as a whole is peculiar to itself and obeys its own internal grammatical forms. At the same time, each idiom is a way of grasping the relations between people and between people and their environment and models the communication process on its own terms. We will begin our analysis by taking a brief look at the 'relational idioms' of witchcraft and food before concentrating on that of the word. All of these are complex metaphors with many dimensions, and the sources are only capable of tantalizing us with what is possible. Modeling communication takes place in a concrete social world of kinship, neighborhood, and village, with each actor providing his own partial understanding or misunderstanding of the situation. Our problem is to discern the argument of the subject contained within the argument of the text – the double aspect of any historian's viewpoint.

The first idiom, namely witchcraft, is what ostensibly the whole case is about. It draws together issues of neighborhood and kinship, youth and adulthood, village and individual. In general a distinction can be drawn between kin and neighbors and, within kin, between blood relatives and affines (those related by marriage).[12] There were many hints in this case that witchcraft or the desire to become a witch was inherited or ran along blood lines. It was not that all relatives were susceptible, but that the chances were much greater that the corruption or seduction necessary would come from within the family. The common phrase to express this was, 'She did not purchase that', meaning that a specific trait was not obtained in exchange with non-kin, or 'learned', but rather inherited.[13] The general structure of the myth here is repeated in current explanations of drunkenness in Württemberg, for which two quite distinct stories are given.[14] One says that if you look in the genealogy of a drunk, you will find another tippler somewhere in the family, perhaps an uncle. The other story – related by the same person with no sense of contradiction – maintains that men frequent taverns and learn to drink when their wives do not prepare good meals or meals on time. This emphasizes the affinal side of the issue, the exchange rather than the inherited.

Thus there was a general tendency to lump consanguineal relatives together. Anna Catharina and her younger brother both had the devil's mark, although there was no suggestion that the brother had been in contact with Gall Baum's wife. Not only was the latter a witch, but her son had followed her lead. One might note here that there was no hint that Gall Baum himself had anything to do with magic or witchcraft. In fact the son by cursing and swearing – carrying on discourse in that dangerous sphere of magic – 'oppressed' the father. In an earlier case in Gerlingen in which Gallassin had played a role, there was also a suggestion that a daughter had been brought to witchcraft by her father, whose mother and sister had, in turn, been burned earlier as witches.[15] If there was danger to be had from relatives, it was generally along the lines of corruption/seduction. Also there is the possibility of unintended harm, illustrated by the lice from the mother that were supposed to be poisonous for her child.

By contrast, it is from non-kin (or from affines) that aggression/ seduction was to be feared. Anna Catharina was responsible for the death of chickens belonging to the schoolmaster's wife. In the earlier case referred to, the girl made a neighbor's calf sick.[16] In part, such aggression was linked to the neighbor's expectation of envy, demonstrated in the latter case by the girl's exclaiming how pretty the calf was. Anna Catharina expressed her fears of aggression in singling out a neighbor who obviously had been central in the village power game and probably still was. In the earlier case twenty-five years before, she had organized public opinion to get the girl involved expelled from the village.[17] Anna Catharina's own fantasies of aggression towards her charge were not put in kinship terms, which may be significant. She carefully labeled all the people she dealt with whom she considered relatives as 'cousins' (*Base*, *Vetter*), but failed to do so in the case of the child. On the other hand, she only referred to her temptation and suggested the evil intent of the non-related Gallassin or the unintended possibility of poisoning by the child's mother. The neighbors were always suspected of envy, and possible evil intent was underlined by the practice of neighbor women taking communion with a dying woman. In one instance, for example, neighbors entered a house for the first time in order to undergo the ritual of proving their innocence.[18]

There is a frequent argument in the literature on witchcraft that witches were generally marginal figures, usually old, isolated women, or as in this instance young children.[19] The issue put in these terms suggests from the outset that it is one of power, and the argument is made that the weak are somehow feared by the strong or that displaced feelings of guilt make people feel aggressive towards their victims. This is not the place to solve the problem of the struggle between the powerful and the weak, but it might be useful to make a few distinctions and suggestions. Gall Baum's wife had probably been suspected of being a witch for some time, which would explain why Anna Catharina turned to her as the natural candidate for her seducer. On the other hand, no adults in the village chimed in to second Anna Catharina's suggestion. It was clear that in a contest between Gallassin and Anna Catharina, the latter was on the weak side and was defined as the loser from the very beginning. Furthermore, she had no status in either Gerlingen or Leonberg, was not 'one of ours' and therefore subject to communal protection in any way. In many cases, witch accusations stayed among the villagers, or at least they, together with their own officials, tried to keep the struggle local.[20] It is not that weak marginal people are the witches but only that in a contest in which magic playes a role, the powerful win. Frequently, for example, one sees in a witchcraft case that the old woman who is at long last brought to court has been a witch all her life.[21] Testimonies of neighbors relate incidents over as much as a forty-year period. In all that time no one made any attempt to bring her to the authorities – or perhaps no attempt was successful – but waited until there was nothing more to fear from her or until the balance of power tipped. In the case of Gall Baum's wife, she was still part of the reputation-dispensing group in the village, a powerful personality who had nothing but contempt for the young girl who had entered the lists on such uneven terms.

If the witchcraft idiom was one way of defining the community, suggesting the manner in which envy, aggression, and fear were to be territorialized, so the food metaphor suggests another way of viewing community, another way of getting at relationships and the process of communication. Unlike images of communication centered on the spoken word, those based on the metaphor of food are inherently mediated ones. Cooking, sharing, offering, and consuming food take place in a more-or-less complex context of exchange between people.[22] Grasping society in this way is to begin at once with relationships and not with the individual or a view of society which can be reduced to a composite of needs.

Those who share food define a moral community, which can be structured in many different ways. It was a common custom in rural Württemberg, for example, for a young, unmarried woman to bake a cake for the annual parish fête. She would hold the cake out in front of various lads to her liking, who were expected to draw their knives from their sheaths and take a slice.[23] Under no circumstances was a married man allowed to dip into her cake. In fact for a married man to take food from any woman at all, apart from his own wife, could be interpreted as having an illicit sexual relationship with her.[24] Thus food and food rituals gave information about relationships, were part of a process of the incorporation of groups, and suggested social boundaries.

Implicit in the sharing of food is, of course, trust. And the issue in social relations often lies right here, for trust may be rewarded with treachery and food with poison. It was not uncommon in rural Württemberg for a husband or wife to suspect the other of poisoning him or her through magic.[25] In fact the charge of sorcery was often a charge of poison, and neighbors exchanging loaves of bread with each other were likely to throw bits to the chickens first before they ate it themselves.[26] In community lie dangers, the more so as one is often unprepared for attack. Food/poison, therefore, offers the metaphors for sharing/treachery inherent in community. Just this set of images served Anna Catharina's purposes for expressing her fears, but more, her position of marginality. Relationships which she had sought with her married brother and various 'cousins' had either resulted in exploitation or rejection – at least she kept running away. The story of meals never shared made the central point for her that she had not yet become part of any community, and that the approaches she kept making were always eventually denied, the relations broken off – until finally she could eat nothing at all. Unlike the idiom of witchcraft, which offers to us one view of that society, partial but shared to the extent that Anna Catharina can be seen to have been part of a discourse about social power, the metaphor of food brings us to a more personal view of Anna Catharina's situation, down to her subjective experience. Yet both are part of a more complex whole. With the metaphor of the word, we enter into the world of hierarchy and Herrschaft and begin to see some of the connections between the village and the state, between the culture of the local community and that of the religious establishment.

The particular issue around which the 'word' was centered was schooling, which seems to have amounted to the oral recitation of prayers. By contrast, the references to Anna Catharina's barbarous recitation (barbarian meaning stutterer) was apt. It was important to get the prayers letter perfect, like reciting the catechism, which was also not distinguished from praying (*beten*). What the superintendent was trying to do becomes somewhat clearer if we consider what education can mean in an oral culture. One has to make a distinction between verbatim and thematic memorization from the outset – the memorization of words rather than things.[27]

Unlike the education of poets and pastors, Anna Catharina was not being provided with topoi (*loci communes*) but with a text to learn. When memorization involves schemata or themes, then the oral performer can be part of a creative process, working the themes but showing his own skill in the variation.[28] By confining her to a text, by expecting her to get it letter perfect, it is clear that she was not expected to talk, or to enter oral discourse, she was not to be a producer but a receiver.[29] In the intent to bind her to the text, the superintendent sought to cut her off from spontaneous production of her own meaning. Of course, the more general issue here has to do with the meaning of schooling for the society as a whole. By expecting word for word memorization, the state/church was making a serious inroad into the ability of communal culture to generate its own terms. Fixing a text is to transform it from a 'living' word, to kill its dynamism.[30] In a sense, one is creating here in the vernacular its own 'archaism', making the word into an object, which then becomes a kind of magic and by its mere repetition a powerful tool against the devil.

It has been suggested that memorization as the central aspect of education implies a sustained adult discipline upon the child.[31] It also has the effect of substituting for or attacking the formulae by which the community 'organizes' objects and fixes the response to objects. Oral education and memorization were part of a long term program of the state to discipline rural society and make its culture dependent. We have seen in chapter 1 how the ritual of communion was also part of the disciplinary process, and in chapter 2 how much churchmen–administrators were concerned with the problems of discipline. By the program of attack on oral culture, they were also in this way mediating between village and state.

All of the actors in the drama around Anna Catharina associated the word with power, whether one looks at the town dwellers in Leonberg, who feared for its contagion, or at the superintendent who offered the magic of the established word, or at Anna Catharina herself, who refused to fetter her own power with the superintendent's constraints. After all, she had a whole town and two villages apparently running in absolute terror of her, and a brigade of adults were spending large amounts of time trying to counter her influence.

The 'word' had been a central aspect of the Reformation. For Luther and Melanchthon, there was no knowledge of God without the word of proclamation and the sacraments.[32] Even the latter were seen under the aspect of the Word of God – there was and could be no wordless salvation. Both of these reformers, as well as Brenz, the Württemberg reformer, stressed the external word, in contrast to the internal word of the enthusiasts and sectarians.[33] In the Church Ordinance of 1559 published in Württemberg, it was announced as a false opinion that God could communicate his gifts without the 'preaching office of the external word'.[34] All the reformers understood the importance of the preaching office, especially in its ability to organize culture. As Calvin said, 'the church is built up solely by outward preaching'.[35] He even went so far as to warn against private reading of the Bible and meditation as radically individualizing and isolating practices. They would allow the individual to escape from the discipline of the external word and break 'the sacred bond of unity'.[36]

In all of this, the reformers grasped the central importance of the spoken word for community. They understood what Walter Ong has pointed out, that sound unites groups of people in a different way from the written word, in that the spoken word is at once communication and act.[37] It is difficult with oral words to participate in the thought of others without commitment. With such a view of the word and with the experience of living in oral culture, it is possible to see the word as powerful and dangerous. The contagion that the town dwellers of Leonberg feared testifies to a sense of the word as act.

The possibilities that lay in the new understanding of oral culture discussed so intensely in the Reformation were also seen by secular officials. In Württemberg the foundation of the Protestant church with its preaching office, the establishment of schools for handling the rudiments of oral discipline, and the development of a state-directed secular oral discourse at the village level went hand in hand. In 1559, it was laid down in law that every Sunday after the sermon the pastor should repeat the Ten Commandments, the Apostles' Creed, and the Lord's Prayer from the pulpit, and that everyone should repeat them verbatim, so that 'one word might be won thereby'.[38] At the same time the ordinance for the village schools was promulgated which centered on memorizing the catechism. Stress was put on learning not to 'swallow the last syllable'.[39] During these years, it became the practice to read the law codes and ordinances publicly to the assembled Bürger in each village and town.[40] Thus at the same time as the word was seen to constitute the community, new techniques were developed to introduce the word as discipline, to strengthen the component of domination inside community. An army of officials trained in the written word were at war with oral culture, and they chose the point of attack with care. One thirteen-year-old girl in a lucid moment saw where the breakthrough was taking place, and she set a guard on her tongue.

4

Blasphemy, adultery and persecution: Paranoia in the pulpit (1696–1710)

As for you, do not pray for this people, or lift up cry or prayer for them, and do not intercede with me, for I do not hear you.

Jeremiah 7.16

Lead me, O Lord, in thy righteousness
because of my enemies;
make thy way straight before me.
For there is no truth in their mouth;
their heart is destruction,
their throat is an open sepulchre,
they flatter with their tongue.
Make them bear their guilt, O God;
let them fall by their own counsels;
because of their many transgressions cast them out,
for they have rebelled against thee.

Psalms 5.8–10

He who digs a pit will fall into it, and a stone will come back upon him who starts it rolling.

Proverbs 26.27

The story we have to tell in this chapter is about a Württemberg pastor at the end of the seventeenth century, who was pushed from pastorate to pastorate, each time getting into unsolvable conflicts with the secular authorities.[1] The High Council file on Georg Gottfrid Bregenzer began in 1696 and ended in 1710 with his dismissal from office and his 'permanent' exile from the state of Württemberg. In fact, he managed to get a pastorate in the village of Truchtelfingen eight years later, but the details concerning that appointment are no longer to be found.[2] His career illustrates a number of themes central to rural and small town

113

society: the relationship between the pastor and civil officials, the nature of the pastor's power, the nature of political metaphor, the concepts of sin, blasphemy, enmity, and reconciliation. Above all, the activities and conflicts surrounding Bregenzer gave rise to a rich vocabulary of abuse, whose metaphorical structure offers clues to the central social categories of the time, no analysis of which can fail to deal with the notion of 'enemy' and the category of 'adultery' and still pretend to an understanding of their dynamics.

> The first mention of Bregenzer in the records came from a report filed by the superintendent of Heidenheim, who enclosed a letter from the chief magistrate from the town of Heubach (population 700–800), dated 12 October 1696. According to the Vogt, Pastor Bregenzer had lately taken several unauthorized and apparently scandalous trips. He had absented himself from the town without any excuse for fourteen days and most recently had spent the day with a Catholic nobleman from Leinzell. More serious was the fact that he was going around the town slandering various people and on the previous Friday, the monthly day of Penance and Prayer (*Buss- und Bettag*), had held such an obscure and slanderous sermon that he shocked all of his hearers. He took the text from the litany about forgiving and converting enemies, persecutors, and slanderers and made the following points: (1) He himself had to suffer persecution from inside his community (*Gemeinde*). (2) He was forced to deal with the issue this time because it arose in the course of the litany and he trusted it would bear fruit in the land. (3) The teacher (*Lehrer*) had been offended by the bearers of the sword (*Wehrer*). (4) In the teaching estate (*Lehrstand*) there are spiritual (*geistliche*) enemies, while in the military estate (*Wehrstand*) there are persecutors, slanderers, and civil (*weltliche*) enemies. (5) On the one side stands the man and on the other the wolf. (6) The persecutors and the slanderers of the clergy should ponder the words of Christ, 'Whatever you do unto the least of these, you do unto me.' (7) He wanted to ask God to forgive his persecutors, slanderers, and enemies for their simplicity and weakness. (8) The persecutors he was talking about were the civil magistrates against the teachers. (9) Those who persecute the clergy will be rejected.[3]

Bregenzer, at least as the Vogt reported the issue, had underlined an important distinction in the power apparatus of the town, namely that between the spiritual and temporal. He denied any spiritual power to the civil authorities *qua* their civilian status and emphasized the gulf by the images he used: *Lehr/Wehr* (or teaching versus defence-word versus violence), man/wolf, persecuted/persecutor, offended/offender, slandered/slanderer, spiritual/worldly. On the side of civil power, he ranged the use of armed force and aggressive behavior, and quite specifically attached all of these images to the civil magistrates in the town of Heubach. By contrast to the power of the sword, that of the teacher 'bears fruit', that is, is not subject to the forces of man's understanding. In the end the two sides were unequal, and his enemies were subject to simplicity and weakness and in need of forgiveness. Offences against someone on the spiritual side of the equation were also against Christ and would be suitably punished.

Much of what Bregenzer preached was linked to the standard Lutheran distinction between the spirit and the sword, but it is fascinating to see how the theological distinctions could be embedded in concrete preaching and how, in what appears to have been a dispute between civil and church authorities, the pastor drew strength from his charismatic status. In fact, of course, he used his preaching office to attack his opponents in the presence of the whole assembly of villagers. But much of his message appears to have been structured around defining social, moral, and spiritual dichotomies and suggesting the laws of their interaction.

One of Bregenzer's sermons included in his dossier was preached on the twenty-second Sunday after Trinity.[4] It was too long to deliver, so several passages were crossed out, but in a preface Bregenzer expressly acknowledged the whole text as reflecting his opinions. Apparently, the superintendent had discussed the sermon with Bregenzer, and the latter subsequently inserted marginal notes contradicting the position of his superior. Basically, the theme and structure of the sermon follows the distinction between the spiritual estate and the magistrates, making clear the priority of the former. In the relationship between the pastor and parishioner – between the father-confessor (*Beichtvater*) and the confessing child (*Beichtkind*) – there can be no state of brotherhood. The relationship remains one of father and child. Bregenzer implies that where the relationship is equal, between brothers, either party can seek reconciliation when one offends the other. But when a son offends a father, it is not up to the father to seek reconciliation. The son has to show remorse and demonstrate the genuineness of his regret. Without naming names, in a series of sharp attacks Bregenzer preached that the 'shepherd of souls' in Heubach was being relentlessly persecuted, and that the whole community sighed to God to see him under such torture. The persecutors were preparing the rope for their own necks, were citing themselves to the last judgment. With breathtaking leaps, Bregenzer pointed out that hate was tantamount to murder, and quoted Jeremiah 7.16 to the effect that one could cease to pray for those whose hands were full of blood. He argued that public sins had to be repented of publicly and that an apology before the community was necessary for sincere penance. Until such time as those with 'false hearts' showed true remorse, the pastor could refuse them access to the chair of confession (*Beichtstuhl*) and refuse them absolution. After all, Christ gave the clergy the keys to the Kingdom of Heaven and expected them to be used. Reconciliation was not the pastor's business – the father is not obligated to jump at the wishes of the son or daughter.

> Complaints from the Vogt, Franz Ulssheimer, caused the superintendent to undertake a thorough investigation of the pastor's behavior. At the meal which followed a shooting match, the pastor behaved with the Catholic noble from Leinzell in a disgraceful way. He cited I Corinthians 15 to the effect, 'but by the grace of God I am what I am', and said that the nobleman was also what he was by the grace of God. Thereupon the two of them drank brotherhood to each other, spoke to each other in the familiar 'Du' form, and the nobleman referred to the pastor as a priestly brother (*Pfaffenbruder*). The nobleman drank to his 'filthy, nasty health' (*gar wüste unflatige Gesundheit*). There were complaints about Bregenzer's sermons and the kinds of analogies and 'types' which he drew. He often exercised his authority arbitrarily. According to the Vogt, the pastor's maid was expelled from the town on suspicion of repeated adultery. On his own authority, Bregenzer brought her back and reinstalled her. He often treated his wife meanly because of the maid and once on the open field struck her in the maid's presence. At the end of one sermon he took leave of the community, and one can see in his text outline the words, 'adieu, valete'. He left the town without telling anyone what he intended to do, and the rumor circulated that he had gone over to the papists. He was a very poor manager of his household, having gone through his wife's dowry and piled up debts.[5]

The Bürgermeister, court, and council all requested a new pastor. In the meantime, Bregenzer wrote several highly confusing apologia and requested an investigation of the Vogt, refusing an offer of reconciliation from the pulpit. For a while a vicar was brought in, but the conflict became even worse, so he was removed. Not confining his activity to the town, Bregenzer traveled to the surrounding villages preaching against the Vogt. After viewing all the evidence the superintendent came to the conclusion that the pastor was not altogether sane.

As far as the Vogt and the town magistrates were concerned, Bregenzer was guilty of confusing important social and political categories. The town existed in a larger context of a Protestant/Catholic dichotomy, and this distinction was absolutely essential to a perception of social differentiation and to the symbols of social control. The seriousness of scandal was measured by the degree of satisfaction it gave to the other side. The scandal of having lunch with a Catholic nobleman and the suspicion that he had run off to the papists suggested for the magistrates Bregenzer's inability to keep the central categories straight, and was part of the demonstration of his incompetency. In his disgraceful action at the shooting match banquet, he went so far as to use the most intimate sign of friendship, the familiar 'Du', in his relationship with the Catholic nobleman. After they drank brotherhood to each other, the nobleman appropriated a kinship image by referring to the pastor as *Pfaffenbruder*, and further crossed the bounds of social distance by drinking to Bregenzer's health in a crude style. Thus the pastor's image of enemy and persecution was countered by the Vogt's argument that he was not able to keep straight who the proper enemy was, and in fact quite inappropriately used the images of kinship and friendship where they did not belong. He also was unable to keep the rules of 'friendship' straight, demeaning his wife in front of the servant, and refusing an offer of reconciliation from the Vogt.

The situation continued for about a year until finally the officials tried to establish a new pastor, but Bregenzer and two deputies of the Gemeinde drew up a memorial accusing him of bigamy. (This typical attack on the part of Bregenzer will be returned to later.) After one of his sermons, Bregenzer read a list of all the names of people he had served: the sick he had visited, the children baptized, the young people confirmed. Although all of the magistrates thereupon left the church, the *Bürgerschaft* (village members) stayed and signed an attestation in his favor. The Vogt suggested that if the pastor remained in the village there would be a collision between the magistrates and the villagers, which would give all of the surrounding papists cause to slander the ministry and the Protestant religion. He should be removed for trying to win the common people illegally to his side.[6]

> In May 1798, the whole town (*Bürgerschaft*) was questioned one by one about the issue of the pastor's removal, which the magistrates claimed everyone wanted. Not one person knew anything about the demand nor could give any reason why they thought he should be removed. In fact, they all said that Bregenzer fulfilled his office

dutifully and in good temper. All of his sermons were preached to their satisfaction and, in teaching the youth the catechism, he carried out his task faithfully. He visited the sick, cut no corners in his duties, and demonstrated many charitable deeds. No one could think of any time that he had acted in a silly manner, foolishly, or abusively. His behavior was quiet, and he gave no offence by his private life. Some had seen him drunk, only the one time, at the banquet following the shooting match.[7]

The picture that emerges after the village testimony is full of contradictions but offers some important insights into the dynamics of that small town society. First of all, that the Vogt, supported by most of the magistrates, and the pastor were in open conflict seemed to disturb the sensibilities of none of the townspeople. No one said that they wished for one side or the other to demonstrate more charity or that such conflict was disturbing or shameful. Nor did anyone take offence at the pastor's persecution mania, his image of enemies, or his use of the sermon to plead his case. All of this demonstrates how central the category of 'enemy' was to that society and how usual it was to see people engaged in a struggle of power. To know that you were being persecuted held no hint of clinical paranoia in the popular mind. Bregenzer struck the right chord and edified his hearers by putting the concrete experience of aggression into the context of spiritual power. In one of his sermons, he had used the text Luke 22.24–7, which dealt with the dispute of the disciples about which one of them was to be regarded as the greatest. He pressed Christ's answer into service, which distinguished between those with authority and lordship and those who 'serve', suggesting that real – spiritual – power and eventual reward lay with the latter. He also read James 3 from the pulpit, which argues that jealousy and ambition are 'earthly, unspiritual, and devilish', and applied it to his enemies.[8]

Some of Bregenzer's actions have to be understood in the context of the play between the two corporations of Gemeinde or Bürgerschaft and magistrates.[9] The position of a pastor was ambiguous from the beginning, for he shared some of the aspects of a magistrate, yet he was not part of their corporation. For one thing, he sat on the church consistory and took part in the judgment of the villagers, dispensing punishment. He was also a conduit for passing on announcements, ordinances, and 'wanted' posters from the state. On the other hand his spiritual power was great, being able almost daily to define publicly the symbols of power, the nature of reality, and the relative moral value to be given to this or that action. It is significant that Bregenzer was much more interested in confession and communion for maintaining church and moral discipline than he was in the church consistory, in which he had to share power with several magistrates. Being even less a part of the Gemeinde than they were, he was the key mediator between it and the world of spiritual power, just as the magistrates mediated the authority of the state. Although he could exclude the civil authorities from the realm of the spirit and use that exclusion as the cutting edge to his critical activity, on the other hand he was never fully out of the realm of the 'flesh', as the dispute itself shows. For after the conflict had waged for over a year and a half, the town magistrates (Bürgermeister, Gericht, and Rat) explained to the commissioners that the whole dispute was rooted in a conflict over how the lesser tithes (on garden produce, flax, hemp, fruit, and sometimes hay) were to be divided between the pastor and the Vogt.[10]

As it turned out, the disagreement between the pastor and the Vogt reached back 'before human memory', which argues that it was already part of communal life before Bregenzer took over the pastorate. Apparently what was new in the situation was the way Bregenzer used the pulpit to carry on his struggle. In this manner he tipped the balance of power in the town by making the Gemeinde party to the dispute. The town magistrates, as a result, became worried, because this posed a threat to their position and caused them to break out of their neutral position between Vogt and pastor on the issue. But it was not just a matter of playing party politics. Bregenzer was making innovations in the way he preached and the nature of his message that were in themselves interpreted as a bid for power.

Bregenzer had brought specific charges against the previous and present Vögte.[11] He alleged that Johann Conrad Bruckh, by then an official in Leonberg, had punished a servant for mixing sawdust in with flour, and had kept the fine for himself. An examination of the financial records found no grounds for this. More seriously the Vogt was supposed to have lent money to townsfolk at thirty per cent interest. Most of the cases involved went back to the bad harvest and inflation of 1693. In that year, the Vogt had advanced seed and half the costs of cultivation in return for half the crop. All those who made a profit supported the Vogt, but those who ended up in financial difficulty had serious complaints, since he forced them to pay interest on the loan and used the power of his office to put people into stocks, to force them into bankruptcy proceedings, or to garnishee their land. Other charges included setting an inflated price on oats sold to quartered troops, and pocketing part of the profit. When the new Vogt, Ulssheimer, arrived, he knocked down the price. Various specific charges against Ulssheimer did not seem too serious. For example, he forced a woman to sell all her property, but since she was well over seventy and deaf and the money was put into trust, there did not seem to be much to the matter.

In the details of the quarrel, one can see how the pastor became a conduit for all kinds of complaints against the two chief officials. His own dispute over the tithes became part of a web of gossip, suspicion, and ill-will. There was no question but that the Vögte used their positions to their own advantage and exercised the tools of domination systematically and successfully. For them, Bregenzer's chief crime was that he stole the 'affection' of the villagers – he unmasked the relationships of Herrschaft, suggesting that authority was based on the arbitrary exercise of force, and that its claim to justice was compromised by self-interest and the persecution of all those who refused to bend to it.

Pastor Bregenzer was apparently dismissed from his pastorate in Heubach. He next appeared in Pflugfelden (in September 1699) but soon got involved in a strange affair with a treasonous official.[12] After that he was briefly pastor in Mauren and, following a four-year gap in the records, went to the village of Hattenhofen in the district of Göppingen.

> Once Bregenzer became pastor in Hattenhofen, his bizarre behavior immediately caused scandal, and the first investigation was already instituted in October 1705. It had been reported that he had behaved in an unseemly manner in an inn in Göppingen. According to one story, he had come in around 8 a.m., sent for an official (the *Amtmann*), and upon his arrival demanded a horse to conduct some business. Since it was a private matter, the request was denied, at which point Bregenzer called him a 'godless official' (*heilloser Amtmann*), an 'ill-mannered lout' (*Flegel*), and a 'dog's ass' (*Hundsfutterei*). Another witness testified that after two hours in the inn, the pastor was roaring drunk. He drank brotherhood with the Baron von Closen and said he was a dog's ass just like himself. To the waiter he kept saying, 'fool, drink some down', and the waiter kept pushing him away. As the Esslingen consul got into his coach outside, Bregenzer called, 'Your excellency or my most honorable Sir, I offer you my great respects'. To which the consul answered, 'and I offer you little respect'. Bregenzer then slammed down the window and said he would go out to the dog's ass and say what needed to be said. He went out and fell down the stairs.

It was alleged further that he gave all the servants silly jobs and titles. One he called 'shoe and boot polisher', another 'valet and bed-fellow' (*Beischläfer*), a third 'language instructor'. Then he said they could all speak French and called for more red wine. Mocking them with having weak stomachs, he poured wine on their hands and heads and smeared it all over them. He soon fell dead asleep and in the late afternoon awakened, said 'Good morning', and refused to accept that it was evening. Eating with the servants, he picked up a noodle that fell from a servant girl's plate with five fingers and shoved it into his mouth. He also stuck his five fingers into her bowl and took pieces out. By midnight he was calling for more wine, saying that he was drinking for a cure. Finally he was put into a room and locked in. But he broke out, yelling 'thunder could hit him, he would not stay under arrest'. In the morning, he called the innkeeper 'brother-in-law', in contrast to the previous day when he called him a 'coarse Bavarian' and a 'pig'. That day he opened his shirt to show everyone a wart, which was supposed to mean that he would become stinking rich. He told everyone not to call him 'Pastor' but simply, 'Monsieur'. Later on, he toasted the servants, and they called each other 'fool'.[13]

By early the next year (1706), Bregenzer was again being inves-tigated, this time for having thrown a scandalous party in the parsonage. One of the musicians testified that he and his brother were called to the pastor's house by the maid, who said the Scribenten were tearing the house down.[14] Upon receiving them, the pastor warned them not to tell anyone that he had called them. He offered them wine and said it was no sin to be in the parsonage. If they sinned so little, they could go right to the Kingdom of Heaven. Music and dance followed. At one point, everyone made a ring and Bregenzer stood in the middle with a glass full of nuts, calling for everyone to drink brotherhood. Then he addressed everyone in the familiar 'Du' form, embraced both the mu-sicians and kissed them. He said, 'You know, dear boys, I am a good ser-vant. When I stand in the pulpit and tell the peasants my opinion, then I am a good servant.' By mid afternoon, the party moved to the street. In the barnyard across the way where green nuts dried in the sun he danced, still wearing his dressing gown, sometimes with his wife and sometimes with his sister-in-law. At one point he got two passers-by to hoist him over a wall. Later, they alleged that he had approached them with a club in his hand and forced them to drink, whereupon he threw their glasses over the wall. Back in the parsonage, the Scribenten played a lot of games and broke a lot of plates. Around 11 p.m., the musicians were paid off and left.

In his own defense, Bregenzer admitted that he had invited the Scribent Dilleny and a few friends, the duke's pensioner, Kerner, the cadastre surveyor, Fink, the Substitut, Lutz, and the young merchant, Lutz. He drank brotherhood with them all, giving them offices – Kerner would be his successor and the others, councillors and officials of one sort or another. But he would not admit that he drank with a dry mouth from a glass full of nuts. Asked whether he said, 'Little brothers, kiss my wife', he said that as good friends he had brought all of their heads together with that of his wife. That happened completely with 'theological modesty' and did not mean that he 'prostituted his honorable theological wife as a common slut'. His wife would not have stood for it, especially with the blasphemer Fink. He held Fink for nothing but a 'defiler of the ministry', who had probably written to his brother, a high official, and got this conscience-less, sneaky investigation started. Although Fink had 'carried the skin to the furrier', he would be given over to God and the authorities (Herrschaft) as a blasphemer. Bregenzer refused to make himself party to other people's sins – to their blasphemy. Asked whether he had danced and was merry, Bregenzer wondered with all due 'theological modesty' that such profane natures could think him, Master Bregenzer, so profane as themselves and think him to be equal with their godless natures. The godless, ungrateful cuckoos related the greatest pollutions about him, such godless pipers, drummers, and coarse musicians as were known in the whole district for their excesses and abominations. Indeed it really was true of them, as the *canon diábolus* says, 'dancing is a circle whose center is the devil'. The pastor made it clear that he had protested loudly against such abominations.

The superintendent asked if he had acted in 'Spanish gravity', a reference to his alleged dancing style. He did not know anything about Spanish gravity, which Spanish sins, abominations, and vices the sneaky tattletale must be acquainted with. One knew that the calumniator was the devil as one knew the lion from his claws. Bregenzer referred to his 'theological gravity' and 'humblest modesty', which guaranteed his belief that his guests were honorable people. However, among brothers, a 'Judas brother' was ominously present and blasphemed not only the ministry but also God himself. Such scoundrels would be left to God's judgment at the right time and would be shown to the whole world as a formidable example of how one should treat ministers (*Geistliche*), laymen (*Weltliche*), and women honorably. That Bregenzer allowed his wife and her sister to dance with the Scribenten came only from his calumniators. As for the musicians, he did not know anything about the maid fetching them nor did he invite them into the living room. They were a devil-band and masters of the dance. The blasphemers of God used his expressions blasphemously against God. They were murderers of his soul.

He denied supplying any wine and, in any event, given the fact that there were twenty-one people there, there was not more than a *Mass* (about 1.8 liters) per person. He himself did not drink much. In other parsonages where the pastor was paid partly in wine, there was leaping, dancing, fornication (*huren, buben*), adultery, abortion, and all the sins of abomination. He wondered that his empty barrels made so much noise when others were hushed up. He was quite ready to tell how many whores' children (*Hurenkinder*) and adulterous children – altogether over thirty illegitimate children of ministers – he had reported to the consistory.

He was then asked if he had tricked the maiden daughter of the pastor in Übenhausen into joining the party. It had been reported that he sent for her on the pretense that his wife was dying and wanted her at her deathbed. When she arrived he said to the Scribenten: 'Little brothers, I recommend my cousin to you. Don't do anything dishonorable to her because she is a lovely girl.' He blamed the invitation on his wife's unmarried sister who did it as a joke. As it turned out, his wife was unhappy that there were ill-raised guests in the house. He pointed out that he had had the measles – his soul killers were sick in their souls, he in his body.

Apparently he had been in a great fight with the Scribent Fink. All he said was that he tried to get the musicians to leave five or six times. He sighed to God to give him a sign or clear out the house. He hoped that the blasphemer (*Lästermaul*) would perish. That Fink lay now on his deathbed was to God's praise.[15]

One of the guests at the party, Substitut Lutz, testified that all of the young men had been at matins.[16] The pastor invited one of them to lunch and later came to get them all at the Rathaus when they showed themselves reluctant. Dilleny sent for roast chickens from the inn, and because there were no clean plates, the pastor plunked them on the table. They began to dance with the pastor's sister-in-law while Fink played the harpsichord. After a while, over the pastor's feeble protests, musicians were fetched. During the dance, Bregenzer kept jumping up from his chair and taking a partner and dancing away with her. But he kept returning to his chair. Once he stood still and had his wife dance around him to the laughter and surprise of the crowd. He got everyone to drink brotherhood from a glass of nuts. Lutz was not sure how they got to kissing. The pastor said, 'Little brothers, kiss my wife.' Although the pastor pushed his head, Lutz said that the former could see that he had no desire to do so. She had been sick and looked terrible. The pastor tricked several girls into coming along by telling them his wife was ill. During the party he acted quite familiarly with the musicians, sitting and drinking with them.

Dilleny recounted the altercation with Fink, who had related how a neighboring pastor had given a sermon on the Passion, in which he said that the Jews had not spit normal spit in Christ's face but cleared their throats and spit green mucus (*grüne Dicke*).[17] Bregenzer told Fink not to say any more, for he was making fun of the merit of Christ, which might not be offered him even on his deathbed. Fink said that the other pastor had no scruples about saying it. At that, the pastor got extremely angry and ordered him to leave. Fink laughed and told him not to be a fool, took his coat and left.

There seems to have been a distinct pattern to Pastor Bregenzer's drinking. It was not that it happened so frequently, only that when it did it took a particularly spectacular form. It is not the place here to discuss the nature of drunkenness and what it reveals – the old *in vino veritas* theory or the notion that alcohol breaks down inhibitions to construct relations without the artificial veneer of civilization. It seems that drinking does not lead to any kind of universal behavior but takes place in contexts of specific cultures and societies and follows certain conventions.[18] Here the issue is to examine what people chose to comment on, and what scandalized them, so that we can see a bit more clearly what Pastor Bregenzer was mocking, what social relations he was underlining and, by implication, some of the dynamics of village society.

A recurrent pattern to his drinking seems to have been the erasing of polite distinctions inherent in the formal 'Sie' and the familiar 'Du'. This went together with clinking glasses and swearing 'brotherhood' with those around him. In all the examples so far, this meant crossing boundaries of social hierarchy and age, whether with the noble from Leinzell, the Baron von Closen, or with the various journeymen scribes and notaries living in the village. In each case, the language of kinship was adopted, such as 'brother', 'cousin', or 'brother-in-law'. In one instance, he explicitly denied his clerical status for a time, requesting to be called 'Monsieur'. Despite the foolishness in much of what he was doing, the pattern of establishing the participants for the moment on a footing of equality was the issue. Handing out silly offices seems to be a part of the breaking down of hierarchy by mocking it. Further, certain sexual boundaries and formalities in sharing food were played with. He would grab food with all five fingers instead of the polite three, eat directly from the table, or dip into someone else's bowl. Sometimes, he would conspicuously waste food or property, pouring wine on his drinking companions or breaking glasses. He would suggest the possible impropriety of the occasion by warning the young men to treat the girls with honor, would kiss and embrace men, and call on everyone to kiss his wife. An ultimate moment in the establishment of the mood of equality was the use of improper language: the frequent use of 'fool' and terms such as 'dog's ass', and drinking to each other's 'stinking health'.

If we consider such moments to be transacting something, the problem is to see exactly what. It is useful, although perhaps a little banal, to say that such 'rituals', by reversing everyday distinctions and hierarchies, reinforce them by the very fact of their being extraordinary occasions. However, we ought to take a close look at how they were structured. In every instance, the central character in the drama was Pastor Bregenzer. Criticism was not directed towards the various noblemen; rather Bregenzer either put himself into a position to be ridiculed or crossed boundaries himself, which for those judging the situation was seen as illegitimate. He continually played with his position as clergyman, for example, as at the scandalous party. For instance, he told his guests not to let people think he had sent for the musicians. After all, he could have forbidden them entrance. During the dancing he sat observing as if outside the activity, jumping in to join, and then leaving again. He adopted a dancing style meant to emphasize his position and age, described as 'Spanish gravity', or stood while his wife danced around him. In short, in every instance he was playing with his clerical status, underlining it by playing with the improprieties consonant with his standing or with the specific areas of danger to his soul, calling on the thunder to strike him or joining in the dance of the devil. He positioned himself in the center of the dancing ring and later quoted to the effect that the devil stood at that spot.

Part of the issue is to know just how extraordinary his behavior really was. In Heubach, after all, he was in a genuine struggle over the right to take in the tithe. Those who brought charges were out to show how oddly he acted. But many townspeople noticed nothing strange and said they had only seen him drunk once in the seven years he was pastor there. As we shall see, he was in conflict in Hattenhofen too with the village magistrates. It could be that his drunken behavior, which had occurred twice in two years, was not all that extraordinary, but part of a ritual in which the social distances of the actors and the specific social quality of the clergy were emphasized by coquetry or temporary abolition of rules. Possibly he was just extreme in his behavior under such ritualized conditions. In any event he provided ammunition for his enemies, who used his excesses to good effect against him.

The investigation brought Bregenzer's sense of persecution into the open. He kept associating himself with God in very specific ways. By analogy – Fink, the Judas among the 'brothers' – he put himself in the place of Christ, as the innocent, subject to direct attacks by his enemies, whose evil will was satanic. Bregenzer was convinced that one could read in the events surrounding him an indirect communication from God – the event as sign, readable by the enlightened, the spiritual, those who belonged to God. Towards the end of the party, he waited for a sign from God and considered the fact of Fink's illness as revelation that the latter was the traitor in the midst of friends and blasphemer of God subject to fearful warning. An important aspect of Bregenzer's argument was a distinction between the spiritual and the clerical estates. It was no good calling on the judgment of other clergymen in his case, because many of them were party to a string of sins beginning with dancing and ending with abortion – a demonstration of their lack of 'theological' morality and understanding. There is, then, something of the religious enthusiast in Bregenzer's conception of the world, for he was more-or-less explicitly denying the importance of the community of clerics and stressing the direct relationships to God based on the inspired ability to read the signs. In Heubach, the magistrates made precisely the point that by his typology and interpretation of symbols, he was engaging in dangerous procedures.

With such a notion, he was vying for power by providing a methodological procedure closed to the non-spiritual, whether that was to be understood as clergy versus laymen, or genuine Christians versus hypocrites. Since Bregenzer made such an issue of his clerical status, despite criticism of other clerics, it seems that it was absolutely central for him. In that respect, he was by no means unusual for the pastorate at that time. It was not yet possible for laymen to challenge the spiritual reading of their lives through their own introspective pietist exercises. The power of the clergy lay partly in their ability to read the signs and assign meaning to the everyday experiences in village life. They tried to create an unassailable methodology, clearly differentiated from other ways of wielding power. They could lay out the meaning of a scripture and apply it to the social and political practices of their village, or read the practices themselves as communication from God.[19] Perhaps that was the danger in the challenge offered by Fink, the layman providing interpretation which properly belonged to the clergy. Or it could be that as Bregenzer waited for a sign from God, it came in the way Fink handled the theme of violation of Christ's sacrifice by the spitting Jew, revealing himself as a blasphemer. In any event, the pastor warned him that his salvation was in danger. Clearly Fink had moved on to territory Bregenzer properly considered his own, and since, as was reported, the latter was no longer drunk, he reasserted his authority as pastor and interpreter of the Word and of the actions around him.

> In the investigation, several other charges and accusations were brought against Pastor Bregenzer, many of which turn around the themes of adultery, fornication, and marriage.[20] Johannes Jaus, lawyer in Hattenhofen, testified that about a year before, the pastor, out of boredom, invited him over to the parsonage after vesper services. There he encountered the unmarried servant, Maria Maurrot, who at the time was pregnant. Since she refused to say who the father of her child was, Bregenzer advised her to say it was a soldier.

> Johannes Rindt from Hattenhofen related that a year previously Bregenzer came to his inn in the company of a barber. The pastor began to tease their daughter, suggesting that the barber wanted to marry her. Taking ink and paper, he made out a contract, put their hands together, and poured brandy over them. At the conclusion of this *scena ludicra*, he said they were now half married.

> Anna Maria Gutschneider, eighteen, reported that she had helped prepare flax at the parsonage. Bregenzer invited her upstairs and grabbed at her skirt, but she defended herself and went back to work. Several days later she was delivering nuts at the parsonage when he again grabbed her skirt and put his hands on her breasts. Several days later as she was dropping off some letters, it happened again.

> Christina Übelin, twenty, the daughter of the Schultheiss, related that as she was alone with the pastor in the living room of the parsonage, he took her by the collar, laid his hand on her breast, and reached under her skirt all the way to her vagina. She defended herself as a virgin and as menstruating and ran away. Informing her mother immediately, she did not tell her father until a week before the hearing.

> Barbara Holl, twenty, alleged that in the previous autumn the pastor
> sent for her. He told her that he knew of two marriage prospects for
> her, a widower with five children and a single young man with a
> good property. She should marry the young man. Under the pretense
> that his wife was in the bedroom, he sent her in and then followed
> and put his hands on her breasts. She ran away.

To Jaus' accusation Bregenzer referred to reports he had filed about
Maria Maurrot in which he said that she refused to give the name of the
father. He, however, wrote that he suspected Johannes Übelin as
adulterer. It is not clear from the text who Übelin was, but he carried
the same surname as the Schultheiss and was probably related to him –
perhaps his married son. As for the story of the mock wedding, Bregenzer
said it was just a joke. Anna Maria Gutschneider was put up to her story
by his enemies. She also slandered him because he had sent her drunken
mother away from confession (*Beichtstuhl*) and mentioned a friend of
hers in a witchcraft protocol. As for the Schultheiss's daughter, she had
been raised badly – just like the sons – and he had often had to suffer
with her over her shameful conduct. But because of her good prospects,
he had suggested many good marriage possibilities despite the fact that
her father had said that the fellow who married her would be 'crapped
on' (*beschissen*) because she was of so little use. Bregenzer could attest to
that 'theologically', because of her indocility, ignorance, godlessness,
and disobedience. In fact she already had her belly full *ex praematuro con-
cubitu* and would have to wear the whore's crown of straw at her wedding. He had asked the superintendent to order that the wedding be
delayed until she could recite the catechism and morning and evening
benedictions. That he ever did anything untoward, may God be his
judge. In the presence of his wife and sister-in-law, he had brought all
of their heads together and kissed her but with no serious intent. Barbara
Holl was the granddaughter of the previous pastor, Sartorius, and
brother's daughter of the Schultheiss, and part of the faction that the latter had built up against him. This all came about because the previous
pastor had hushed up cases of witchcraft and sorcery (including milking
cows through the mouth and false lard making) by putting them in the
church consistory protocols instead of reporting to the district officials
as was proper. All of the people involved were still living and had gone
unpunished. Bregenzer had sent the protocols of the church consistory
to the High Council in Stuttgart, and since then those involved had all
become his enemies and said that he was bringing the village into dis-
repute. Instead of the honorable defending themselves honorably, they

feared that other enormities might be discovered. All the witnesses against him were from among the Schultheiss's relatives (*Freundschaft*). Although Bregenzer had performed nothing but good deeds, he was being attacked by Satan's hellish hordes. If he had had evil thoughts concerning Barbara Holl either in the living room or in the bedroom or outside, then he would wish all damnation and punishment to be his lot. He certainly did not touch her with his hands or grab for her breasts, but in fact lectured her, extracting an oath that she would keep herself honorable, avoid whoring young men and not creep off into corners with them.

> Bregenzer wrote a document entitled, 'Protestando contra falsa prae-judicia', in which he lamented the fact that the Schultheiss had taken the affection of the people away from him, although: his son's father-in-law was an adulterer, his brother's son was an adulterer, his wife's sister's husband was an adulterer, his wife's mother was an adulterer, his wife's mother and sister were in the witchcraft protocol: what the Schultheiss is he does not know.

The mixture of accusations and counter-accusations in this set of testimonies all turn around marriage, alliance, family, and sexual activity. Such matters reveal themselves as part of the everyday political life of the village but also as part of the political symbolism, the way enmity, partisanship, and action were organized and given expression. Several of the stories related by the witnesses either turned around marriage negotiations or had them as central elements. Bregenzer had been involved in such arrangements for the daughter and niece of the Schultheiss. Retrospectively, his heavy-handed humor in the mock marriage scene was brought as a charge against him, the ridiculous element deriving from his toying with such central symbols of village life. It seems likely that everyone at the time enjoyed the joke, even if it had a worrying edge to it. But as the story became part of village discourse, it fitted into the central problems of alliance formation, partisan negotiation, and political give-and-take. If one element of Bregenzer's power lay in his ability to publicize the sexual transgressions of the villagers in the church consistory, in preparation for communion, personal counseling, marriage negotiations, gossip, and abuse, then the point of attack from his enemies was directed precisely there. As he flung charges of witchcraft (sexual delicts with the devil), adultery, fornication, and immodesty, they countercharged with accusations of lechery, confusing lines of paternity, mock prostitution of his wife, and meddling with marriage alliances. All of this must be seen in its proper context – the confusion of sexual lines and those of paternity/inheritance were parallel to other social confusions. As Bregenzer said in his testimony, when he came to the village no one wanted to believe what he said about adultery, about the great scandals in the consistory protocols, about the plundering of the tithes, about the wages of the Schultheiss – in fact he threatened not to mount the pulpit again until God gave him a sign regarding the sodomitic abominations in the village.

> The Schultheiss, Johann Jacob Übelin, related how he had invited the pastor and his wife to the parish fête a year before. At the table where the pastor sat with Übelin, the former brought up the matter of the old consistory protocols and said that the pastor from Rosswälden had falsified them. Reluctant to talk about the matter, the Schultheiss thought that the superintendent and Vogt had probably reported the details to Stuttgart, and everyone just had to wait for an order. He accused the pastor of extracting suspicious points and reporting them directly to Stuttgart. Denying it, the pastor said that only a scoundrel would say such a thing; the Schultheiss was a scoundrel, as was the lawyer, Jaus. He attacked the honors of those about him and said many times that 'thunder should strike him, the devil should take him', he would indict the superintendent, the Vogt, and the Schultheiss from the pulpit. Intervening, the Schultheiss's married son suggested letting the old matters rest and instead eating and drinking together, to which the pastor responded by yelling, 'You dog, you lazy slob (*Bernheuter–Bärenhäuter*), you snot-nosed monkey (*Rozaff*), you dumb face (*Loippmaul–Luppelmaul*), you should have your teeth knocked down your throat.' He shook his fist and then took a chair, which he smashed to pieces against a door. The next day, the Schultheiss entered a full room in the inn. He went from table to table drinking from the guests' glasses and having them filled again. Proceeding past Bregenzer he wordlessly tipped his hat. Thereupon, the pastor sent the sacristan to have Übelin bring him some wine, but the latter declined. By custom those already there offered latecomers a glass of wine. Then Bregenzer came to the Schultheiss's table, demanded that they toast each other and clink glasses. When the Schultheiss refused, Bregenzer hit the glasses together so hard that his broke, pouring wine all over the Schultheiss's trousers and jacket. Having another glass brought to him, he forced himself in and sat next to the Schultheiss. Then he tried to kiss him, but Übelin said he did not kiss women let alone men. With a knife in his hand, Bregenzer said if the Schultheiss was

not satisfied with him he should stick it into him, otherwise he would
do it to the Schultheiss. The latter suggested that they were not up to
the point of massacring each other. Bregenzer then stood up and forced
a woman to dance with him and when his own wife came in sat on a
chair in the middle of the room, put a hat on his wife, and had her hop
around him. At one point, he took a chair, smashed it against the
ground, and said, 'a scoundrel says I dance – the chair dances, and my
wife'. He often jumped around dancing, to the scandal of the room.
He finished by emptying a glass of brandy, saying he did not feel well
and had to drink the devil down.[21]

All five of the witnesses called said that there had been so much
whistling and hollering that they had not been able to hear a word.
Bregenzer himself either denied swearing or tried to reinterpret what
he had said. He had not wanted to clink glasses with the Schultheiss, but
rather the glass by itself quite ominously broke apart ('may God be a
witness') so that everyone was amazed at how the bottom simply
dropped out. He thought then that God had to be honored that the bottom fell out, revealing the Schultheiss publicly for what he always was
secretly, namely his enemy. As for kissing the Schultheiss, the latter
rather liked to kiss the pastor's wife from Rosswälden. He called the
Schultheiss 'murderer' and 'soul murderer' for the story of the knife
and called on him to take a physical oath. He himself had criticized
everyone for dancing with coarse jumping about and showed them how
to do it in a seemly fashion.

> Pastor Bregenzer composed a document with a short parable
> followed by a diatribe against his 'forty-nine persecutors'. There
> were once three Bürgermeister who greatly offended the clergy and
> curers of souls, but God punished them. The first was knifed when he
> was drunk and did not have a chance to say, 'miserere mei deus'. The
> second became blind, deaf, and dumb and could not read, hear, or
> speak. The third went mad, raging like a dog, and could no longer
> understand God's word. All three deserved punishment from God.
> There is no more dangerous wound than the one that cannot be felt.
> Among his forty-nine persecutors, the first was the mid-wife who, as
> was well-known, tried to kill him. That was prompted by Satan, the
> original child murderer. In his student years, two persecutors were
> Pistor and Sigel – Pistor became a hussar and Sigel seduced the
> shoemaker Birenmann's wife into adultery. He eventually became a
> Catholic and apostatized. Others also became apostates, and the
> superintendent in Heidenheim, an adulterer. In Grünbach, his first
> pastorate, the Heiligenpfleger was bitten by a mad dog and his family

was reduced to poverty. In Heubach, the Heiligenpfleger absconded with 206 fl., and a whole list of others stole grain. One man had to be exiled for sodomy, and both of the Vögte got palsy.[22]

In the autumn of 1705, Bregenzer apparently was drunk again on the open street in Göppingen with the Scribent Löhr and the bookbinder Frank, two of his former pupils.[23] Frank testified that as he entered the inn the pastor was already with Löhr and not behaving 'theologically'. A Catholic peasant sitting at a nearby table was laughing at him. Late in the afternoon, he embraced the barber and kissed him. Another witness said he met the barber again and kissed him a second time, and then he played with his dog as if it could understand French. A flock of laughing children followed him up the street. At the well, he drew a circle on the ground around the barber and told him that if he stepped over, the devil would fetch him. To all of this, all Bregenzer would say was that Frank proved himself a bookbinder and not a book reader. He belonged to the 'ninety-nine'. Playing on Löhr's name, he said he was empty (*leer*) of reason. All of his adversaries were empty of honor and teaching (*leer an ehr und Lehr*) and good conscience, empty of God's honor (*leer an Gottes ehr*), empty of salvation, as blind and as hardened as his predecessor Sartorius (previous pastor in Hattenhofen), empty of teaching (*leer an der Lehr*) but full of damnation.

> During the previous May, Bregenzer was with a furrier and his wife in an inn in Oberbergheim. A servant girl saw the pastor kiss the woman several times. If it did happen, alleged Bregenzer, then because she was a relative it probably happened in *charitas*. As they parted, he joked close to her face: his whole life long he had always heard that women with red hair had very white skin on their bodies, and it would be a shame if she had club feet. She replied that she would not want to go alone with him over the field. He protested that she was afraid to show her feet. The woman herself could not remember if Bregenzer kissed her; certainly there had been no improper behavior. He said to her: 'Red haired people normally have white bodies if they do not have club feet stuck in their ass.' Bregenzer testified that the kind of kiss he gave his 'cousin' was the kind he would not be ashamed to give to the wife of the court preacher. He had held a discourse over red hair and talked ironically about club feet but did not say her club feet were stuck in her ass.[24]

Bregenzer tended to play all sides of his spiritual power. He sprinkled his conversation with such phrases as 'God be my witness', 'God preserve us', and read the signs as direct revelations from God. He was able to show that all of his enemies in one way or another were sealed and revealed as the devil's. He was able to call on God to deal with his persecutors, revenge according to his parable coming in the form of an attack on their ability to speak or hear the truth, the sudden death making repentance impossible at the last moment. He called on them to take a physical oath, which would put their souls in direct danger, and he himself pointed to his attackers as 'murderers of his soul'. But at the same time, Bregenzer played with the darker, more dangerous side of power. He frequently challenged the thunder to strike him or the devil to take him and even chased the latter down with a gulp of brandy. In such actions as drawing a circle around his companion and warning him that to step outside would bring the devil, he toyed with the unease in the culture and suggested that those in the power sphere of the spiritual had more forces than commonly acknowledged. And in his joking relationship with his 'cousin', again the play on magic and witchcraft was suggested. It was a common idea that red hair and witchcraft were associated, and one of the chief physical characteristics of the devil was his club feet.

> When Bregenzer first took over his pastorate in Hattenhofen, he sent a memorandum, a *vitae curriculum*, to the pastor in Göppingen. It contained an outline of his biography. He was born on 28 March 1656 in Göppingen where his father, Petrus, was pastor. His mother, a daughter of a pastor in Besigheim, was worth 4000 fl. In 1665 he went to Cannstatt to the Latin school. While he was there, his mother died and his father married again. His step-mother was able to steal the inheritance from his mother and give it to her children – as a dowry for his step-sister and an apprenticeship for his step-brother. He was able to get a 50 fl. stipend to study, but the capital was largely used up by his step-mother. With the remainder, she purchased a vineyard for his step-sister, which a cloudburst washed away, a revelation of God's revenge. No one helped him to obtain his rights.
>
> In 1670, he went to Kloster Hirsau and a year later to Tübingen to study. In 1681, when he was preceptor in Neuenstadt, his step-mother was still cheating him over his stipend. In 1683, he married, an act which displeased the superintendent, who wanted him to marry his wife's sister's daughter. As a result the superintendent became his persecutor. To spite him, Bregenzer sought a job elsewhere and was first in Cannstatt (1683), a year later in Waiblingen, and the next year in Dornstetten. In 1689, he became pastor in Grünbach in the district of Wildberg. Following that, he

was from 1691 to 1698 in Heubach. For over a year, he received no salary, but he defended himself vigorously and brought many delicts to light. For a year (1698–9) he was in Pflugfelden but was fired because of the adulterer and traitor, Stock. He and his Heubach and Pflugfelden supporters all prayed for Stock's death, and because God heard their prayer, he sent alms to the consistory for the poor. In 1704, he got a pastorate in Hattenhofen where he again expected to be thrown out.[25]

The superintendent in Göppingen sent in a summary report together with all of the testimony.[26] Since Bregenzer had been in Hattenhofen, he had shown himself to be quarrelsome and turbulent in the public sphere (*rei publicae*). He had piled up debts and managed his own financial affairs badly. He treated everyone as adversaries and devilish calumniators. He himself predicted he would be thrown out of office. He told the chief peace officer in Göppingen that he wanted to scandalize all of the magistrates in the city and district of Göppingen so that all the children and their children would talk about him for years to come.

By the end of February 1706, the High Council gave its judgment.[27] Bregenzer was often totally drunk. He was quarrelsome and called people 'dog' and 'scoundrel'. He had drunk brotherhood with Scribenten and servants, hollered, yelled, slandered, and rioted. He was violent, fell down stairs, and cursed. He kissed young women, touched their breasts, and reached under their skirts. He was called 'fool' and 'pig' (*Saumag*) by servants. Often he was not completely sane. He offered to let the Scribenten kiss his wife and her sister. He was familiar with musicians in the parsonage. He kissed men and often danced foolishly. He called the consistory protocols a 'book of scoundrels' and called people 'witches', 'adulterers' and 'fornicators', and sent people from confession. Because he had no money to support such a punishment, he was not to be put into prison but exiled. By 1710, he petitioned to become pastor in Heubach again now that the new pastor was dead, but was refused.[28] According to the records he again got a Württemberg pastorate – in Truchtelfingen from 1712 to 1718.

The story of Georg Bregenzer offers a number of leads to a number of problems. Each reader will have his own reaction to that more-or-less complicated, difficult, and angry man, but I suspect that most will side in the end with the magistrates. They were saner, more reasonable, more embedded in the realities of practical life. Although they feathered their nests and looked out for their own interests, they more-or-less fit into the mores of their time. Bregenzer was too much of a *Querkopf* to offer the historian of popular resistance much solace – he never questioned the structure of authority, led a revolt, or organized any kind of recognizable protest. Still there is a great deal of appeal in his extremeness, in his inability to stop when it was good for him, and in his sheer desire to go out making a racket.

It is always difficult for the historian of popular culture to assess the meaning of a career like that of Bregenzer's. He was not a popular preacher who spoke to crowds or wrote tracts distributed in their thousands to the faithful. He was just a pastor in a few villages and towns, none of which was larger than 600 or 700 people. He may have gained a little regional notoriety for a time, but that just provided some interesting gossip and scandalous material for good stories. It is also not very helpful to ask about whether Bregenzer was really representative. If some contemporaries thought he was crazy and if I have chosen the term 'paranoia' for alliterative effect in the title of this chapter, that still does not tell us which aspects of his behavior distorted reality. He may have made people particularly uneasy precisely where he revealed the most about well-established structures of power and authority. Yet it still seems far-fetched to expect much from Bregenzer as a demystifier. Perhaps we can learn most from him by seeking to understand the metaphors by which he sought to grasp his reality. His peculiar logic was constructed from elements common to his society, and however distorted his lens might have been, he was still looking at the same things as his contemporaries.

Among the issues presented by Bregenzer's life, there are some insights into the problem of the formation of political consciousness: the sense of shared interests, the conception of practical performance, the experience of concerted action. In its simplest form, the problem has to do with how people explain to themselves the things that happen to them and what particular constellation of forces are thought to be present in action. To begin with, Bregenzer never sought for his own destiny inside his own personality, moral capacities, or character. The exercise of spiritual introspection which characterized Protestantism in the eighteenth and nineteenth centuries was not part of Bregenzer's religious practice nor that of his parishioners.[29] Such exercises radically individualize personal destiny and make it difficult to imagine a nexus between structures – whether economic, social, or political – and the person.[30] The battle is within, the successes and failures in this world

radically tied to the relative ability of a subject to divine his own character and take steps to remove the stumbling blocks to his enlightenment,
improvement, or sanctification.

Bregenzer provides an example where the explanation for events lies
outside the person. It is not a question, perhaps, of the logic of everyday
events, the ordinary chain of cause and effect. Rather, there were basic
turning points and general trends for which meaning was sought outside
the individual and his moral capacities. In this instance as well, no
interest was shown in the general structure of economic facts or change.
Nor did Bregenzer invest much energy in explaining the conditions of
Herrschaft as a system of exploitation. Rather the individual was caught
in a web of kinship relationships and a world of partisanship largely
congruent with the dynamics of interfamilial rivalries. In his
autobiographical sketch, he showed the keenest interests in the internal
workings of his own family, the crucial pivot of which was inheritance.
Not surprisingly, the specific point from which aggression was to be
feared was the step-mother, who posed a threat to the dowry which his
own mother had brought with her into her marriage. From the outset,
Bregenzer was centrally concerned with the distribution of rights
following from the rules of marriage alliance and the lines of
succession.

In the autobiography, the other side to family and alliance emerged
as well, not the internal tensions and conflicts but the formation of
interest groups and coordinated kin networks. In his refusal to follow
the superintendent's wishes to marry one of the latter's relatives lay the
conflict between them. Since he did not become part of that network,
he could only expect aggression, a struggle for scarce resources, and
'persecution'. In Bregenzer's construction of the world, family group
stood against family group, and when some issue arose over which they
might enter into struggle, they became 'enemies'. Nothing could be
more natural than to expect persecution from the other side. In
Hattenhofen, he found that the Schultheiss coordinated various relatives (his *Freundschaft*), some of whom had been affected by the pastor's
zeal in ferreting out witchcraft and the like, in a concerted effort to
break his power in the village. In one way or other, one central
framework for Bregenzer's thinking was constructed from family
dynamics, interfamilial feuding, and partisanship. What happened to
the individual came about in the ever continuing pitting of will against
will and person against person. God was of course part of the drama but

was never independent, never really subject to His own will, never outside the history of the direct personal confrontations involved in
village life.

As his central political metaphor, Bregenzer took up the charge of
'adultery', which in essence is a charge of illegitimate paternity and
false alliance. The personal force of the image was buried in his own
biography, the robbery of his inheritance, the decision to reject a proffered marriage alliance. But the image goes far deeper than Bregenzer's
psyche, and one can see in the counter-attack of the Hattenhofen magisterial clique charges which led to the same thing – adultery, *mésalliance*,
and scrambled lines of paternity. In fact, the air seemed to be charged
with sexuality. In the way the metaphor became so central, there seems
to be a problem because from everything we know in the now considerable literature on illegitimacy, there was at that period little premarital
practice of sexuality that led to conception, despite the examples
alleged by Bregenzer.[31] It seems unlikely that restraint before marriage
gave way to a flood of free floating sexual practice once nuptials took
place. Leaving aside the problem of the nature of sexuality for the
moment, the question still remains why adultery should have been such
a central concern and attained such symbolic value in the sixteenth and
seventeenth centuries. Later on in the eighteenth century, when a real
rise in premarital sex and illegitimate births can be demonstrated and
when, if ever, extramarital sex might have been on the rise, the abusive
term, *Ehebrecher*, lost all its force. The clue to the symbolic value of
'adulterer' lies in the concern for family politics, the understanding that
the person was not divorceable from the family of which he was a part.
But it is also at this point that the early modern state entered into the
lives of its subjects.[32] A large part of law-giving and codification of law
at that time was concerned with inheritance and the nature of the family
estate or 'marital fund'. The great series of French provincial law codes,
concerned almost with no other problem than family property and its
devolution, were all published in the second half of the sixteenth
century.[33] And in Germany, as well, the smoothing out of regional differences, codification, and continual innovation in family law took
place at the same time.[34] In every Württemberg parish and village, the
long series of documents concerned with marriages, births, and deaths,
marriage inventories, *post mortem* inventories, and land sales, going back
deep into the sixteenth and seventeenth centuries, attest to the intense
concern of the state with the family holding of property. As far as the

state was concerned, the issue was a clear and unambiguous tax responsibility based on viable farms. It therefore reached its rational hand into the core of family interest.

'Adulterer' as a symbol of political life took its force from the penetration of the state into the family, the intense rivalry of coordinated kinship networks, and the inflection of individual interest with the dynamics of family life. Freund and Feind – friend and enemy – defined the parameters in which one lived; 'friend' was not distinguished from family and 'enemy' was subject to all kinds of abominations.

In Bregenzer's perception of the dynamics of society as composed of competing groups and individual strategies of aggrandizement, there seems to be no room for self-criticism. Just as in power struggles centered on witchcraft and sorcery, where it is usual to be able to point to the witch or the sorcerer but impossible for the sorcerer himself to admit that he or she had the alleged power,[35] so Bregenzer could locate persecutors and enemies but not perceive himself as such. Aggression belongs to the person who is trying to take away rights or destroy reputation, but there was no perception of his own activity as the pendant to that imputed to others. By associating himself with God, the boundary between praying and cursing was erased. Even if he had conceived of himself as surrounded by enemies, he could have prayed for protection without supplying God with specifics and names. To move over to naming the enemy already comes close to exorcism, but to call down the judgment of God is not distinguishable from seeking a person's damnation. In practical life, Bregenzer, like many a peasant, surrounded himself with powerful forces to counter the attacks of the envious and ill-willed. Everyday life was a continual struggle, with reputation, respect, and material well-being at issue. Fearing the illegitimate and nefarious attacks of adversaries in league with powerful forces, one publicly secured one's own position by unmasking the culprits, labeling their behavior, exposing oneself to danger by swearing, and sapping the other's strength by 'recommending' him to God.

Just as a person's destiny was tied to familial politics and not so much to internal personal capacities, so one read not internal but external signs. There was no communication from God directly, no inner light – in this Bregenzer was a completely orthodox Lutheran. The signs lay about in the external world, in illness, a storm, a broken glass, adultery, or palsy. Here an important shift had taken place in the notion that the external world was significant in that respect. No longer was the revelation of God tied to the Word alone as it had been for the Reformation. As the early reformers saw it, the discourse on the Word, either in terms of the group responsible for studying and teaching it or in terms of those assembled together to hear it, was above all an act of community. Their faith lay in the working of God inside the hearers of the Word and partakers of the sacraments – which in turn were subsumed under the Word – that is, in the construction of the *communio sanctorum*. When the world becomes significant, however, the Word becomes significant in another way. Bregenzer drew far-fetched types from the Bible – which made some of his hearers uneasy – and that was part of his methodology of locating meaning in the occurrences around him. A case in point is the sermon he held in Heubach at the occasion of a shooting match.[36] He found correspondences between the Trinity and the three steps which a marksman was supposed to take after each shot. He also drew an analogy between the Lamb of God and the marksman's prize of a sheep covered in red satin. The whole contest to determine who was the best shot was seen as corresponding to the dispute among the disciples as to who was to be the chief among them. Christ was the *Oberschützen-meister* – the referee. Just as the marksmen sat together to eat and drink, judging one another's prowess, so in heaven there is conviviality and judgment over the twelve tribes of Israel.

To understand the context in which this way of thinking was developed, we have to take note of some of the theological trends of the seventeenth century. Bregenzer was very much an orthodox Lutheran, but was concerned like many of the theologians and pastors of the time with the problem of the connection of right belief to Christian living. One of the people he most admired was Johannes Arndt, whose popular devotional work, *Vom wahren Christenhum*, achieved wide circulation, but who was thought by many orthodox ministers to be 'enthusiastic' (*schwärmerisch*) – informed by a fanatical, sectarian spirit.[37] Both Arndt and Bregenzer centered their theology on remorse and repentance and sought to develop a notion of the living word, which would generate the proper internal change, as against the dead letter. They were still orthodox Lutheran in the way they considered grace to be God's work and man's nature to be totally corrupted with sin. God's grace was necessary to lead sinners to inner repentance. Arndt wrote against the impenitent who confessed Christ with the mouth but who lived an unchristian life.[38] It was not enough to believe in Christ, but one had to be penitent from the innermost ground of the heart.[39] Bregenzer in his *Apologia* said that the greatest failure of Christianity compared with other religions was that most teachers taught according to the external letter and the external man, but gave no insight into grace and the battle of the spirit against the flesh. He was a 'doctor of souls', not a 'soup preacher' (*Suppenprediger*), and he considered it his task to warn his parishioners against the fires of hell.

This notion of the dead letter and the living appropriation of the Word in faith and spirit was central to both Bregenzer and Arndt.[40] True faith was intimately tied up with penance and conversion.[41] One had to die to sin in order to be considered a Christian, and that was something which did not happen often.[42] Bregenzer argued that most of the preachers who preached reconciliation did so with unreconciled hearts. He considered only people who did good works and practiced virtue to have true faith. For him, it was improper to allow those who were not reconciled with their neighbors to take communion.[43] One of the papers included in the Bregenzer dossier was a set of notes he had taken from the theologian Josua Stegmann.[44] Stegmann encouraged pastors to consider how they could impart the living power of faith to their hearers. Preaching was not for consolation but for awakening remorse. There should be more 'thunder and lightning' than 'water and air'. Above all, parishioners should be reminded of their sins before the Lord's Supper, because if they did not partake in repentance and remorse, the bread of life would become their bread of death.

Closely related to the notion of the Word as internal and tied up with action rather than just belief was a departure in hermeneutics. Arndt said that everything that is external in the Word should happen in men through spirit and faith. For example, the story of Cain and Abel is something that one finds in oneself – the battle of the old man against the new, the flesh against the spirit. The flood has to be in the Christian and drown out the corruption of the flesh. Just as Abraham fought against five kings, so the Christian fights against the five kings in himself – flesh, world, death, devil, and sin. God established the whole Bible in spirit and faith and everything has to happen spiritually in the Christian.[45] Arndt gave a 'spiritual' reading not only to the Bible but to nature as well. For example, in a long passage on the character of the ocean, he drew a set of spiritual meanings, which were not just analogies, but in the spiritual structure of nature itself. The world and life are like a wild sea. Just as the ocean is never still so the life of the Christian is subject to frequent storms. As sweet water runs into the sea and becomes bitter and unpalatable, so all the sweet things of life flow into an ocean of disappointment. The sea always throws up bodies, and the world will eventually spit us out. As deep as the ocean, so deep is our wretchedness.[46]

This way of dealing with scripture and nature involves a method of interpretation called typology, but of a kind which departs from its use in the Bible and the greater restraint of the Reformation.[47] The basic procedure is to find a likeness in two separate facts or events, and to treat the one as prefiguring the other or grasping its essential nature. It is more than just analogy, in that the meaning of the prototype is really and prophetically in the original event or person. For example, many different types were drawn in the New Testament from the Old Testament. Baptism was seen as corresponding to the flood – just as eight people were saved by water, so now water saves the Christian (I Peter 3.21–2). Adam was seen as a type of Christ – as sin and death came into the world through one man, so they were abolished by one person (Romans 5.12–17). Or 'as Moses lifted up the serpent in the wilderness, so must the son of man be lifted up' (John 3.14). In general, the structure of the story provides the correspondence in typology. It is different from allegory, where the deeper meaning is found in the story itself, or from prophecy, which sees a fulfillment rather than a repetition.[48] There is much that can be said about the history of biblical interpretation and homiletical practices here, but for our purposes a few points need to be stressed. Luther saw the prime meaning of the Word in the literal sense and suggested that all prophetic meaning in the Bible should be strictly subjected to its discipline and, furthermore, that all prophetic meanings were to be derived from the central facts of the incarnation, sacrifice, and resurrection of Christ.[49] With Arndt and Bregenzer, there was a shifting away from the objective interpretation inside the Bible to a widespread finding of correspondences between scripture and life, and between nature – under scriptural interpretation – and life. Such a way of interpreting the 'text' was radically individualizing because the text was no longer discreet. It either expanded outwards to cover the world or inwards to develop symbolic meaning directly connected to current happenings. This kind of explosion of metaphor at once breaks community and reintegrates it at another level. Meaning becomes subject to radical partisan interpretation, and the community of the Word alters to become based on competing patterns of interpretation of external signs. On the other hand, rival groups attain tighter integration in the strengthening of partisanship through a more fractionalized symbolic structure.

In Bregenzer, we have one concrete example of the way the mediation of Christian texts, everyday life, conflicting senses of the person, and different interpretations of the structures of Herrschaft took place. He provides an insight into the process of centering explanation for personal and collective destiny on the internal rivalries of town and village. As long as people personalized the forces in which they were caught, then 'envy and hate' were better tools to think with than failures in their own characters or abstract forces of the economy. Attention to the evil intent of neighbors or relatives could shift the glance away from the system of domination from the outside, the requirement to pay the tithe, the organization of the money market, or exactions to support the military apparatus.

A further dimension to Bregenzer's thinking had to do with the dichotomy between the spiritual and the temporal, the relative value of each, and the way they were connected to each other. In some way, those who lived in the realm of the spiritual were powerless in a direct way in the temporal order. Spiritual enemies could attack each other in the realm of the spirit, but the spiritual were above all subject to attacks by the worldly. In part this was due to the aggressive behavior against the children of God by the devil, who began particularly early with Bregenzer. The problem lay in the means of counter-attack. All that the spiritual could do was expose the wicked, call attention to their sins, bring adversaries who practiced their hatred in secret to public attention. None of this was conceived of in terms of practical activity – as a counter-attack in the political and social theater. Exposure of this kind was meant formally to induce conviction of sin and to bring about penance. But real revenge and punishment of wrongdoers belonged to God, who heard the prayers of the godly and brought storms, palsy, and death. Bregenzer's fundamental despair for this-worldly justice was expressed in his thought that no one had helped him to obtain his rights. Despite his orthodoxy, most of his discussions about the spiritual and temporal remained at the level of the clergy and magistrates, and there was no general appeal to or acknowledgment of a community of saints. In some way, his struggle was that between two estates in the general apparatus of Herrschaft, with the village Gemeinde always as an appendage to one side or the other. Nonetheless, his kind of thinking was another link in the transmission of the notion of a gulf between the two realms, together with a consequent negative judgment on the world of the 'flesh'. The ability to judge and to read the signs remained with those in the spiritual realm, but the alienation with the other was more-or-less complete. The values in the one were not transmissible to the other and no vision of a corrective cooperation was possible. Pietists were aware of Herrschaft as arbitrary, cruel, heedless, and wasteful – as in and for itself without any legitimacy other than God's toleration. One day it would be all set to right, but meanwhile one could see the hand of God in the death of this or that ruler, in the sickness of this or that Vogt, Amtmann, or Schultheiss, in military disaster, epidemics, or harvest failure. The pietist way of determining and reading texts is the reverse side of their sense of being powerless vis-à-vis political authority. It echoes their despair.

It is, of course, not necessary at all that a world-view be consistent. Much depends on the level on which one is operating. It is possible in general to see the problems of the time as the result of corrupt officials, illegitimate violence, or wasteful court life and at the same time to find the explanation for personal destiny or failure in the hatred of one's enemies, whose attacks can take various forms, from cheating and slander to witchcraft and sorcery. Given this way of dealing with reality, solidarity with one's fellows extends only so far as it is a question of excluding the outsider, but a practical plan of action based on a perception of a link between events in the everyday life of the village and more inclusive political and social structures remains elusive.

5

The conscience of the poor:
A village detective story (1733–43)

Simeon and Levi are brothers;
weapons of violence are their swords.
O my soul, come not into their council;
O my spirit, be not joined to their company;
for in their anger they slay men,
and in their wantonness they hamstring oxen.
Cursed be their anger, for it is fierce;
and their wrath, for it is cruel!

Gen. 49.5–7

The Lord is a jealous God and avenging,
the Lord is avenging and wrathful;
the Lord takes vengeance on his adversaries
and keeps wrath for his enemies.
The Lord is slow to anger and of great might,
and the Lord will by no means clear the guilty.

Nahum 1.2–3

Dramatis personae

Vogt Wippermann – lazy chief magistrate in Kirchheim unter Teck; led the
    cover-up
The Superintendent – supported the secular officials
Friederich Wilhelm Breuninger – pastor, alchemist, and lecher; the victim of foul
    play?
Jacob Ochsenwadel – Schultheiss, part of a plot?
Hans Jerg Weber – Bürgermeister, broke the silence
Hans Jerg Drohmann – brutal, successful, diligent; a killer?
Michael Drohmann – his brother and accomplice, a profaner of the sabbath
Hans Jerg Bauer – drinker, gambler, biblical student, and man of conscience;
    the source of accusation

144

Matthes Plessing – blasphemer and rumor-monger; in collusion with Hans Jerg Bauer

Jacob Bauer – counterfeiter and convict; crony of Plessing and Hans Jerg Bauer

Pastor Mauchard – stage-managed the attack on the Drohmann faction; feared becoming the next victim

Georgii – *Vogt from Urach*, investigator and prosecutor, sought revenge

Hans Jerg Lutz, Jr – well-to-do; a link between gossip and accusation

Jacob Geiger – 'friend' of Hans Jerg Drohmann; told his sister to drop dead

Dorothea Geiger – his wife; broke family solidarity over a will

Hans Jerg Mayer, Sr – helped draw up the will

Hans Jerg Mayer, Senninger – heard nothing

Johannes Geiger – beaten bloody by his son-in-law, Hans Jerg Drohmann, with whom he always got along

Adam Geiger – pubkeeper; his deceased nephew, Hans Jerg Geiger, accused the Drohmanns

Friederich Drohmann – carried on the family affairs

Michel Authaler – dealer in butter; met Hans Jerg Drohmann on the way

Hans Jerg Renz – had a fading memory

Ursula Renz – tippler, enemy of Ochsenwadel; cleared her conscience

Michael Bauer – superstitious windbag, thrifty, and honest; met Michael Drohmann near the scene of the crime

Frau Renz – organist; object of Christian love

Schultheiss Greiner – part of the cover-up

In this chapter, we will relate the story of an investigation into the murder of a village pastor.[1] It will allow us to take a close look at the way village political life was structured in the second quarter of the eighteenth century and will provide some insights into how local life was connected with the wider set of state institutions. Because the list of characters in village dramas tend to be the same from the sixteenth to the nineteenth century, namely the village Schultheiss, Bürgermeister, Richter, pastor, peasant, vintner, artisan, laborer, the regional official – the Vogt, the superintendent – or the central representatives of Herrschaft, such as the commissioner, ducal counsellor, or consistory member, there is the danger of generalizing too soon from one case or period to the others. When motives or power relations are under consideration, it is easy to reduce a conflict to the simplest generalizations about needs, power drives, and inconsistencies in social structure. But if notions such as Herrschaft and domination are to have analytical usefulness, they must be able to deal successfully with the issue of time and the historical discipline of context.

If we just take the officials of Herrschaft, who appear most frequently, for example the Vogt and the Schultheiss, superintendent and pastor, we see that their relationships are constantly shifting. A Vogt, for example, long in office might get used to dealing with a particular Schultheiss. A change of personnel could significantly affect the relative success which direct complaints from villagers at the Vogt's office could have. In a period when official ideology was concerned with the good householder, or the economy of the viable farm, the Schultheiss's own wealth and the assessment of other villagers in terms of their property or working habits would weigh heavily in his assessment. In some periods, there can be a shift in ideology and thus in political argument with no social change, or there can be significant changes in the composition of society which call for subtle or not so subtle changes in symbolic language. A change in theological fashion or modes of reasoning can bring significant shifts in the people susceptible to a message, and the message in turn will be received in a specific social context and make up part of the elements of that context. As the message changes then so too does the relationship of the pastor with his audience and therefore with coordinating or competing authorities. In addition, the various officials and kinds of officials can be unified with regard to one thing and at odds with regard to another.

Sometimes the analysis of political relations among elites resolves itself into issues of personality and fashion. A particular pastor may be overwhelmingly concerned with one issue, just as an age can provide particular focal points of interest. Audience response is important, and one problem is to see how the peculiarities are part of a continuing process, for the disappearance of an issue may be linked to a changed language for discussing it, its suppression from public discourse, or from the fact that it was symbolic for another problem, and another symbol has taken its place. It may be that a local pastor attacks surface abuses and leaves the foundation alone. Sometimes behavior is the chief concern of pastoral care, while at other times it is suffering. Indeed the very ability to make certain kinds of connections is learned and changes significantly with time.

All these considerations are part of the problem of sources. They arise particularly when the historian tries to be specific about context, to understand how events, issues, and struggles were experienced, to consider the dialectic between external reality and the notions which people had to grasp that reality with. They arise also when one tries to see history as a continuing, changing process. For example, the way a society 'maps' the person or takes a fix on community will vary according to family structure, social class, and cultural discourse. Such are the issues that we want to take up in this chapter. We want to investigate a rather modest difference in the way people talked about conscience and a peculiarity in the way they described relatives. We want to show how changes in village social structure fit these conceptual items and how the latter were part of concrete social learning experience.

On 9 May 1733, the two chief officials of the town of Kirchheim unter Teck, the Vogt and superintendent, reported to the Württemberg duke that the pastor of the parish of Zell unter Aichelberg had died suddenly on his way home from a theological disputation, which had been held in the district town of Kirchheim.[2] He had apparently stopped for a rest by a stream not far from his village, and overcome by the heat had fainted – as had happened to him on several occasions before. He fell into the brook and was found there dead the next morning. The officials wanted to know whether they should proceed with a regular autopsy and requested a rather prompt answer, since due to the summer heat the body was rapidly decaying.

Appended to the report were a few details about the dead pastor – Friederich Wilhelm Breuninger. In Zell almost eight years, the forty-two-year-old man left behind four sons and three daughters, a pregnant widow, and a great many debts. The parish, composed of four hamlets, had a population of 757 inhabitants. In a final note, it was mentioned that the pastor had been in conflict with the community, but with this appendix, the matter rested. The officials had taken pains to suggest that Breuninger had been unwell. His problems with the villagers were not linked in the text directly with his death.

> Ten years later the same Vogt reported to the duke a second time about the matter.[3] At his annual court in the village, the forty-nine-year-old Schultheiss, Jacob Ochsenwadel, reported that several people had informed him that Pastor Breuninger had been murdered. One of the informants was Hans Jerg Weber, Bürgermeister in Pliensbach. At the same court session, two brothers, Hans Jerg and Michael Drohmann from the hamlet of Aichelberg, complained that several 'debauched and malicious' people had spread the godless gossip (*Geschwätz und Plauderei*) that the two brothers had murdered the pastor. Various people said that if the brothers were innocent they would have to 'demand proof or satisfaction'.

The term used by both of the Drohmann brothers – *Geschwätz* or gossip – refers to the kind of information that circulated in a village that one did not have to take seriously as long as it remained mere 'gossip'. Sometimes the term was denigrated one notch by calling it 'female gossip' – *Weibergeschwätz*. It was clear from the reports that the gossip had been around for a long time. Something had brought matters to a head and prompted several people to report all on the same day information that had been known about or discussed among villagers for quite some time. At one point a letter about the affair had even been read from the pulpit but had not brought forth any kind of an official report.

One accuser had tried to raise the issue above gossip by suggesting that the Drohmann brothers ought to take anyone to court for defamation who accused them. In fact, this kind of thing was a common mechanism in village life, for people held anyone guilty who did not seek 'satisfaction' for libel before the court.[4] In the everyday play of power, it was usual to allude to delicts in some sort of a veiled way – or directly if the accuser felt sure enough of his grounds. The accused either had to take the verbal abuse or demand that the opponent make clear his accusation. With such clarity (before witnesses), the offended party would then demand before the court that the accuser either produce evidence of his accusation or provide satisfaction – which most often involved a fine and an apology. Even when the offended party had committed a particular offense, it was up to the accuser to provide sufficient evidence. In a round of gossip, a particular target of abuse had only to find someone whom he could prove had made an allegation. This person in turn either had to reveal his source before the court or provide the necessary evidence or satisfaction.[5] Nonetheless, the expression 'gossip' offered a gray area, for no one had to take offense at something so trivial. This was the point of the Drohmanns' choice of the term. They had not been required to seek satisfaction before the court for gossip – that is, not required according to the rules of public opinion. But the problem was whether only gossip or something more serious was at issue. One of the villagers was challenging them by his demand that the brothers seek satisfaction. He was also suggesting in his testimony to the Vogt that the matter was one of village *knowledge*, as would soon be discovered if the corporate body was examined one by one. But in his report, the Vogt gave his opinion that the whole matter was one of silly gossip (*Plauderei*) started by godless and wicked people.

Appended to the report were two documents, which help set up some of the issues. First, was the report by the village Schultheiss to the Vogt's court (Vogtruggericht), in which he referred to the rumor going around, using the word *Geschrei*.[6] It is important to distinguish this term from *Geschwätz*. As soon as the information circulating in the village rose above common gossip and became 'rumor', it was a matter for action, and the Schultheiss could not avoid reporting it to the higher authorities. What in his eyes made it Geschrei was the fact that the Bürgermeister in one hamlet and a substantial landowner in another had reported the matter to him. The Drohmanns, however, continued to use the word Geschwätz and to refer to the anonymity of the round of gossip.

> A second document lists the various actors in the drama, giving their 'wealth' and an opportunity for the officials to offer hints as to their characters. The chief author of the round of gossip was an inhabitant of Aichelberg called Hans Jerg Bauer. He was characterized as a poor householder (*Haushalter*), who while heavily drinking had once gambled away a cow. He let his *Haushaltung* go, and his property was constantly diminishing. Matthes Plessing, a blacksmith, the second key link in the rumor-mongering, had been sent to prison fifteen years previously as a bad Haushalter. Another rumor-monger, Jacob Bauer, a wheelwright, had been tied up with a counterfeiter and ended up in jail for three years, subsequently going bankrupt. He was a poor Haushalter and worth nothing. Those were the people on one side. On the other were the subjects of the gossip. Hans Jerg Drohmann from Aichelberg could only have one negative thing said about him and that was that he sometimes ran around with Hans Jerg Bauer. He was a good Haushalter – sometimes fresh with his advice – and had a substantial property. His brother Michael, worth even more, had never acted with impropriety or been punished.

In this manner, the officials – the Schultheiss, the Vogt, and the local Richter – set up the sides in the case. On the one hand were jailbirds, gamblers, drinkers, coiners, bankrupts, and poor householders. Such people had been circulating gossip out of evil will, godlessness, dissolution, and perhaps envy. Both the nature of the activity and the nature of those carrying it on were not worthy of comment. Their gossip had been part of an underground struggle within the village, known to everyone but not yet in the public domain, not subject to official report. Something had happened to raise the matter to the level of the village public, yet all the officials seemed to have been agreed that the outcome would be a punishment for the rumor-mongers. After all, the other side was composed of substantial, diligent villagers, the one occasionally loose with his tongue, but the other well-behaved and quiet.

Important contemporary categories for making social distinctions were the notions of the 'house' and the 'householder' (*Haus* and *Haushalter*).[7] Throughout all the reports and testimony, the Vogt and superintendent, and many of the village magistrates and more substantial Bürger, evaluated the characters of various people in the drama according to their abilities to manage their 'households'. The positive value put on the aggressive characteristics necessary for maintaining or increasing an estate was apt to mask the fact that they were most likely to go along with wealth. In other words, 'good householder' and 'bad householder' were code words for the system of domination. They suggested from the outset a strategy for dealing with the people distinguished by their defining power. In the ideology of the household, we can see a central connection between the state and the internal dynamics of village life. As far as the state was concerned, a primary assumption of its existence and smooth functioning was a system of viable farms as tax objects, and by the mid eighteenth century such needs were grasped under the category of the 'house'. This fact characterized the particularly strong relationships between the Vogt and the Schultheiss and explains how the Schultheiss stage-managed so much around such values. The Drohmanns, not Bauer and Plessing, were the foundation of the state.

As the Vogt was filing his report, Breuninger's successor, Pastor Mauchard, had decided to send his own version of what was going on.[8] He started by saying that by almost universal *bruit* the two Drohmann brothers had done the deed. Not only that but the Schultheiss, a bosom friend (*Hertzensfreund*), was tied up in it. The Vogt had displayed a singular lack of diligence in the investigation and was plainly biassed (*parteiisch*) from the very beginning. Pastor Mauchard felt in need of protection because those people were used to shedding blood. In fact, the Schultheiss had hinted that he would end up the same as the last pastor. He wanted to make it clear that there was no evidence that the old pastor had died a natural death. In the ditch where he fell, there was so little water that no one could have drowned. It was observed that he had a large bump on his forehead, which could not have been caused by a stone or a fall. There had been no water in his nose or mouth and no water or mud on his shoes. Although the Vogt had once told him that the pastor's mouth had been covered in mud, Breuninger's wife said that this was simply not so.

Mauchard reported that as the body lay on the table in the schoolhouse, the pastor's shirt was suddenly raised to reveal his naked bottom – to the scandal and consternation of all of the women gathered around. In the confusion, the Vogt announced that the pastor had not been murdered (*todgeschlagen*). A surgeon from Weilheim who had come along by chance pointed out a few things, but the Vogt told him to keep his mouth shut; it was none of his business. No one then dared to ask about any further indications of foul play. In short, there were many irregularities, and the Vogt played a central role in covering them up. During the *post mortem*, the Vogt spoke Latin to the other officials and told the doctor not to bother with an autopsy. Above all, the large contusion over the eye was not investigated.

> Pastor Mauchard suspected that the Vogt had painted a black picture of Hans Jerg Bauer, the author of the rumor, in his report. Mauchard, when he first suspected that Bauer knew something, talked to him sharply and spoke to him from God's word. It was clear that his heart was beating fast. Still he would not answer for fear of the Vogt and the Schultheiss and the two Drohmanns, all brutal and violent people, who always carried everything through and won. On the same day that the pastor spoke to him, Bauer attended communion, and his conscience was awakened even more, so that he had to reveal the truth. Since he did not have the courage to come personally, he wrote a letter and slipped it under the parsonage door. As for his general conduct, it cannot be said that he had an impenitent heart or a habitus in wickedness and vice. Whenever the pastor talked to him, he was able to get a confession and tears in his eyes. During the last ten years Bauer had only appeared before the consistory six times – for gambling, drunkenness, and marital conflict.
>
> Mauchard then dealt with the Drohmann brothers. They were impudent, brutal, and bloodthirsty in word and deed. One time Michael, a shepherd, spent a weekend drinking and gambling – including on Sunday. He plotted with several people and almost murdered someone. Hans Jerg also had a reputation for violence. He once lay in wait to kill his father-in-law and another time beat him so that he was covered in blood.[9]

The Vogt added some details to his own report about the rumor that Drohmann had watched out for his father-in-law and that Drohmann at that time had admitted to killing the pastor.[10] Plessing, who was at first sure that the incident had taken place, admitted that his memory had been shaken by Pastor Mauchard. Bauer and Plessing contradicted each other about who first told whom that the Drohmanns had killed Breuninger. It was also pointed out that Michael Drohmann had complained to the office of the Vogt many years before about Plessing spreading the gossip that he had killed the pastor. Plessing got five weeks labor in prison as punishment because his allegations were found to be completely false. It also had to be pointed out that he was a shady character. Sixteen or seventeen years before, he was in prison for blasphemy and shameful misuse of the hymn, 'Komm heyliger Geist' (Come Holy Spirit), by making a pun on the name of a fellow villager, Adam Heylig. The Vogt was unable to find any indication of this in the records but noted that Plessing admitted it. Plessing was a wicked, useless person. For his godless and drunken life, he got ten weeks in prison in Stuttgart in 1732.

During the interrogation, the Vogt caught up Plessing, Hans Jerg Bauer, and Jacob Bauer in a series of contradictions. He referred to them all as people who run around (*liederliche Aushäusers* and *Herumläufer*). Both Plessing and Jacob Bauer had been involved in counterfeiting and had been subject to interrogation by torture. Obviously, there was collusion among them, and their accusations were based on Feindschaft.

Because the Vogt and the pastor had lined up on different sides and because there were so many discrepancies, the duke ordered a fresh investigation and appointed the Vogt from Urach, Georgii, as a commissioner to conduct hearings and make a report. Georgii began his report by noting that everyone was agreed that it was impossible for Pastor Breuninger to drown where he was.[11] His hat, walking stick, and handkerchief had been neatly piled up on the bank. On his head above his eye and behind his ear there were contusions. Because of this evidence of foul play, Georgii decided to question all the witnesses in an effort to get to the bottom of the matter. He asked each witness to begin by telling if he or she was related to the Schultheiss, Plessing, Bauer, or the Drohmann brothers. The way they answered will be significant for our analysis.

The first witness was Hans Jerg Weber, Bürgermeister and pubkeeper in Pliensbach, one of the hamlets of the parish. His wife and the mother of the two Drohmanns were the children of siblings (*Geschwisterkinder*). He was the conduit of information to the Schultheiss that forced the report to the Vogt. Because Drohmann never brought a complaint, he considered the rumors to be true. Hans Jerg Drohmann had told him that he had never complained because he did not know whom to complain about. As for the Drohmanns' characters, they were both *brutal* with their mouths, but he knew of no actual quarrels.

The next witness was Hans Jerg Lutz, junior, thirty-three, a substan-

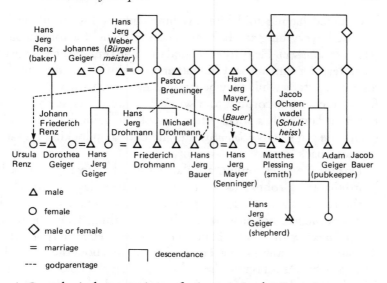

4. Genealogical connections of witnesses in the Breuninger
   murder case

tial landowner. He was not related to any of the chief actors. He had
heard from Plessing and from Dorothea Geiger, the wife of Hans Jerg
Geiger, that Hans Jerg Drohmann had killed the pastor. Dorothea was a
sister-in-law of Hans Jerg. Drohmann's wife, when she was dying, had
wanted to make out a testament in favor of the children of her siblings
because she did not know what the future would bring, since her husband had killed the pastor. In any event, that was what Dorothea Geiger
said. Previously Lutz had heard the general gossip and thought that
Michael Drohmann had done it because he failed to make a complaint.
The gossip (*Geschwätzwerk*) had been going around for a long time.

Matthes Plessing, a blacksmith, forty-five or so, said his grandfather
and that of the Schultheiss were siblings. His wife was a siblings' child
with Hans Jerg Bauer. He did not have any Freundschaft or Verwandt-
schaft with the Drohmanns. Right after the pastor was found, his death
was discussed because the barber who was there said that he had not
drowned but had been choked or beaten. He did not know the cause of
the rumor but only repeated what he had heard, as others did. He had
heard from his sister-in-law that the two Drohmanns had done the
deed, passed the information along, and ended up having the mus-
keteers come to get him. He ran away for three-quarters of a year but
finally came back and went to Kirchheim to be punished. His sister-in-

law denied having told him anything, but in any event he had not repeated everything she had said because he held it for female gossip (*Weibergeschwätz*). He further related that one time at the village of Boll, Hans Jerg Drohmann and his father-in-law were in the inn drinking together. After a while they began spitting at each other. Drohmann left for a time and, according to a witness, waited outside the inn for his father-in-law with a stick. After a while he came back in and asked where the pig's belly (*Saumag*) was and ended up locking his father-in-law in a back room.

During the questioning, a villager rushed in to report that he had heard that the Drohmanns wanted to burn the village down. The origin of the report, Jacob Geiger, upon being questioned said he only said that they might, not that he had heard anything from them himself.

The next witness was Hans Jerg Geiger. Hans Jerg Drohmann's deceased wife was his sister. He had heard a lot about the matter but had let it pass by. As a Freund, he did not pass on the talk (*Rede*). As a *close* friend, he did not concern himself with the matter. He related, however, that by the recent testament of his dead sister, he and the children of his other sister had received considerable damage. He had to admit that his brother-in-law was an insolent man and that if he had not been present seven years previously there would have been a slaughter between Drohmann and Geiger's step-father, Johannes Geiger. Questioned about the testament, he said that he had already been punished for speaking his mind when he heard that he had been disinherited. He told his sister she should go ahead and die.

Dorothea Geiger, forty-one, his wife, was then questioned. It turned out that she had been the one to take the information furnished by Bauer and Plessing and pass it on to Lutz, Weber, and others, who then reported it to the Schultheiss. It happened just after her sister-in-law (*Geschweyh*) made out her testament in front of the Schultheiss. She had left everything to her husband, thereby disinheriting Dorothea Geiger's husband and their children. Dorothea had gone along to the sick bed and told Drohmann there that if the property were made over to him, it would come out that he had killed the pastor. The Schultheiss threw her out.

Hans Jerg Mayer, senior, *Bauer* (farmer) and member of the Gericht from Aichelberg, around fifty, said he was not born in the parish and was not related at all to any of the relevant people. He had been called in by the Schultheiss to witness the making of the testament. He questioned Drohmann's wife about her wishes, and she said that everything was to go to her husband for his life-long use. Only after his death would anything go to the other relatives. The Schultheiss wrote it all down, and the three witnesses signed the document, but none of them were willing to take it to Kirchheim. Therefore, the Schultheiss went to Kirchheim to get a Substitut to come and make out another testament. Mayer did not know what happened to what the Schultheiss wrote. He considered the Drohmanns *brutal* with their mouths, but for the rest they worked hard and were diligent (*hausen*) and therefore both had considerable wealth.

Hans Jerg Mayer, Senninger (not related to Hans Jerg Mayer, senior, although the latter was his godparent), thirty-four, was the next witness. His wife was sibling's child with Hans Jerg Bauer. He also was present at the testament. He admitted that he said to Bauer that if a report were made and the matter came to light, he believed that the Drohmanns would be judged guilty (*durchgehen*). By that, he only meant that it would cost them their lives. He was asked how he could say such a thing if he had not heard it from Hans Jerg Drohmann himself (they lived in the same building). Their living quarters were so separate that nothing could be heard between them.

Then Hans Jerg Bauer was questioned. He and Matthes Plessing's wife were children of siblings. Hans Jerg Drohmann was his godfather (*Gevatter*). He related that he had been afraid of the Schultheiss and the Vogt. The Schultheiss had threatened him by saying that he would teach him to shut his mouth – he would kill the 'priest'. He now had no fear because he had cleared his conscience.

Four or five years previously, he went with Drohmann to another hamlet to drink, where they met Drohmann's father-in-law, Johannes Geiger. After they left, Drohmann tried to get him to lay in wait for the father-in-law with clubs to 'beat the dog to death'. They were to throw him in a ditch so that people would think he had drowned. 'No, god-father, you hold my children at the baptismal font and should warn me against such things.' Bauer expressed fear for eternity and pointed out that they only had a short time to live in the world. He then said to Drohmann that everyone said that he and his brother had killed the pastor. To this Drohmann answered that it did not matter if one beat the dog to death – it was not a sin. On the way home, he asked Bauer if he supposed that his brother Michael would be shepherd if they did not have the Schultheiss. The two brothers and the Schultheiss had an alliance with each other that no one of them might say anything against the other even into eternity. As long as Drohmann was with him, he had nothing to fear. Bauer pointed out that Drohmann had often quarreled with Geiger over his wife's maternal inheritance.

The commissioner then tried to establish a motive for the murder of the pastor. Bauer knew that the Drohmanns were the pastor's enemies. When Hans Jerg was single, he was caught in bed with the pastor's maid and had been excluded from confession and communion. He also heard that Michael had been corrected during confession for swearing. Another time when Hans Jerg had been excluded from the sacrament, he had sent the pastor a bottle of wine in reconciliation. Then he had told the story all over the village.

Jacob Bauer, wheelwright from Aichelberg, fifty-seven, was related to Hans Jerg Bauer 'zu dritten kind'. At the time of the death of the pastor, he was in jail because of counterfeiting (of which he was innocent). As for his knowledge of the case, even the birds sang about it, so great was the noise. While he was in prison, all the guards were gossiping about the Drohmanns having killed the pastor. He first heard that the Drohmanns admitted it from a soldier there.

Adam Geiger, pub owner in Eckwälden, sixty-one, was siblings' child with the Schultheiss. He related that his deceased nephew (brother's son), Hans Jerg Geiger, shepherd, had become involved in a dispute with Michael Drohmann. Apparently the young Geiger's sister had been made pregnant by Michael's other brother, Friederich. They got into a quarrel because of it, and Geiger used the occasion to accuse Drohmann of killing the pastor.

Michel Authaler from Zell, sixty-six, said he was not related to any of the chief characters. He had lived in Zell only ten years and before that in Ohmden, from where he traveled around buying butter. He was in Zell on the night that the pastor was murdered, and started for home with a load of butter on his back just as people were lighting their houses. About twenty paces from the village, he met Hans Jerg Drohmann who told him that he was coming from the Remstal where he had fetched some wine. When they said goodbye to each other, Drohmann proceeded towards the village. Drohmann had left the wagon on the road and had taken a short cut along the footpath where he met Authaler. The path led straight from the road where they met, and Authaler could hear the wagon continue above them. Since that encounter, Authaler had never spoken another word with Drohmann – until the recent Vogtruggericht. After leaving Drohmann, Authaler continued on his way. He encountered Pastor Breuninger half way between Zell and Ohmden in the Bodenwiese, a field's length away from

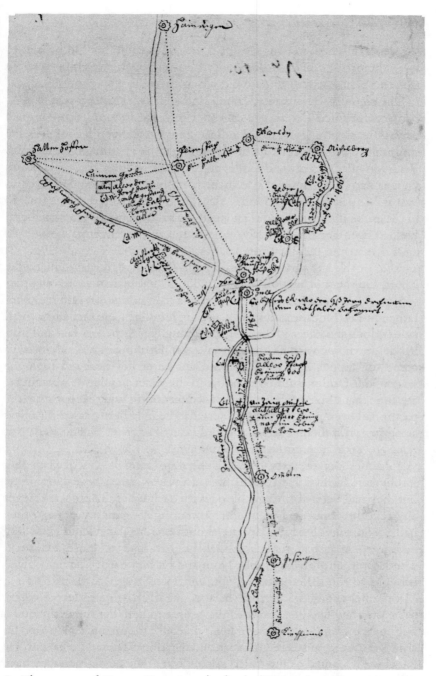

5. The scene of Pastor Breuninger's death (*Württemberg Hauptstaatsarchiv Stuttgart, A214 Bü 476*).

the ditch in which he was found. It was impossible for Drohmann to meet the pastor where he died, and it was impossible for him to know that the pastor would be coming along there.

The commissioner wanted to interview Hans Jerg Renz, senior, who had accompanied Drohmann on the trip to the Remstal and who had driven the wagon along to the village after Drohmann left to take the short cut. Unfortunately, he died just when the commissioner arrived. Renz was over seventy and senile, but when he still had his senses, Jacob Geiger had taken down a statement from him, which he delivered to Pastor Mauchard. Renz said that Hans Jerg Drohmann did not come to his house that evening and then leave for his own home in Aichelberg. He had been persuaded by the Vogt to tell a different story before. As an old man the memory often fades.

One of the key witnesses was Ursula Renz, daughter-in-law of the baker. On the morning of the trip to buy wine, she had visited the parsonage. The pastor asked her to borrow a half gulden for him from her father-in-law, but she said he had already left. She gave him a few small coins which she had with her. That evening, her father-in-law and husband came home with Drohmann's wagon. Drohmann was supposed to come for supper but never showed up. Later her husband took the wagon and Drohmann's oxen home to the other hamlet. It was during the time that Drohmann could not account for his whereabouts that the pastor had been murdered. Hans Jerg had begged her to say that he was at supper with them. Having cleared her conscience, Ursula Renz was ready to take an oath on her testimony.

Johannes Geiger, sixty-five, was the step-father-in-law of Hans Jerg Drohmann. He said that Drohmann had always wanted more inheritance, but they had been able to get along with each other. There were never any real threats from Drohmann. About eight or nine years ago they had become involved in a dispute about the inheritance, and Hans Jerg had used such bad language that he had had to raise his stick. Thereupon, Drohmann grabbed him and hit him hard. The matter was brought to the office of the Vogt, and Hans Jerg was fined 53 fl.

Breuninger's wife said that she was one of the first to arrive where the pastor lay. She pleaded with the people to help her move the body, but no one would take pity on her. Michael Drohmann, who stood up above the ditch, answered in scorn and derision. 'There you have it. He has always damned us and called us children of the devil. Now you have it.'

Michael Drohmann, forty-three, testified that he was distantly

related to the Schultheiss but did not know how. As he was being questioned, Pastor Mauchard interrupted to say that there was fresh
evidence from Michael Bauer from Zell. Bauer said that he was a
stone's throw from the Bodenwiese on the night of the death, getting
some grass for his cattle. He saw Michael go over the road towards
Ohmden near to where the pastor was found. Drohmann came along to
ask Bauer if he planned to remain there long, and then asked if the pastor
had come along yet. Drohmann then went along the way that the pastor
had to come. At that moment, they saw Authaler two field lengths
away, and Drohmann, referring to the load on Authaler's back, said that
he was carrying the devil out. According to Bauer, Authaler was not a
very trustworthy witness.

Bauer then said that about two years ago he had had a dispute over a
meadow with the Schultheiss. They had had to go to Kirchheim to settle
the matter. Afterwards as Bauer went into a pub, he encountered the
Schultheiss with Michael Drohmann. Bauer made himself scarce and
hurried home. He was relieving himself on the other side of a wall in
the village when the two of them came by. He heard the Schultheiss say
to Drohmann that he was counting on him to stand by him and 'clean
up' Michael Bauer. But Drohmann answered that 'by thunder', he
could not do it because he had encountered Bauer 'on the meadow'.
The Schultheiss warned him not to admit it and said that he would help
him as long as he could.

One of the documents which the commissioner appended to his
report was a fresh copy of an earlier report from 1733 about Breuninger
sent by the Vogt and superintendent.[12] It stated that the pastor had been
unable to deny that he had carried on intense theoretical investigations
of chemistry and alchemy and that he had put a great deal of time into
the study of mines and minerals. He had wasted a lot of money and
gained little profit. He was accused of spending a lot of time with the
vagrant counterfeiter, Rauschenberger, who was then in exile. In fact,
the latter had stayed in Breuninger's house for some time. Breuninger
had been accused of drunkenness and was also under suspicion of carrying on with the organist, Frau Renz – but he covered the accusations
with the mantle of Christian love.

A report from the law faculty of the University of Tübingen summarized the whole testimony, assessing the guilt of the Drohmanns.[13] It
started by saying that Friederich Wilhelm Breuninger had become pastor
in Zell in 1725. From the beginning, he had come into conflict with the
community over unnecessary experiments, neglect of church services,

drunkenness, and flirting with women. A commission had been appointed to investigate, and it was expected that Breuninger would be sent to another parish. During that time, it was reported that he had died of apoplexy. After the burial a murmuring arose among the people suggesting that the two Drohmann brothers had killed him for the Schultheiss (at that time, Greiner), who had helped lead the commission against the pastor. After examining all of the evidence from the exhumation, it was concluded that the pastor had probably been brought to his death by someone other than himself. Although he was not respected by his community or by almost anyone else, and although through his own bad management and costly experiments he had become quite poor, there seemed to be no evidence that he might have committed suicide. The document then takes up the character of the various witnesses. Plessing did not seem to be a false witness, but on the other hand he had been before the courts for his godless and drunken life. Once he had thrown his parents-in-law and wife out of the house. He also ran away from home for a long time to escape arrest. Young Geiger and his wife could be considered enemies of the Drohmanns and not qualified to give information. Indeed, they had been fined for their hard language during the time when Drohmann's wife was sick. Hans Jerg Bauer had a reputation as a drinker, gambler, and bad householder, but there were those who thought that he was not so bad. Furthermore, there was no evidence that he was a liar, and his knowledge of God's Word was far from small. Ursula Renz was a bad housekeeper and often drank. She had been punished several times with jail. She argued that she had never done anything very bad, but she had been deceived by her enemy, the Schultheiss Ochsenwadel. Although there was no suspicion that she was lying, because of her sex she was not able to give information in criminal matters. As for Michael Bauer, it was alleged he was not in his right mind. He was a liar, a windbag, and carried a charm against the devil with him. He had once accused his brother-in-law and his neighbor, Rosina Ochsenwadel, of witchcraft. On the other hand, he was hard-working, thrifty, upright, and honest. He had never been summoned before the village church consistory. Only his enemies called him a fool and an idiot (*simpel*). Still, he was not very reliable as a witness. Jacob Bauer was a counterfeiter and had been to jail. It was hard to use his testimony, and without it the proof against the Drohmanns was difficult. Both of the Drohmanns were insolent when it came to words, and often, when drunk, they were brutal in deed and brawled and fought. No one was happy to deal with them, since from nature they were so violent.

The report went over the evidence against the Drohmanns. It questioned whether the single dismissal from communion was enough to cause the brothers to seek revenge. The law faculty was not in agreement with the state prosecuter, the commissioner, Georgii, who conducted the original investigation, who wanted the brothers condemned to death.[14] Even if there was evidence that the pastor had been killed, there was no proof that the two brothers had done it.

Finally, the brothers were called before the city court in Urach and after a trial were dismissed and left to their own consciences.[15] They were warned that physical freedom did not mean freedom from conscience.

This material offers us three general areas for comment. It tells us first of all a great deal about the experience of Herrschaft and power, second about the dynamics of family relations, and third about the nexus conscience/domination.

It is not possible from the evidence to say whether pastor Breuninger died a natural death or not, but it seems clear from the actions of the Schultheiss (Greiner), the superintendent, and the Vogt that none of the authorities wanted to clear up the matter. They failed to undertake an autopsy, and the superintendent covered up by asking the duke if he thought it might be necessary, suggesting apoplexy as the cause of death. Nevertheless, from the beginning, many people were convinced that Breuninger had been killed by some villager or other. There were the marks on the body and the position of the personal effects at the top of the ditch.

The drama at the grave determined the nature of future suspicions and the positions of the various people in the village round of gossip. Although the pastor was by no means isolated in the village, as witnessed by the fact that Ursula Renz had visited on the morning of his death, and he had expected to be able to borrow money from her father-in-law, no one was willing to help the widow move the body from the gully. The drama of the scene with her screams had shaken a number of people, but with the Schultheiss, the central opponent of the pastor, present, and with Michael Drohmann pouring his scorn from the crowd around the top of the ditch, no one had the ability to detach himself from the crowd and help – especially as the power balance had definitely tipped in favor of the pastor's enemies.

We can see at that point some of the party making up the group opposing the pastor. Schultheiss Greiner had led the move to get him removed from the pastorate and had worked closely in that with the

Vogt Wippermann and the superintendent in Kirchheim. His successor as Schultheiss, the then Bürgermeister Ochsenwadel, appears from all of his actions to have been a member of the party. It seems from the behavior of Michael at the scene of the accident and from the symbolic issue of excommunication that the Drohmanns, as important landholders, substantial Bürger, tied up closely with the village officials, were also part of the party. Hans Jerg was godparent for Ochsenwadel, and everyone saw the brothers as willing to carry on the dirty work that the officials wanted done. Thus their reputation for violence and their integration into the power structure was enough to point suspicion in their direction. No one was able to suggest a sufficient personal motive of the Drohmanns to do the deed, and all that village discussion could come up with along those lines was a reprimand to Michael for swearing and the exclusion from communion for Hans Jerg a few times for being in bed with the pastor's maid. Information here was vague and contradictory – whether the exclusion happened only before his marriage or several times, for one or two services, or for an extended period. What brought the suspicion was the very fact of the pastor's death, the belief that he had been murdered, and the lack of any other context to fit the facts in other than the pattern of enmity and friendship which structured village relations.

The outlines of the other 'party' are harder to see. Breuninger was godfather for Ursula Renz and apparently had good relations with old Hans Jerg Renz (a baker), Ursula's father-in-law. Still Renz had cooperated with Hans Jerg Drohmann on the very day of the death as they all drove to the Remstal to buy some wine. If we can see a more-or-less firm connection between the pastor and the Renzes through godparentage, we can see the continuation of village fault lines in the continuing conflict between Ochsenwadel and Ursula Renz over the subject of her housekeeping and drinking habits. She considered him an 'enemy'. That is, what he interpreted as purely administrative practice, she put into the context of enemy/friend. She also provided the key testimony against Hans Jerg Drohmann, some of which she 'recalled' only in the days before testifying before the commissioner.

As for those who provided testimony and were key people in circulating the rumors, some of them can be linked to the pastor through the rather strange phenomenon of counterfeiting, the outlines of which are not at all clear from the sources here. One of the charges brought against Breuninger was being a friend to the counterfeiter Rauschenberger, and indeed his alchemical activities were thought to have been tied up

with false coining. Jacob Bauer, in whose house Hans Jerg Bauer and
Plessing wrote the incriminating letter, had also been tied up with
Rauschenberger and had indeed spent three years in jail for suspicious
behavior in the affair. Plessing had also been tied up in the counterfeiting 'gang'. Both Jacob Bauer and Plessing had been tortured in the
investigation. None of this establishes any motives but helps suggest
some lines of force. Vogt Wippermann alluded to their activities as
collusion, thereby recognizing their common position, and alleged
Feindschaft as their motive, thereby recognizing their common
interest.

The evidence does not offer a clear indication of the conflicting
groups and individuals in the village, but does point to their existence.
Motive was attributed to Feindschaft, to kinship, and to fear, the latter
growing out of the web of social relations and the threat of violence or
revenge. While there were perhaps competing families and landholding groups in the village whose exchanges and competitions were based
on rough equality, the grand cleavage running through the village
seems to have been that between the substantial landholders, integrated
into the power structure, and a group of artisans, smallholders, and farm
laborers. What integrated the group of landholders was not so much
direct consanguineal ties (at least beyond those between immediate
family members – brothers, fathers and sons, etc.), as relations of
marriage alliance and fictive kinship (godparentage). Many of the people
on both sides of the cleavage were related in some way through blood
ties and could trace that relationship, but by itself it was not an integrating force.

The relations between the two groups were often characterized by
violence, either actual or threatened, an important point being how the
relationships were conceived and the various actors understood. The
words that always cropped up to characterize the Drohmanns were
'brutality' and 'violence'. There were various stories going the rounds
about Michael being drunk for several days at a time and 'intriguing'
with others to attack this or that person. The stories of Hans Jerg kick-
ing a man in the head or beating up his father-in-law also seemed to
symbolize his penchant for physical violence. The pastor referred to
both Drohmanns as insolent, brutal, and bloodthirsty, giving Michael's
drinking spree and Hans Jerg's treatment of his father-in-law as examples.
Nonetheless, when everyone brought in their stories, the actual events
of violence were few and far between, stretching over a long period of
time. More often, the word *brutal* was coupled with the way Hans Jerg

talked.[16] In his first report, the Vogt admitted that Hans Jerg Drohmann was sometimes impudent (*frech*) with his advice. Hans Jerg Weber referred to the two brothers as *brutal* with their mouths but not apt to quarrel. Hans Jerg Mayer, senior, used the same phrase, '*brutal* with their mouths' but coupled that with the fact that both worked hard. Michael Bauer called Michael a 'godless man'. Taking all of the assessments together, it would seem that the two Drohmanns were apt to drink and brawl a bit, but that was a danger only to others drinking and brawling with them. The only other people ever in physical danger were close relatives. Yet the impression remains that the Drohmanns were capable of violence – even of burning the village down – and this is precisely the image which they themselves presented. They demonstrated the power of the word – which had the capacity of being *brutal* – which gave their fellow villagers a sense of incalculable violence. The direct coupling of the 'brutal mouth' on the one hand and a large property and successful management on the other, which was made by several persons assessing their characters, makes precisely the significant link between the two practices, namely presentation of the self as powerful and the successful management of property. As the pastor said, the Vogt, the Schultheiss, and the two Drohmanns were all brutal and violent people who always carried everything through and won.

In this way, one can see that the relationship between the two central groupings in the village was determined by a matrix of fear. That was always there, whether openly stated or simply understood, which did not mean that integrative ties of another kind were not also possible, such as the link of godparentage between Drohmann and Hans Jerg Bauer, who eventually was a key figure in setting the rumors going the rounds. Or take the relationship between Hans Jerg Drohmann and the Renzes. The father and son went along with Drohmann on his wagon, using his draft animals. In return they were expected to offer him supper – which he failed to show up for. The son took the wagon home for Drohmann but knew that he would not get a glass of wine from Drohmann's wife, who would not 'give anyone anything'. The relationships here express ones of patronage/clientage, just as did godparentage with Bauer – a carefully balanced set of reciprocities, mutual aid and services, the symbols of social difference and deference.

Hans Jerg Drohmann's playing with his dangerous status and with his suggestion of how power worked in the village – a collusion of office holders and large landholders – were part of the practice of the everyday exercise of power, and this was a game shared by the Schultheiss. It is difficult to assess whether Drohmann was serious about killing or beating up his father-in-law in Eckwälden. In any event, he impressed Bauer probably more than he meant to. In suggesting but not actually admitting that he was responsible for Breuninger's death, he himself was helping to reinforce his reputation for violence. Calling the rumor mere gossip and refusing to do anything about it helped to keep the reputation of bloodthirstiness alive. In like manner, Schultheiss Ochsenwadel let the schoolmaster think that Pastor Mauchard might also be the object of violence. The Schultheiss threatened Bauer when Bauer began to come under the influence of Mauchard – in the nearby presence of Drohmann. The story that Hans Jerg told to the credulous Bauer about the Schultheiss and the Drohmanns having a league (*Bund*) together played on the way Bauer himself perceived the power structure. The coordination between those in power was close enough for them to seem like a league – just as the disaffection of the dominated appeared to those in power as a collusion. Michael Bauer's description of the Schultheiss and Michael Drohmann also fit the popular perception. Bauer felt himself under pressure from the Schultheiss and feared Drohmann as the Schultheiss's executioner.

Such a description of village life suggests a separation into two loose factions determined by access to landed property. The relative importance of this dichotomy in Württemberg varied from place to place and over time, but by the mid eighteenth century was coming to play an ever more central role. In an analysis of one village not far away from Zell, it has been found that artisans might rank among the wealthiest members of the village at the beginning of the eighteenth century and were likely to serve on the village Rat and Gericht and hold such positions as Bürgermeister and Schultheiss.[17] By the end of the century, they had been almost completely squeezed out of office-holding and were seldom to be found among the top quarter of the wealthy. During the eighteenth century, a process of social differentiation had taken place in which the struggle for landed resources intensified and in which the village separated into two general factions characterized by wealth and occupation. In this process, violence and the threat of violence came to play a part integral to the social process. It appears that Zell was typical in this respect both in terms of social differentiation and in the way that social relations became increasingly characterized by 'brutality' and fear. Even then the villagers had their 'myth of origins' and could locate people on a map of descent. Such a reckoning points to a group of ancestors where equality reigned – brothers and sisters – from whom the present unequal set of contemporaries descended. It provided one set of coordinates along which social relations could be presented, but the sense of being 'one family' could only have exacerbated the harshness of the processes which radically differentiated first and second cousins from each other. With this aspect of family conceptualization in mind, it would be useful to examine the nature of family relations in the village.

In the ten years that rumor circulated in the village, no one had effectively brought about an investigation. Plessing had been accused by Michael Drohmann and had been punished by Vogt Wippermann in Kirchheim. But the issue then had not been whether Drohmann had done a killing but the source of Plessing's information. Since the relative who told him was never even called for questioning, it is clear that the Vogt simply treated the matter as slander. For the rest, over the years nothing had ever emerged worthy of court action. All the bearers of information were dismissed as drunks or dissolute (*liederlich*), and the rumors discounted as common gossip. Not even the public reading of Bauer's letter from the pulpit had led to an investigation. Although the Schultheiss fulfilled his obligation to report to the Vogt, the latter said that without personal knowledge of the content of the letter, there was nothing to report; therefore the affair remained local knowledge – or even regional knowledge – but not something that ever became officially investigated. What broke the unity in official response was a fissure in the dominant faction in the village – a family quarrel. At that moment the gossip became rumor – Geschwätz became Geschrei.

Apart from the general context of Feindschaft and violence, the only concrete story about the Drohmanns stemmed from Hans Jerg Bauer. He in turn told Plessing. The two of them then related the story over a relatively long period to various people including Hans Jerg and Dorothea Geiger. What seems to have brought the matter to a head was the family dispute over an inheritance between the Geigers and Hans Jerg Drohmann. This broke the unified stance of the landowning peasants vis-à-vis the 'gossip', and made the family split the pivot on which its new use as rumor or common knowledge turned. Dorothea Geiger immediately informed a member of the Gericht, Hans Jerg Mayer, as soon as she lost the struggle with her brother-in-law, Drohmann. She also used Hans Jerg Lutz as a conduit to Bürgermeister Weber. Once the information was going around within these circles, there was no choice but for Ochsenwadel and the Drohmann brothers to report the matter to the Vogtruggericht.

Since family dynamics played such a central role in the conflicts in the village, it might be helpful to examine them a little closer. A central pivot of family relations had to do with inheritance. Tensions could get so great that father and son-in-law could sit in a pub together and spit at each other, or the son-in-law could attack and thrash his father-in-law. This relationship between Hans Jerg Drohmann and old Johannes Geiger was of course extreme, but it demonstrates clearly one of the points of most tension in family relations. One can see that the discussion and quarrel between the two men went on over a very long period, flashing up from time to time in violence or extreme behavior. The issue between them needs to be explained. Johannes Geiger, called Schnell, said he was Hans Jerg Drohmann's step-father-in-law. Since Hans Jerg Geiger was only seven years younger than his 'father', it would appear that Drohmann's wife and young Geiger were full siblings and that Johannes Geiger was their step-father. The fact that Drohmann had fought over both the paternal and maternal inheritance of his wife meant that both her father and mother were dead. In this area of Germany, full partible inheritance prevailed, with women inheriting land equally with men.[18] Women also had full testamentary rights. The property brought together by a couple was under the administration of the husband, but there was a complex set of institutions to protect the wife from alienation of her property or having it encumbered with debts. How efficient such machinery was is not at issue here, rather the fact needs to be stressed that both partners to a marriage played the same role in inheritance. The 'marital fund' stayed together as long as the couple was married. In the event of the decease of one spouse, the whole estate of both husband and wife was inventoried, with the various inheritance rights specified. The survivor kept what he or she brought into the marriage, received an inheritance portion from the deceased if any children had been born in the marriage, and shared in the gain or loss of the marital community.

Various issues arise from such a system. Upon remarriage, the survivor could only take his or her inheritance into the next marriage, creating a new marital fund. This kept the children of two marriages separate, and they often ended up in radically different social positions. The children from both marriages shared in the inheritance, however, from the common parent. As for the timing of the reception of an inheritance, that lay in the hands of the surviving parent, who had lifelong use-rights to the property of the deceased spouse even though it had been apportioned on the books to the surviving children. A final hitch had to do with marriages which produced no children. In the case

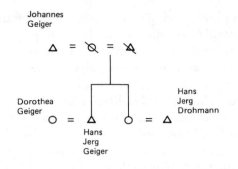

6. Genealogical connections between the Geigers and Drohmanns.

of an intestate estate, the spouse received no inheritance from the deceased, and everything went to the collateral heirs.

Drohmann had had two separate quarrels with his step-father-in-law. The first was over his wife's paternal inheritance. Presumably Drohman's wife's mother was still alive at that time and exercised the use-rights over the inheritance of the dead father. Geiger, as her new husband, administered her property and had the use of it, and Drohmann was anxious to have it passed along, or more of it passed along than had already come in the dowry. A second quarrel had to do with the inheritance from the mother, some of which had come along to Drohmann's wife, while apparently some still was held by Geiger in usufruct. Similarly, the quarrel between Hans Jerg Geiger and Drohmann came about because the Drohmanns had no children, and therefore the Geigers had claim to the inheritance so long as Drohmann's wife did not dispose of the property by testament. Drohmann and the Schultheiss had brought extreme pressure on the dying woman and threw out her sister-in-law, whose sole interest in being there seems to have been to secure the succession. Once they had succeeded in gaining the woman's assent, they called in members of the Gericht to witness her will, but none of them were bold enough to take it to be registered in Kirchheim.

The issue of descent and succession was crucial to the society, for it was the chief way in which social differentiation took place. Although each village had a land market by this time and more and more land exchanged hands by purchase – in ever smaller parcels – still, far more land changed hands through the process of devolution than through sale.[19] Thus interest in the facts of marriage, descent, and inheritance rights had the same keen edge that other societies might put on wages, employment, interest rates, or inflation. In fact, there were two ways of expressing kinship: with the words Freundschaft and Verwandtschaft. Sometimes used synonymously, they usually referred to affinal and consanguineal relations respectively. When villagers reckoned 'Verwandt-schaft', they did so in a peculiar manner. Rather than saying that so-and-so was a 'cousin' or a 'cousin twice removed' or the like, they traced lines upwards to a set of siblings and then back down to the present generation, as if retracing the lines of property devolution. So, for example, Plessing said that his grandfather and the grandfather of the Schultheiss were siblings. Or as Hans Jerg Weber put it, his wife and the mother of the Drohmanns were siblings' children. In other words, to map blood kin was always to map property devolution at the same time, and to stress the way that current social structure was the outcome of the way property had moved through the generations. The knowledge of kinship links did not seem to imply a set of moral relationships where people had mutual claims on each other. Much more, it was a statement about destiny.

The other coordinate of kinship relations were those cemented together by marriage. This kind of kinship was not reckoned step by step but was given specific terms. Thus Hans Jerg Drohmann's wife was Dorothea Geiger's *Geschweyh*, and Hans Jerg Drohmann was Hans Jerg Geiger's *Schwager*, Johannes Geiger his *Stiefschweher*, and Ursula Renz was Hans Jerg Renz's *Söhnerin*. *Freundschaft* or affinal relationships were more subject to comment and given a 'moral' sense, precisely because they were so negotiable. Hans Jerg Geiger gave as the reason why he had not passed on any talk (*Rede*) the fact that Drohmann was his Freund. Close affinal relatives did not do that sort of thing – although I suspect that Geiger's use of the term *Rede* suggests that for him the rumors were village *knowledge* and not mere gossip. It should also be pointed out that the chain of in-laws often made up the coordinated set of equal property owners, putting class and family interests in the same territory and allowing the language of family to mask the language of mutual self-interest in the play of power within the village. Geiger had solidarity with Drohmann as a 'Freund', despite the fact of important clashes over property. Geiger had even gone so far as to tell his sister to drop dead if she persisted in drawing up a will. A final point should be stressed, namely about the ambivalence of family relations. Conflict goes together with solidarity. Old Geiger and Drohmann had sworn at each other, spat at each other, fought until bloody, and Drohmann had threatened to kill Geiger. Nonetheless, Geiger said they always got along and passed off his beating as a minor disagreement (a 50 fl. fine would have been levied only for a very severe beating).

What has been presented here has been a picture of village politics along two axes. One is the interplay between close family members and the network of affinal relations, largely centered on the issue of the access to property but probably also in the background the organization and control of labor. The other axis had to do with the shifting position of loose groupings, not necessarily directly coordinated, characterized by landholding, occupation, and the ability to work and manage. These groupings were criss-crossed by blood relationships, which may or may not have played much of an integrative role. At least in the evidence examined, there do not seem to have been many moral claims or obligations based on the wider network of blood relations. In fact, the word 'Feind' was more likely to be used to describe relations between people connected by blood than those connected by marriage. Thus the Freund/Feind axis was at least *in potentia* an overlap of the affinal/ consanguineal axis. Whatever characterized the relations between the coordinating set of affinal equals – and as we have seen the conflict was integral and mediated by property – the operative word in the structure of domination between the propertied peasants and the marginal landholders, artisans, and day-laborers was 'fear'. And an analysis of that emotion will provide us with an opportunity to examine the theology and political economy of 'conscience'.

When one examines what role 'conscience' played in village discourse and the moments when it came into discussion, it is difficult to elude the fact that it was part of the everyday practice of power. Hans Jerg Drohmann only mentioned his conscience once, and it was never alluded to at all by the Schultheiss, landed peasants, or members of the Gericht. They spoke from their positions of respect and honor, and 'conscience' was not a word that they often referred to. Even Drohmann's one use of the term was different from other uses – for him it was a state; he had a good conscience or no knowledge of wrongdoing (and he probably did not choose the term himself but only answered a question about whether his conscience was in order).

One can contrast the wealthier villagers with Hans Jerg Bauer whose conscience was variously described as 'awakened' or 'cleared'. Ursula Renz had also 'cleared' her conscience. For them the relationship between the person and conscience was an active one, and the practice subject to specific occasions. Bauer first decided to write a letter about

Drohmann's relations to him when he attended communion. As he described it, his conscience was then awakened. He saw communion as an ordeal, and his notion only makes sense if one understands the fear he experienced in undertaking the ordeal. The incident suggests that the idea of conscience was still that of the Reformation, something which offers judgment and hindsight, is retroactive, but not a control mechanism along the lines of a 'superego'.[20] Bauer continually balanced the fear he had for the Vogt, Schultheiss, and Drohmanns and the role conscience played in erasing that fear. As he himself said to Drohmann, one had to balance this life on earth with eternal life. What the pastor was doing in speaking 'sharply' to Bauer or to Plessing was to balance spiritual fear and the hope for eternity with temporal fear. He assessed people's characters by their susceptibility to the fear of God's Word, by their contrition, and by the external signs of awe – tears and trembling. Conscience was the point on which the pastor's position turned in the village, and it was set in the village economy of fear. The pastor labeled as 'godless' those members of the community who seemed immune to the message of contrition, those for whom fear was not experienced in the everyday practice of village politics. By contrast, the Vogt characterized as 'godless' those whose behavior was irregular, those who sinned, or those who were not good householders. The issue was whether the godless or those who showed no 'contrition' were the 'sinners'. One can see from this how the power base of both these pastors, given their message, tended to be rooted in the poorer half of the village. Michael Drohmann expressed the hatred of his class for Breuninger at the scene of the death: 'He called us children of the devil.' In part their struggle was over the religious sanctions of village political life. And what would have been the point of excluding Hans Jerg Drohmann from the sacrament unless he demonstrated no proper sense of contrition? For him to have shown contrition would have meant adopting the characteristic posture of the dominated within the village. Thus there was a kind of dialectic between the pastor and his power base. Contrition, fear, and conscience were rooted in the context of village social life and were part of its political and theological discourse. The lines of cleavage between dominated and dominating running through the history of the village at that time were recapitulated in the tensions between pastors and Schultheiss and Vogt.

If 'conscience' had a specific meaning in the practice of village Herrschaft, there was also a discourse over conscience among the learned theologians and state officials. While the state felt it necessary to acquit the two Drohmanns on the evidence, it did not 'free' them from their consciences. In fact, at their last appearance before the court they were subjected to a sermon by the superintendent Lang, which, judging from its recorded length, must have taken well over an hour to deliver.[21] He pointed out that the sentence meant that they were neither found guilty nor acquitted, but let go and left to conscience and God's judgment. Lang's job was to explain what conscience meant. meant.

He argued that their conscience in this matter was either good or bad; good if they had nothing to do with the murder and bad if they either took part or had any knowledge of it or communicated falsehood to the high magistrates. The point of this argument was to lock them into a position no matter what their particular psychological state, and to tie conscience to God through the state. For Lang, conscience and a particular relationship to authority were coordinate matters. A bad conscience could never be made good, right into eternity, unless a public recantation took place. To explain this, the image of piling sins on sins was used; that is, to the original crime was added lying to the authorities, and that precluded a good conscience (murder was eventually forgivable but lying to the state was not). By such an action, one offended the honor of the magistrates, whose office was carried on in God's name. In all of this, the orthodox Lutheran position was expounded – the office of the magistrates as representative of God's justice. What is interesting here is the way the issue was hung on conscience and the way state officials used conscience in the practice of authority. Individual responsibility and public confession were the central theological concepts buttressing state power. Lang pointed to David, who acknowledged his sins to God because he had no greater lord or magistrate over him. However, that kind of private repentance was excluded for those under public authority. Prayer would be of no avail because a prayer heard by God could only proceed from a state of grace, and to attain that state, true penance was necessary, and that entailed public confession. It was also not possible to hope for reconciliation with God through inner confession and communion, since if one denied one's sins before the magistrates, such confession would be rejected and one would never receive absolution.

The thrust of Lang's harangue was to deny all subjectivity to the Drohmann brothers. It was not how they felt, or whether they felt justified or reconciled, hardened or chastened. It was no good to temporize – to put off repentance to a death-bed confession. Conscience was the knowledge pure and simple of a misdeed. It was not a mechanism for self-control or self-direction. Conscience was still tied to grace and not yet tied to virtue, although it may well be that the specific context of Lang's sermon brought the particular emphasis he laid on conscience. He did briefly say that never to sin was the best penance, but his heart was not really in that concept. It was the coupling of the state and grace, public exhibition and private conscience, eternal life and the duties of the subject that were central to his thinking.

At the level of learned discourse, the meaning of conscience was integrated into the practice of domination, with the theology of grace being the node at which the magisterial and the divine met. In village discourse, conscience turned on fear. It was not so much grace that was at issue as countervailing power. It was through conscience that the individual could create a space for himself given the power structure in the village – with more or less tight linkages between landholders, the local representatives of Herrschaft, and the higher magistrates of the crown. In this discourse, conscience was also linked to the public but not so much to established authorities as to village knowledge, its *fama*, *Geschrei*, *bruit*, and *Rede*. It allowed a mechanism for mere gossip to become public rumor, for individuals without property, respectability, or 'honor' to support their individual claims to public attention.

6

••

The sins of belief: A village remedy for hoof and mouth disease (1796)

For the life of the flesh is in the blood; and I have given it for you upon the altar to make atonement for your souls; for it is the blood that makes atonement, by reason of the life.

Leviticus17.11

Beutelsbach, Zwiefalten, Napoleon,
What's the rhyme and reason?
In Beutelsbach, they bury the bull,
In Zwiefalten, they play the fool,
And Napoleon is not – notoriously extravagant.
That's the rhyme and reason.[1]

The people from Beutelsbach are called 'bull lynchers'.[2]

In 1796, the villagers of Beutelsbach in the Württemberg District of Schorndorf, faced with an outbreak of hoof and mouth disease, decided to make a sacrifice to the epidemic.[3] They buried the communal bull alive outside the village under the crossroads leading to Endersbach. Rumors of the outbreak of superstition and cruelty reached the officials in Stuttgart, who in due course sent a special commissioner in the person of *Canzlei Advocat* and *Amtsschreiber* Bolley from Waiblingen to investigate. He took evidence from various villagers over the period 24 October to 5 November, finally turning in a 209-page summary of the testimony together with a report.[4] Conflicting testimony, unexpected lapses of memory, evasion, and prevarication made it impossible to get at the 'truth' of the matter, which for the commissioner amounted to assigning clear responsibility to the actors in the drama. However, what was a problem from Canzlei Advocat Bolley's perspective is for us particularly helpful, because the multilayered testimony provides a great deal of insight into the processes of village decision making and the

174

workings of popular culture. There is no better way to begin than by simply relating the testimony as it was taken down by Bolley, letting the story emerge bit by bit until we can see how he himself put it together.

The first witness was the twenty-seven-year-old Lieutenant Johann Friedrich Reinhard, at that time Substitut in the village Rathaus. According to him, the burial took place at the insistence of the villagers (Bürger), who believed that the same means had been used to bring a cattle epidemic to an end in Neckarrems a hundred years previously. The deed took place in Beutelsbach on 4 September and was carried out by three men, the cowherd Hans Jerg Becker, Hans Jerg Knauer, and Friedrich Ritter. Although they had shared one and a half *Mass* (a little more than two liters) of wine together, they were by no means drunk. The Schultheiss ordered that when the bull was brought to the grave, it was to be shot in the head and then buried. Although Reinhard was not a witness, he heard that 200 people attended the event and that apparently the bull had not been shot. In fact, it took three attempts to get the bull into the grave. Feeling so sorry for the animal, the lieutenant had not asked any further about the matter, except to enquire why it had to be done. The cowherd, Schultheiss, and Bürgermeister had all told him the story about the cattle epidemic in Neckarrems a hundred years previously. In addition, the cowherd (Becker) had also reported several days before that the bull had contracted the disease. Everyone thought that the burial had to happen in the way it did in order for its magic (*zauberisch*) power to have effect (*äussern*). The lieutenant felt he had to point out that no one had ever thought to bury a sick cow alive. In fact, the central government had ordered that sick cows be slaughtered and buried with skin and hair.

The next witness was the sixteen-year-old Incipient in the Gerichtsschreiberei, Abraham Mayer, son of the pastor in Steinenberg. He testified about the three men coming to the Rathaus to get some wine. The cowherd appeared a while later to fetch a rope to tie the bull with, at which time he told Lieutenant Reinhard that the Schultheiss had given the order to shoot the bull. Nothing else was said then except that the animal was sick. Four days later, the *Feldschütz* Knauer told him that as the cowherd Becker was leaving, the Schultheiss, standing in the doorway, had cancelled the order to slaughter the animal first.

One of the members of the village Gericht was the fifty-year-old surgeon, Christoph Barchet. When it came time to discuss the issue in the Rat he had left the village rather than take part in the resolution. He

7. Burial and monument in Beutelsbach (*Württemberg Landesstelle für Volkskunde, Stuttgart*).

was aware that as a surgeon, well versed in physics and philosophy, he could be expected to oppose superstition. In fact, he had had a set-to with the Schultheiss on the Rat over just that issue. About eight days before an official from Stuttgart had come to give instructions about the epidemic, the *Dorfschütz* had been sent to a blind shepherd in Kirchheim to get him to help heal the cattle.[5] Barchet expressed the opinion that the shepherd could not be of much use unless he came to the village, to which the Dorfschütz replied that he had helped other people already even when he was not present – one did not have to worry any more. As far as sympathetic means were concerned, the surgeon held them for useless, and the notion that they could have effect as pure superstition. But the Schultheiss in a very offensive manner said that Barchet did not know everything. One of the Räte present noted that a French doctor at Endersbach had ordered the burial of a bull after it had mounted a sick cow. And then the Schultheiss mockingly said, 'That, of course, Barchet would believe.' Although Barchet did not stay around the village to discuss the matter further, he was able to say that the decision was taken in the Rat on Sunday after the morning church service. Customarily during the church service, the Schultheiss invited Rat members to gather together when there was anything to discuss.

Johannes Schwegler, aged forty-three, another surgeon in the village and member of the Rat, testified that over a hundred head of cattle had died so far in the epidemic. At the meeting of the Rat on Sunday after church, the Schultheiss had informed them all that the bull was sick. He also related that various villages in the region had learned that if a bull was buried at a crossroads, the epidemic would be snuffed out. The question was put as to whether Beutelsbach should give the method a try. Some were of the opinion that it would do little good, but it would not hurt to try anything. In any event, there was no decision, and Schwegler was no longer able to say who in the Rat was for the measure and who was against it. Furthermore, he never heard anything about the burial of a *live* bull and was sure that it had always been a question of killing the bull first. It could be that he had missed something, since as a member of the Rat and not of the Gericht he did not attend all of the meetings. He also did not attend the execution of the bull. When Bolley expressed great skepticism over his testimony, he noted that all four of his cows had died, and he therefore had little to expect from any action. In all probability, he had thought to himself that such means would not be of very much use. He had to admit that the official document about superstition during a cattle epidemic had been read in church before the burial of the bull took place.

In order to clear up a few details, the surgeon Barchet was recalled. He said that in one assembly of the Gericht and Rat, a live burial had been discussed. He could not say whether pressure for the burial came from the villagers (*Bürgerschaft*) or who was responsible for starting the idea in the first place. He observed people going by his house on the day of the event itself with buckets full of earth to bury the bull, but he could not recall any particular names. He also heard that two members of the Rat were there but did not know which ones.

The schoolmaster, Matheus Eberhard Hammer, happened by chance to be in a field near the burial. He heard a noise and saw a lot of people, but by the time he came along to investigate, the bull was already buried. In any event he heard absolutely nothing about the stupid prank beforehand. Except for the three men who did the deed, he could not think of anyone he saw at the time. The schoolmaster then said that he was against the deed but was of the opinion that once the sacrifice was made, that would bring an end to the matter. He also did not think that the burial place was a real crossroads. One of the 'roads' was more of a path that lost itself among the fields. He heard later that the Schultheiss had been asked by several villagers to do what had been done.

The court recorder (Gerichtsschreiber), August Ludwig Billfinger, had been absent from the village when it all happened. According to him, it was the general opinion (*Gerücht*) that such a burial was a means of curing a cattle epidemic.

Johannes Kuhnle, thirty-seven, son-in-law of the oldest Richter, Bernhard Koch, actually attended the burial. He noted that it was very dangerous to try to kill a bull in an open field. Even though several people had axes, it was found to be too dangerous to use them. But as luck would have it, the bull slipped into the grave accidentally – otherwise it certainly would have been slaughtered.

Michael Ellwangen, forty-five, was in his field but came along when he heard the noise. By the time he got there, the bull had already been buried. It had slipped into the grave. All there was to observe was a great tumult of women and children – nothing important – so he went on. Although he had never heard the story about burying a live bull, he had to say that he ignores all such tales anyway.

Already having lost eight cattle, the miller and Richter, Augusten Raff, was against the decision to bury the bull. For him, the epidemic was a judgment of God that no one could escape. He was also unable to say how anyone voted, although most did vote in the affirmative. It was not decided under which crossroads the bull was to be buried, nor was it expressly said that it should be buried alive. The story was that the 'sympathetic' means involved would have their effect after the bull had mounted a sick cow. At the time of the council discussion, the bull was not yet sick. He further said that he did not approve of the magistrates being called together to a meeting on Sunday, which happened all too often in the village.

Friedrich Koch, son of the Heiligenpfleger and himself Richter, came along once the bull was in the grave. Because it had fallen in by itself, it was impossible to slaughter it. He had never heard anything about such a burial being able to prevent a cattle epidemic.

One of the village butchers, Leonhard Vollmar, fifty-six, had gone along to slaughter the animal and was there from the beginning. Indeed the bull had slipped into the grave, but it was then dug out because it was standing up. He could not say what happened after that because he left. Not having been asked to slaughter the animal, he had no other reason to be there.

At this point, the commissioner Bolley went to view the spot where the burial took place and concluded that it really was a crossroads. He then continued questioning various people, several of whom had passed by at the time but were unable to say anything about the matter.

One of the oldest members of the Gericht, Wendel Gaupp, seventy-seven, said that he was out there in the field at the time. He wanted to get a look at what was happening, but there were so many people that he could not get to the grave. He had indeed heard the superstition about a live bull and had in fact believed it. The Schultheiss certainly had a good intent, and many people would have held it against him if he had not carried out the burial. People would have been able to say, 'so was it with the Philistines, they did not believe'. Gaupp was not able to point to any individual who demanded the burial, rather it was a question of a rumor (*Sage*) in the village.

Further testimony was taken from various villagers. Jacob Vollmar III, who was getting potatoes from his field, was not believed when he said that he had not been interested enough to go along and see what was happening. He said he was not as curious as other people. As for the rest, there were the same contradictions about who had helped and who had seen what. Michael Ellwangen said it was quite unreasonable to expect the truth from a single villager. One would risk having one's windows broken in, and no one would pay for them.

Then Bolley got to the actual men who had carried out the deed. The cowherd Hans Jerg Becker, thirty-two, had been the caretaker (*Pflegevater*) of the bull. He buried it so that the cattle epidemic would stop. This method had been suggested by David Langenbach, who had worked as a journeyman mason in Schwetzingen. There, an epidemic among the swine had been ended by burying one at a crossroads. Since the bull in Beutelsbach was sick, he had been told by the Dorfschütz to take it out and bury it at a crossroads. As for himself, he did not want to watch, but in any event it was never a question of burying the bull alive. After going over all of the steps of the burial, he maintained that it had been impossible to kill the bull. The third time it fell into the grave, it broke its neck. At the end of the testimony, Bolley suggested that he was full of contradictions and that although the story from Langenbach was about the live burial of a sow, Becker now tried to maintain that there definitely was no order to bury the bull alive. Hans Jerg Knauer, fifty, who also took part, similarly denied that there had been any order about burying the bull alive. Friedrich Ritter, mason, forty-four, also related the story about the swine epidemic. According to him, the bull in Beutelsbach was sick. He thought it had broken its neck when it fell into the grave.

Wendel Gaupp was brought back, together with Heinrich Breuning, who had given testimony that has not been summarized here. Gaupp said that the generally accepted story (*Sage*) was that the bull had to be buried alive. That, of course, is why he went along to watch. The bull would have been killed before the burial if the superstition had not dominated. Breuning also said that from beginning to end it was a question of burying the bull alive, for otherwise the epidemic would not end. That was the general opinion (*Stimme*).

Bolley then put the various witnesses together against each other and forced them to tell their versions in the presence of those who contradicted them – a so-called 'confrontation'. Friedrich Ritter finally said that he had offered to fetch his gun when the bull came to the grave, but everyone had said that the bull must be buried alive. All those who were there to slaughter the bull were sent away. Then he contradicted himself and admitted that from the beginning it was a question of a live burial. He had been given his order by Knauer. Bolley put as much pressure as possible on Knauer to get him to reveal who had given him the order, but he talked so confusedly that no sense could be made from what he said.

The source of the story about the buried sow, David Langenbach, said that he had never suggested that a living pig had been buried. Anyway, he had told the story only after the incident with the bull. Friedrich Birkenmaier, member of the Gericht, aged seventy-five, as an old man seldom went to church, and he could not remember anything about an assembly of the council. He seemed to be able to recall something about the burial of a bull. The oldest Richter, Koch, was too sick to come to testify. Hans Jerg Breuning, senior, Richter, eighty-six, was sure that in the council the notion about a live burial had been discussed. He had

ventured the opinion that it would not help very much, but since he had
no cattle himself, he did not follow the matter. In the discussion, the
Schultheiss gave as his source for the story the knacker in
Neckarrems. He himself did not hold much for the idea, but because
the bull was sick and the order had been given to bury it with skin and
hair, he was willing to give it a try so as not to have to suffer from the
criticism of the community. Breuning was unable to say what decision
had been made. Some had argued for the burial in order to keep the
villagers happy. Others said that it would not help. Another Richter,
Jacob Becker, was also at the meeting but did not remember any longer
what was dealt with. Some villagers probably wanted the burial and
some probably did not.

Hans Jerg Knauer was questioned again about the origins of the
order to bury the bull alive. He finally said that the cowherd Becker
gave the order. He had never said anything before because it had only
just occurred to him. After various confrontations and denials, the
cowherd Becker said he gave the first order to Knauer and that he did it
off his own bat. If it had been so wrong to do such a thing, then the
minister and vicar from the village of Schnait would not have watched.
Besides, several other villages and towns had done the same thing,
namely Neckarrems, Schorndorf, and Weiler. Then he said, in a brutal
manner, that the bull was his and he could do as he wished with
his belongings.

The vicar Jäger from Schnait said he happened 'by chance' to be
walking along the path with his brother-in-law, the pastor Bilfinger,
when they came upon the scene. By that time, the bull already had three
feet of earth on it. He said something suitable to the occasion and went
sadly away. Pastor Bilfinger asked rhetorically, 'Do you people think
that brutality exercised on an animal will help you?' Although the
schoolmaster there agreed with his opinion, most of the people told him
it was none of his business.

Another Richter, Philipp Lenz, denied that anyone talked about the
burial place in terms of curing the epidemic. He asked how that method
could help in any way, for the epidemic was a misfortune from God that
one was powerless to turn aside. There was no superstition mentioned
at the Rathaus.

After several others were called to testify, Bolley got to the
Schultheiss, Johannes Schuh, who he was sure was the source of the
order to bury the bull alive. Schuh testified that everyone agreed to
bury the bull with skin and hair according to the law. Some Richter had

related various stories at one meeting or other of the Gericht or Rat about burying an animal at the crossroads. He had said that he did not hold anything for the idea and would not give a pinch of tobacco for it. But the bull belonged to the community, and they could do with it as they wanted. During the epidemic, he had scrupulously followed the orders of the prince, often against the opinion and will of the villagers. As for the magistrates, it was all the same to them whether the bull was buried here or there. Out of necessity people often play false tricks (*Misstreiche*). Some of the Räte and Richter considered the whole matter to be superstition. During the discussion, no record was kept, and there was no real decision taken. It seemed a matter of no import where the animal was buried, and in any case, there was never a question of live burial. The Schultheiss suggested that people had given false information at various times because 'they did not know how to remember'.

The Schultheiss was unable to mention any specific villagers who wanted the bull buried. Among the common people (Bürger), superstition was very strong. He had found himself in great difficulty because so many cases of misfortune were piling up, and they were all simply in despair. Villagers gave many examples where this method had helped: Schwetzingen, Hebsack, Neckarrems, Schorndorf. In fact it would have been impossible not to carry out the burial for the very reason that the animal was already sick. Contrariwise, nothing was sacrificed, and no one ever thought of a live burial, which would have been too gruesome. What the Schultheiss had in mind was to use the burial as a means of stamping out superstition or of preventing an outbreak of it. Furthermore, if various people had not brought the matter up in the council meeting, he would not have mentioned it. He could not remember who had suggested the idea. He himself was far from being superstitious, which brought up the matter of the altercation between himself and the surgeon Barchet over the blind shepherd. Although he had said that Barchet did not know everything, he could not remember what the Dorfschütz had said in the first place to prompt the reply. The shepherd had a great reputation as a veterinarian, but the Schultheiss did not know beforehand what sort of methods he used. True, mistakes are sometimes made, but there is a difference between sins of wickedness and mistakes which one is driven to out of great necessity.

After taking all of the testimony, Bolley made his summary report on 7 November. He had experienced how many difficulties were in the way of anyone wanting to investigate the truth of any happening whose consequences extended over an entire village, especially where the only witnesses were the people from the village itself. He could only find a few people who were capable of telling the truth.

The first conclusion that the commissioner came to was that the bull really had been buried alive. Secondly, there were two men there to bury the bull – Friedrich Ritter and Hans Jerg Knauer. The cowherd Becker was believable when he said that he was only supposed to lead the bull to the grave. In fact, the sad fate of the bull lay on his heart. There were conflicting stories about whether Knauer was there the whole time or not. During the hearing, he got Becker to change his testimony. Bolley suspected some deeper meaning from the fact that Knauer was never willing to admit where he was. Without support from other people, the three were probably not capable of carrying out the deed themselves. According to the most reliable testimony, at least five other men helped throw the bull into the grave. While many of those named denied it, the matter was not pursued, since in most cases it was a question of simply jumping in to help.

Bolley encountered the opinion among many people from Beutelsbach that they were empowered to dispose of their own bull arbitrarily. They were not responsible to anyone. However, part of their attitude stemmed from the great publicity that the matter had received and the constant teasing which the villagers had experienced ever since the event. Their behavior had been shaped by the attitude of outsiders who thought that they lived in the kingdom of darkness, even though at the moment of carrying out the deed, their interest in the event was completely different. But now, because of the impact of the treatment by the more enlightened and intelligent part of the nation, they had become shamed and embittered. This brought Bolley in danger of personal threats, and he had had to be careful and cunning (and threaten the villagers with military force). With this mood in the village, it was somewhat undesirable to make the number of people guilty of the actual execution of the deed very large.

Bolley's third conclusion had to do with whether the bull was buried alive with intent. It was hard to see how it could have happened otherwise. In the end, Bolley obtained confessions on certain points. But the problem was that all the people he interviewed were in constant communication with each other. The facts were these: the bull was taken to the grave by the cowherd. There he was tied by the feet and pulled from the other side and thereby thrown into the grave. Unfortunately, the first time he landed on his feet, which meant that a way had to be dug to get him out. The second time he landed on his back but directly jumped to his feet. The third time, after landing on his back, he was immediately covered with stones and earth so that he could not get up again. As for Johannes Kuhnle's story that the bull slipped in, Bolley did not believe it. He pointed out that he was the son-in-law of the oldest Richter. The other son-in-law, Michael Ellwangen, said that it was too much to expect one Bürger to tell the truth. In the end, anyway, Ritter and Knauer admitted that the intent was to bury the bull alive from the very beginning.

The fourth point of the report had to do with the reasons for doing the deed. Everyone pointed out that the bull had been sick, even those who were against the burial. Bolley was not able, however, to venture how sick – it had certainly not been sick for fourteen days as the cowherd said. At least it had enough strength to get out of the grave, and if it had been so sick, then slaughtering would not have been so dangerous. It seemed clear that the bull was not buried because it was sick. Also there was no doubt that the bull was buried at a crossroads. This was done to stop the epidemic, and no one dared to say otherwise.

Much of the commissioner's interest was taken up with the fifth point, namely how the order was given and by whom. The matter was dealt with at the meeting of the Gericht on Sunday, 4 September. There the Schultheiss announced that the bull was sick and brought up the notions that had been mentioned at previous meetings. From all of the testimony, it was not clear who first put forward the idea. The Schultheiss proposed burying the bull at the crossroads, but he said that at the meeting he made it clear that he did not believe in its curative powers. Several people supported this part of his testimony, although most did not remember. There seemed to be no way to find out who was for or against the proposal. Almost all of them were indifferent to the matter of burial and raised no protest. There was no formal vote or decision taken. Only Hans Jerg Breuning, senior, said that the discussion was about a live burial from the beginning.

The question narrowed down to the events just before the burial and the orders given at that time. The cowherd Becker said that there had been no order at all – it should be noted that he lived in the Schultheiss's house. It is clear that only he came to get a rope from the Rathaus and that only he was given an order to shoot the bull. On the other hand, the Bürgermeister, Heiligenpfleger, and Schultheiss all say that Knauer came and not Becker. Thus the question of whether Knauer stayed at the grave during the whole event is linked to whether he came back for another order. Or, on the other hand, if he was not there, the whole thing could appear as an accident, or a demand on the spot from the Bürger who were present. In the end, however, Knauer said that the intent was to bury the bull alive, and then the whole set of inventions lost their value. However, Knauer still maintained that he had received no order. Scribent Mayer's testimony that an order had been given in the doorway on the way out can be collated with the fact that more than 200 Bürger at the graveside heard Knauer speak of an order. It is unimaginable that Knauer and Ritter would have carried out the deed without an order. Still Knauer denies that he had one.

Many people went to the show because the bull was to be buried alive, and the superstition had to do with a *live* burial. It would seem that since the Schultheiss ordered the burial, he also ordered its exact manner. Since the whole event took more than an hour and several members of the Rat were present, the only conclusion that could be reached was that the live burial was done with the permission of the Schultheiss, Gericht, and Rat. But the actual matter of the order remained full of contradictions. For one thing, many people were there with buckets full of earth and stones, ready to suppress the bull right away. Yet all of the Richter said that they had never heard that a live burial was necessary. One of them said that there was nothing unusual about a great crowd of people; it happened every day.

The Schultheiss said that the demand for burial at the crossroads came from the villagers (Bürgerschaft) with vehemence, and that he would never have made the proposal if he had not lost hope. He was pushed into a corner by their unreasonable expectations. On the other hand, he was unable to name anyone who had made the demand. None of the deputies from the community (Gemeinde) were brought in to take part in the decision, nor was a meeting of the whole village called. Heinrich Breuning maintained that if the village (Bürgerschaft) had been asked, the deed would never have taken place. It appears that many Bürger never learned anything about the matter and most were not even interested in it. Indeed, some were angered by this outbreak of superstition under public authority. Yet one can assume that many people wanted the attempt made, and many were hopeful at the time. And there must have been a large part of the village which did not disapprove.

Canzlei Advocat Bolley reflected that superstition was still common among the educated class of people, and the common man had a very crass grasp of religion. For them, there was little receptivity for purer notions. Both classes demonstrated their superstitiousness in the belief in the magical power of a church in the Remstal. As for the lower stratum, there was a great tendency to be receptive to the supernatural and the extraordinary. They would run after the hawkers of secret remedies, charlatans, and quacks, and were not used to paying any attention to the relationship between cause and effect.

Since the villagers thought that the bull was lost, they thought that by its horrible death their cows could be rescued. When they wondered about the thoroughness of the investigation, they often said that after all it was only an animal. What was done was probably not a violation of the sensitivity of many of them – here Bolley noted that he had a great deal to do with peasants, and so he knew. He was unable to say whether their wishes were communicated to the Schultheiss in any way or if they got him to take the first step. Perhaps there simply existed a tacit agreement between the villagers and the Schultheiss, and necessity led to the decision. The commissioner finished by noting that if the teasing by the neighbors did not stop, there could be a number of serious incidents.

After due consideration by the High Council, the reluctant Bolley was sent back at the end of the year to investigate further.[6] This time he concentrated on the exact events surrounding the supposed order made just before the burial. When he talked to Knauer, the latter was rude, kept wandering out of the hearing to check with people outside, and continually changed his testimony. There was also a great deal of interest in the rope that was fetched from the Rathaus because it was considered that this could have had no other purpose than to pull the bull live into the grave. Finally, the Schultheiss was questioned again and warned sternly to tell the truth. He said that he had been brought up to tell the truth and would continue to do so. Bolley said that all of the witnesses pointed to the fact that Knauer gave the order at the grave and that he had just come from the Rathaus. It was also known that the *Wildschütz* Böhm was there with a gun and would have shot the animal if allowed. There could be no other conclusion than that the Schultheiss had given the order to bury the bull alive. However, the Schultheiss said he gave the order to kill the bull, and began to cast blame on the Heiligenpfleger Koch and a council member, Joseph Breuning, who were both at the burial. There was no way of shaking the testimony of the Schultheiss.

Some of the solidarity of the villagers seems to have been shaken a bit, and a few strange incidents took place. The cowherd had apparently said at one point that the matter would have gone quite differently if Koch and Breuning had not been at the graveside. In fact, Koch's son, when he was drunk, had a document made out saying that those who had carried out the deed would be 'taken care of' for hushing up the problem of who had given the orders. Later, young Koch pleaded that he was too drunk to know what he was doing, and Becker began to fear that he was now going to be the scapegoat. The Schultheiss came along again later in the hearing and repeated his accusation about Koch, and began to suggest that other witnesses were untrustworthy because of deeds that they had committed in the past. Friedrich Ritter, for example, was a knave (*Spitzbube*) who had sat out a term in jail for stealing wine. Finally Heiligenpfleger Koch said that he was not the only one involved in the event. After all, one should believe an honorable man a little bit. Those behind it were the whole magistracy. He came back a few days later and said that the Schultheiss had sent him to Endersbach fourteen days before the burial, to a French doctor who prescribed buried live bull for the epidemic. Not finding any such doctor there, he was informed by the local Schultheiss that it was all empty talk. On his return, he told most of the magistrates that it was a matter of shooting the bull.

On 10 December, Bolley made his second report. He pointed out that Ritter had informed him that as soon as the Schultheiss had told him *where* to dig the grave he knew that the bull was to be buried alive. Bolley considered the Schultheiss to be somewhat of an enthusiast (*Schwärmer*). As for Koch, he appeared to be a good and sensible man but with a tendency to superstition. Both Ritter and Koch considered the Schultheiss to be a knave (*Spitzbube*), while others considered him crafty.

In January of the following year, Bolley again made his way to Beutelsbach, this time to force those who appeared to be principals in the burial to take an oath.[7] The ceremony was preceded by a sermon in which perjury was explained. The Schultheiss, Heiligenpfleger, Knauer, Becker, and Ritter were all warned several times and told how small the gain from perjury was in comparison with the terrible consequences. When they would not be moved, they were forced to take a physical oath. The Schultheiss swore that he had never ordered or intended a live burial. He swore that he told Knauer to kill it. The other oaths were similar in content. Knauer swore that he never received or passed on an order. He had repeated gossip as a mere rumor, but he could not give the origins of it. Becker swore that he had not received an order from the magistrates but thought that Knauer gave the order off his own bat. Ritter swore that from beginning to end the order came from Knauer. He would have shot the bull if allowed to.

With the oath-taking, the affair seemed ended; at least there are no indications in the reports that the men were punished in any way. From later information, the men who actually took part in the 'execution' apparently all received fines. However, in 1801 the whole affair flared up again with various accusations, changes of testimony, and attempts to unseat the Schultheiss. It all began in September when the former cowherd Hans Jerg Becker was put into the tower in Schorndorf on bread and water for six days.[8] He had broken into a neighbor's house in Beutelsbach with an open knife in his hand and carried out various 'excesses'. At the end of his jail term, he took the opportunity when summoned before the officials to say that he had sworn a false oath four years previously. Since then, he had had no peace. At that time, he had sworn that the whole village (Bürgerschaft) in Beutelsbach had demanded a live burial, but it had just been a case of the Schultheiss's order. Ritter and Knauer had also sworn false oaths.

In the several weeks that followed, a faction developed inside the village that tried to bring charges against the Schultheiss. Heinrich Geywitz and Jacob Vollmar petitioned to have the affair opened up again and to let several deputies of the village (Gemeinde) take part.[9] On 5 September, a petition argued that the largest part of the Bürgerschaft requested that the authorities rescue their honor. They wanted the responsible people in the famous bull burial affair to be publicly punished. It was pointed out that the bull was buried alive as an offering to the epidemic. The execution of this work of superstition was an act carried out by the enlightened village magistrates alone, and had no other effect than to bring the village of Beutelsbach into ridicule for a long time both inside and outside Württemberg. They had experienced in the previous investigation how the magistrates tried to pass off the work of superstition and folly on the whole village (Bürgerschaft), and indeed Knauer, Becker, and Ritter were misled into taking an oath that the famous act came from the will of the entire community. Becker now says that he was led astray by the Schultheiss on the grounds that it was only over an animal that they would have to swear. For over five years, people had been patiently waiting for the Schultheiss and magistrates to be punished, but they were still in office with their honor maintained. Finally to rescue what honor could be rescued and to punish those responsible, a questioning of the whole village was requested.

The immediate investigation which this petition caused was, however, into the motives of the two petitioners.[10] Apparently they had not gone through the proper channels, which involved forwarding their petition to the central authorities in Stuttgart by way of the district officials of the *Oberamt*. Unfortunately, they had sent it directly to Stuttgart, and then upon questioning alleged that they did not know about the rules. It was pointed out that the order regarding petitions had been read to all of the Bürger in the village. All that they could reply was that at the time of the publication of the ordinance they had no petition and did not pay any attention. When told that they were responsible for the details of every such communication and that this one had been sent out many times, Vollmar and Geywitz then pointed out that they had not been to church for a long time and so must have missed it all. Handing in a list of 129 Bürger who had signed the petition, Vollmar said that when Becker returned from jail in Schorndorf, he alleged that the whole community would be fined 1600 fl.[11]

Canzlei Advocat Bolley arrived in the village at the end of September and took fresh testimony.[12] The former cowherd Becker now related the story that on the Sunday before the burial, Ritter was sent by the Schultheiss to find a crossroads to bury the bull alive. Having found a place where no one would notice, the Schultheiss then ordered the job to be done late at night. However, Becker had refused to help, and one of the Richter talked the Schultheiss out of it. On the following morning, Becker started to take the bull to join the other sick animals which were to be slaughtered, but the Dorfschütz ordered him not to do anything on his own responsibility. The bull had to be buried alive at a crossroads. Knauer and Ritter, who were to dig the grave, first had a drink in Becker's living room, which was in the house of the Schultheiss. Becker was sent for and given the order from the Schultheiss to take the bull to the grave, tie him up, and throw him into the grave alive. But the cowherd was only willing to lead the bull there. When he arrived without any rope, he got into a dispute with Heiligenpfleger Koch, who then sent the Dorfschütz to get one. As the bull went into the grave the second time, Leonhard Vollmar wanted to shoot it, but Friedrich Koch and Johannes Breuning who came fresh from the Rat would not allow it. But as the second attempt misfired, everyone there called to have the animal shot so that it would not have to suffer any more. Knauer then went to the Schultheiss to get fresh orders, but while he was gone the Richter present insisted on a live burial, which was accomplished before Knauer returned. In any event, he came back with orders to bury the bull alive. The Schultheiss said the bull was to be buried with its feet towards heaven and its head towards the village of Stetten.

Becker saïd that at the previous hearing everyone had been coached by the Dorfschütz before testifying. Before taking oaths, the Schultheiss had warned them all to be firm. They would only be threatened with an oath but would never be forced to take one because of an animal. In any event, the Schultheiss promised to make good any costs to the participants. Becker was threatened with ejection from his house if he failed to remain constant. In the end, he got an 8 Reichsthaller fine, which the Schultheiss did not pay for him. When Bolley suggested that this new testimony came only from hate and revenge against the Schultheiss, Becker maintained that he had not had peace since he took the false oath. Unfortunately for Becker, Ritter remained by his previous testimony and maintained that the Schultheiss had ordered the animal to be slaughtered. Knauer said that he had too strong a conscience to be moved to taking a false oath just for his own advantage.

Bolley's personal opinion was that the whole affair was full of contradictions and no one seemed trustworthy. In his report, he pointed out that Becker had had to pay his own fine. Also, the Schultheiss had kicked him out of his house, taken away his job as cowherd, and recently fined him for some misdemeanor. In addition, Becker could not be trusted because he had sworn a false oath. He seemed to be motivated by revenge and hostility against the Schultheiss. If one decided to expand the investigation to question all the villagers, little would be gained since the problem was not whether the bull was buried alive but who gave the order. None of the leaders of the anti-Schultheiss faction were eye-witnesses. In one of their petitions, they mentioned that Breuning had sworn a false oath, but in fact he had sworn no oath at all. Since Breuning's son got Becker's post as cowherd, it would seem that the entire affair was resolving itself into petty quarrels of personal advantage.

At the end of the file of documents, a short report from the High Council was forwarded to the prince.[13] Bolley was commended for an excellent investigation. It was pointed out (as it had been by the commissioner) that Becker had never sworn that the whole village (Bürgerschaft) had demanded a live burial. With this major inconsistency, his denunciation of the Schultheiss and magistrates was very suspicious. As for the Schultheiss himself, his consistency throughout spoke in his favor – if not for his rectitude, then for his cleverness and subtlety.

It is difficult to compare some of this material with that in earlier chapters because of the nature of the particular investigation and the limits posed by the goals of the questioning. There is a certain eighteenth-century flavor to the discourse between the commissioner and the villagers – enlightenment versus superstition and ignorance. Certain themes which had exercised villagers in the seventeenth century seem to have disappeared, especially that of penance. Although some villagers saw the epidemic as a visitation of God's judgment, none of them seem to have called for a show of remorse and a wave of conversion to ward off the consequences of sin. One pietist seemed resigned to the fact that God's punishment was inexorable, but another suspected that one could get round God and obtain results in another way. However, that would have been an even greater offense. In the earlier metaphor of penance, an implicit exchange relationship was implied. Although Lutherans always had to struggle with the original notion of Luther that there was no way in which people could earn their salvation, the notion of penance, even when it meant mere receptivity, introduced a more-or-less implicit reciprocity. In the story of the buried bull, the dominant theme is sacrifice, which at first glance seems finally to introduce a clear element of exchange, although this time outside the Christian tradition.

To understand the nature of the metaphor of sacrifice, it is necessary to take a close look at the symbolism of the burial. First of all, it took place at a crossroads outside the village. It was from the outside that the epidemic came, and the place of burial represented an open route, a crossroads suggesting communication in general. No one thought of burying the bull under the crossroads at the center of the village; rather the place chosen was acceptable precisely because it was outside. In this way, it was not a metaphor expressing exchange but was a seal against transaction altogether. Nor were the categories of sacrifice those which suggest exchange – not across species but within, a pig for pigs, a bull for cattle. Contrasting sharply with the Hebrew-Christian tradition, the sacrifice involved no shedding of blood.[14] All of the drama surrounding the burial during the actual event centered on the issue of suffocation versus the shedding of blood. No one was allowed to sacrifice the bull by shooting, hacking, or bludgeoning. In short, the nature of the sacrifice differed precisely from the Christian notion in its bloodlessness and consequent lack of exchange: 'without the shedding of blood, there is no remission of sins' (Hebrews 9.22).

By not modeling relationships with the outside in terms of exchange, villagers were expressing the arbitrariness and unpredictability of some of the relationships which the village had with the wider world. And the notion of a live burial was conceived of as a sacrifice made to the disease, not to God. The only time He was brought into the matter was to say that His judgment could not be questioned; there was no use trying to placate Him. Perhaps the conspicuous absence of the Beutelsbach pastor in the whole investigation suggests that everyone saw the matter as simply outside his domain.[15] In any event, the sacrifice was to the disease and was associated by many people explicitly with cruelty and horror. The village was in fact communicating with the outside – with the epidemic – along the model of inflicted pain, a sacrifice, a destruction – through the mediation of the bull. The pastor from Schnait posed the right question when he asked if the villagers thought that exercising brutality on an animal would help them. It seemed reasonable to them because relations with outsiders – the recruiter, the quarter-master, the tax collector, the huntsman, the *rentier*, the debt collector – were frequently modeled along the lines of just such a sacrifice.

Another aspect of the metaphor of the bull lies in the puzzle posed by the story of sows being sacrificed to bring a swine epidemic to an end. In that story, a female pig was thought to suffice for female pigs. But no one considered the possibility of sacrificing a cow for the cows in Beutelsbach – it had to be the bull. The significance of the bull lies in the fact that it stood for the whole collectivity of the village in a way that no boar could do. In the eighteenth century, it was very unusual for a village to have its own boar, while almost every village had a bull.[16] In the transformation from one story to the other, the figure of the bull as representative for the village was therefore emphasized.

A central part of the story as it unfolded in the various testimonies is the notion of the village collectivity. One never spoke of the 'Dorf', the village as such, but of the 'Gemeinde' or the 'Bürgerschaft', often suggesting a corporate group but sometimes just the people who happened to live within the boundaries of Beutelsbach. Most frequently, the corporate meanings of the terms were used for the collectivity as it stood against the Schultheiss or the group of magistrates. Although officials were chosen with at least the partial agreement of the villagers, they were not the 'representatives' of the villagers, that function being left to the *ad hoc* village *Deputierte* questioned from time to time on this or that matter. There was the will of the Gemeinde and the will of the magistrates, both being corporations in their own right. The links between the two are complicated, but the example offered in the documents here helps to make a few points clear.

Perhaps the basic model can be understood by reference to other corporations such as 'master and college', 'dean and chapter', 'abbot and monastery'. Once elected, the head figure fulfills his office without direct reference to the opinions of his 'subjects'; or better, he has the prerogatives of Herrschaft which he can and does exercise. In this case, however, the Schultheiss constantly referred to pressure from the Bürgerschaft, and the way he conceptualized the relationship is a clue to the nature of the community, at least in terms of its internal government and the dynamics of Schultheiss/Gemeinde. Various witnesses suggested that the villagers would have held it against the Schultheiss if he had not carried out the deed. Schultheiss Schuh himself said that before burying the bull, he had been acting against the opinion and will of the villagers. He found himself in great difficulty because so many cases of misfortune were piling up. Indeed, he felt himself pushed into a corner. The problem lies in how he considered himself answerable to the community. Since his position carried life tenure, one would have to look elsewhere than the mere threat of dismissal for the sanctions that could be brought to bear on him.

In fact, the authority exercised by a Schultheiss depended on certain important moments of consensus. After all he was, as most village heads were, a native of the village, a landowner, farmer, and family member. His position was tied up with all of the relationships that bound people together as neighbors and kin. More importantly, the success of his office rested to a large degree on his ability to get people to follow his lead. The denial to any powerful group of what they considered their just demands could make a village essentially ungovernable. A small example must suffice.

It was quite usual for the prince or state of Württemberg to have the rights to the tithes, which once belonged to the church.[17] By the eighteenth century, a usual procedure was to auction off the collection of the tithes to a bidder or several bidders from a village in the following way. Before the harvest, an auction was held with prospective bidders estimating what the size of the harvest was likely to be. They would offer a price for the whole tithe, expecting to make a profit on the margin between the price bid and the actual amount collected.

Whether there was one bidder or several and whether the bid was for the present harvest or extended over two or three years, many people were bound together to make a profit. Sheaves had to be inspected, grain brought in, stored, threshed and delivered, all of which involved administration, policing, and labor. Of course, it was to the advantage of whoever won the bid to keep the price as low as possible. This was done by making an arrangement with the Schultheiss beforehand, so that various interest groups each got their turn at offering the low bid. Although a public auction was held, with perhaps visiting officials as observers, and minutes of the transaction were kept – everything running perfectly to form – in fact the central government was being short-changed. Of course, such ruses were part of the everyday life of a village and could only have been carried out by tacit consent, which in turn rested on a sense of mutual advantage and fair distribution. No faction could be excluded from important resources – at least no faction which 'counted'. The fact that knowledge which was generally available in any community could be communicated to the outside for use in destroying a Schultheiss is not the most interesting point, although village magistrates often left office under such conditions. The more important insight is into how the Schultheiss had to balance between factions, and how his skill was related to his prestige and power. A key word in the village vocabulary was *parteiisch*, rooted in the interest of a complex spoils system.

But the Schultheiss did not just balance different factions, he also balanced different sources of power: the secular and the sacred. By the nature of his position, he carried secular authority. He was the agent of the Würrtemberg state, and its most direct link to the subjects. He was the magistrate whom villagers had to deal with on a day-to-day basis. On the other hand, his power in the religious realm was substantial. He always sat on the church consistory, which among other things dispensed punishments for swearing, violations of the sabbath, and immorality of all kinds. He had the most prestigious seat in the church, was empowered to deliver an annual judgment on the pastor at the superintendent's visitation, and was always a central figure for good or evil in the formation of opinion vis-à-vis the pastor, popular piety, and village moral life. But this is mostly on the formal side; more loosely, his authority and power were related to the way he was tied to the village notions of the sacred and the supernatural.

How Schultheiss Schuh played both sides of his power base offers instruction on the way the system functioned. On the one hand, he seemed to have placed a screen over his 'true' beliefs. No one was sure whether he really believed in the efficacy of the buried bull or not, or whether he was an 'enthusiast' or enlightened, acting from his own beliefs or those of the village. He seems to have planted himself squarely in the area of 'perhaps'. In fact, he stood to win no matter what happened. If the epidemic had stopped, that would have increased the non-secular side of his power base, perhaps emphasizing the charismatic aspect of his official personality. On the other hand, if the epidemic had continued, then he had recourse to the argument that he had not really believed in the magic. He had simply done his best for a superstitious lot of people. All of this, of course, did not take into consideration the interference from the outside. What had been an issue of power and authority was turned into one of belief. As Canzlei Advocat Bolley said, the villagers were not used to thinking about the connection between cause and effect, but *he* was – and about the connection between belief and action. And just there he failed to understand the situation by searching for a belief/action nexus, when the issue was the relative power position of the Schultheiss and other members of the community.

Perhaps we can see the situation a little more clearly by turning our attention to 'knowledge' as it was processed by the community. It always came in the form of generally received notions, rumor, tradition, report, opinion – *Sage, Gerücht, Stimme*. Knowledge in this sense is social knowledge, worked out in the give-and-take of discussion between neighbors, friends, and family members. It is emphatically not a single 'truth', a coherent story with only one version, but rather a continuing discussion around a single theme, a reckoning of the probabilities, a fluctuating judgment. It is by its very nature a basis for *practical action*. It is part of the various strategies which determine that actions of village members are coherent and understandable to all the actors. There was, of course, room for individual interpretation, disguised self-interest, skill, stupidity, and conservatism. Judgment always comes after the fact and is based on the success of an action, whether a person emerged with honor, power, or esteem, and one could choose to lose materially while gaining other forms of capital – symbolic or social. The link between Sage – as social knowledge – and action, and between them both and success should make it clear that this kind of knowledge is always tied to power, and that as 'discourse' is not composed of a discrete set of ideas. Nor can the Sage be the belief of a whole village, as Bolley sometimes seemed to think. Many paid absolutely no attention to the reports, and even those who believed in them took various attitudes and gave them varying degrees of credence.

Given the structure of village knowledge, there was a basis for many different kinds of action. What the Schultheiss did was to throw his 'comment' into a running discussion. He had to be seen as acting from the Sage, for only then would his action have political meaning inside the village. As Gaupp testified, he could not afford to put himself totally outside the range of village reality – to become a foreigner, a 'Philistine', a 'non-believer'. When his conspicuous lack of success emerged as the village became the laughing stock of the whole region and subject to a very irritating investigation, then people tried to deny him the protection of the Sage. Some pointed out that no deputies from the Gemeinde had been consulted, nor had the Bürgerschaft been assembled, suggesting thereby that the Schultheiss himself was not even a part of the culture, which was patently untrue. Those who petitioned for a further investigation in 1801 put the Schultheiss outside the bounds of village discourse by ironically calling him 'enlightened', but more significantly coupled the superstition of the burial to its effect – which was to bring the village into ridicule. That is, the act became superstitious for the villagers in retrospect because of its disastrous outcome. Since such a result could not have arisen from the 'will' of the entire community, then the community could not have been said to be superstitious. Even Schultheiss Schuh could never mention anyone in the village who held the idea which he imputed to them. Although this probably came partly from the fact that he would never reveal something like that to an outsider, it was more certainly from the fact that no one held the idea as a *belief*. Practical knowledge is of the sort: 'one says . . .', 'I have learned . . .', 'I don't think there is much to it, but . . .' It is a basis for action, not for abstraction, and arises from the collective weighing of probabilities and trial and error.

The Sage of the village and the rationalized knowledge of the bureaucrat or journalist, theologian, or academic thus contrast quite sharply. Ideas from which one can stand back dispassionately and analyze on the model of the written text are not part of the world of the village. With this contrast, we can see why the surgeon Barchet, because of his position as philosopher, medical student and 'physicist', rooted in a notion of knowledge not subject to processing in the Sage, had to leave the village altogether when the matter was discussed. The Schultheiss tested his power against Barchet by denying him the sanction of village discourse. When he said that the surgeon did not know everything, he was arguing that his kind of knowledge did not cover all cases. It was not a denial of the effect and usefulness of rational knowledge but a denial that the rational could judge its own terms: it too was evaluated by the effects it produced, by its usefulness for practical action.

Both Canzlei Advocat Bolley and the surgeon Barchet had a model of communication based on ascertainable facts, clear ideas, and a direct access to truth. For the villagers, truth was instrumental, and the specificity of the ideas not so important. Whether the bull first mounted a sick cow or whether it was itself sick – or dead – the exactness of detail was not so impelling as the necessity to act. In a sense there was a truth for normal times and one for moments of desperation, a point which the Schultheiss repeated several times. Similarly, another distinction between implicit and explicit truth is clearly to be made and helps explain an essential problem for Bolley. If the Schultheiss acted on the basis of an internal village belief structure, then there was no 'fact' to be obtained. The search for an explicit order was bound not to end in the location of a 'corpus delicti'. Communication modeled on the Sage is implicit; it shares the structure of the metaphor rather than that of the declarative sentence.

In part, the commissioner was unable to penetrate the village because the knowledge contained in it was not subject to being made explicit. On the other hand, the village systematically denied him access to what they knew because they did not know what use he was going to make of it. They were amazed at the thoroughness of the investigation, which after all was 'just about an animal'. Feeling justified in using an animal for human ends, the villagers nonetheless knew they were not particularly prone to cruelty. The cowherd Becker felt sorry for the animal and was always referred to as its guardian-father (*Pflegevater*). At the grave, many people had had enough when they saw the bull actually suffering. Nonetheless, they quite rightly feared opening their values to inspection from outside.[18] There was a considerable amount of lying in order to create a screen of confusion, although probably no one thought of a concerted plan, even though there had been some coordination of testimony. Confusing the outside was part of a long ingrained habit based on the experience of domination. Since for the villagers there could be no knowledge which was not tied up with power, it would have been foolish to give those in a position of domination something to dominate them with. In addition, it was unclear and unpredictable how knowledge given to the outside would change the power situation inside the village. In the end, a serious fight broke out after the balance of power had been tipped. The faction attacking the Schultheiss could not imagine how the Schultheiss, having so clearly failed in his linking the Sage with action, could nonetheless have emerged with his power and honor enhanced. Whenever outsiders mixed into village affairs, the situation veered off into absurdity.

For the Reformation and for the moral philosophers of the Enlightenment, the accent was always on right belief. Justification, after all, came from faith, which, whatever the nuance of position, brought a noetic element to the first rank. When moral philosophers became concerned with reform, they attacked from the outset crass religious beliefs, uneducated conscience, or corrupting ignorance. Whatever the degree of optimism, it was necessary to attack these matters first before good practice on the part of the mass of the population could follow. Württemberg villagers, on the other hand, were more worldly wise, or perhaps saw under the mask of reforming notions the realities of social discipline and domination; they were more apt to see belief as a kind of matrix from which different sorts of action could flow. This was so because practical action grew out of the situation; it was part of a strategy directed towards maintaining or enhancing one's position in a web of social relationships. A story, a theory, a coherent structure of ideas could be shaped and reshaped in village discourse without anyone necessarily giving assent to them in any specific way. Community members could describe village opinion on a certain point without implying belief or the willingness to take any specific action on the basis of that opinion. What was thought to be the case and what people did were not linked in the definite way that a simplistic hermeneutic would expect. In fact 'mistakes of belief' were considered to be of very secondary importance and carefully distinguished from 'sins of wickedness', the latter being imputable largely to past actions in the light of how they worked out, and in terms of the social relationships that were rearranged.

Conclusion

A central feature of the analysis so far has to do with the dialogue over the nature of the individual carried on between state officials and rural village inhabitants from the second half of the sixteenth to the end of the eighteenth century. I have tried to show how the historian can draw conclusions about the nature of communal discourse on the subject, but I am well aware of the thinness of some of the results of my 'thick' description. A great deal of work remains to be done on all of the issues raised in this book, and I can only attest to the richness and variety of sources available for analyzing the nature of early modern German popular culture. In the discussion which follows, I want to reflect on some of the ways the exercise of Herrschaft introduced particular notions of the person, and in doing so, I want to confine myself largely to the evidence provided so far. The issues are far more complex than will be handled here, but it is useful not to draw broader conclusions until further spadework has been done on how villagers actually formulated their ideas, conducted themselves, and interacted with their fellows. I do not wish at this point to investigate at any great length books, tracts, and broadsheets which villagers and small town inhabitants possessed and presumably read, because the problem still remains how they understood them and how the ideas of churchmen–administrators, devotional writers, preachers, and folksingers actually entered into village discourse. Anyone who has sat in church long enough knows how difficult it is to draw conclusions about the social life of parishioners from the message of the preacher. But even if we take the popular classes as our object for study, we still have to consider very carefully what the actual message delivered in the village was. We have seen that pastors Schertlin, Bregenzer, Breuninger, and Mauchard all communicated notions which cannot be inferred from their theological training or their libraries.

Sometimes in order to handle large, complex issues, it is helpful to simplify considerably, so that the analysis can be sharpened and certain aspects emphasized. In this case, in encountering officials of the duchy of Württemberg, two broad, fundamental aspects of state practice have emerged, which without too much distortion can be labeled respectively the 'fiscal' and the 'sacral'. I wish to suggest that there were two general sources of state ideology in the early modern period and that they were rooted in different needs of the state. Herrschaft did not just involve a more-or-less well run program of expropriation; it was also heavily into the business of pastoral care. In neither instance was the development of ideology crude or simple. Within the terms of Herrschaft, many needs of village inhabitants were satisfied, and the hierarchy of communal power was entangled in its structures in complex ways. Viewed from above, the two aspects of state power involved separate, although related hierarchies. Sometimes officials were delivering the same message, and sometimes they were at odds with each other. We have seen in chapter 2 how the local pastor had emerged as a stern critic of taxation and various forms of official corruption. Between him and the Schultheiss, there had been a long-standing conflict about the nature of secular power. In chapter 5, the conflict between the two sources of ideology formation and between the two sets of officials seemed almost to take on the flavor of class conflict. In any event, both sides of the hierarchies of Herrschaft in the end were concerned with the well-ordering of the state – and at least by implication with its financial well-being – and with the spiritual/moral natures of subjects. Exactly how the state-church and the sacralized state interrelated is worth examining closely, and we will want to suggest a few aspects of that interaction at the level of the village in the ideology of the individual.

What conditioned the fiscal needs of the early modern state were changes in the nature and organization of warfare, on the one hand, and the problem of maintaining internal security, on the other. Fritz Redlich has provided a thorough analysis of the new military situation confronting central Europe in the sixteenth century and demonstrated how capitalist financial institutions within a structure of feudal expropriation created the conditions for the emergence of the 'military enterpriser'.[1] The competitive situation, driven on by ever-expanding cash flows, eventually radically transformed the nature of statecraft. Either the enterpriser was to become the state (Wallenstein) or the state had to set up and rationalize its own organization and recruitment of military force. As far as internal security was concerned, the great example of the problem in central Europe was the Peasant War of 1525, which was able to extend so widely and last so long because most of the German princes had overextended themselves in the Italian wars.[2] A glance at the correspondence between the princes shows that their chief concern was about how to get their hands on sufficient funds to pay for military captains and their hirelings to suppress the revolt. In larger territories, the centrifugal tendency inherent in the transformed military organization, 'bastard feudalism', and the new networks of power cemented by cash patronage, help explain the need on the part of princes and monarchs to create an independent officialdom at the cost of offering them ownership of their offices.[3] When by the mid seventeenth century the extension of state competence to the permanent organization of a military force took place, a further expansion of bureaucratic controls as well as financial sources to pay for them was necessary. Similarly, the state became concerned with the systematic exploitation of its population for military personnel. At the beginning of the process of securing a financial base for the new costs of warfare, subjects often resisted new arbitrary forms of taxation and feudal rent payments. Another period of intense conflict occurred during the depression of the seventeenth century when the great reorganization of military power, together with extensive and expensive warfare, was taking place. In the long run, the economic changes brought about by military organization, bureaucratization, and taxation were considerable, but the issue for us here is the ideological development which came as a result of the reorganization of feudal relationships.

The ideological intervention, which is so important to understand in any investigation of the early modern construction of the person, was closely related to the way the fiscal state gained access to the individual. We must be clear on the fact that many kinds of people remained outside the authority of the state until the professional revolution, led by medical bureaucrats, took place in the nineteenth century. Except as murder victims, small children, for example, practically never fell under the protection of the courts. In 8000 court protocols from one village from 1730 to 1870, there is no case of child molestation on the part of parents brought to official attention, and there are only a handful of cases where parents objected to neighbors disciplining their children.[4] Not every kind of behavior and not every kind of person fell under the jurisdiction of civil authority. The innovative grip on its subjects which the state extended grew out of the logic of an ideology based one way or another on its fiscal needs.[5] In the sixteenth century, this meant clarifying the units responsible for tax payments, assigning correlative rights to various kinds of property, defining more carefully the responsibilities of village hierarchies to outside authorities, and drawing up ever more carefully the rules of property devolution. In fact, one of the greatest innovations of the sixteenth century can be found in its extensive cadastral surveys and inheritance codifications. In the first instance, it was not so much a matter of radically changing any rules as fixing them down in written form. Then one had a way of knowing where some field escaped the attention of the state, or where a bit of waste land could be put to better use, or where the relative production capacity of different plots could be subjected to more sophisticated rates of expropriation. The basis was only laid in the sixteenth century, but the process of remeasuring, revaluing, and optimizing land use stretched over the next two centuries.

In Württemberg, cadastres were first drawn up at the end of the fifteenth century, just about when the crisis in state financing of military power first made itself felt. Tax lists were drawn up on a crude assessment of immovable property in the several decades before the mid sixteenth century, but, on the basis of two cadastral renovations and ever more precise attachment of land to village inhabitants, a first attempt was made at the turn of the century to provide an exhaustive register, not of taxes to be paid but of property valuations on which any particular tax could be apportioned. There is no need to follow the steps of increasingly exact and comprehensive book-keeping represented by the extensive series of marriage and *post mortem* inventories begun in the 1550s, or the records of land sales and mortgages going back well into the seventeenth century. On their basis, whenever a peasant had overextended himself, he could be efficiently put under a guardian or have his land auctioned off, before his creditors suffered or the state watched back taxes disappear on the books. The full implications of the system only developed in the eighteenth century, when this constantly revised form of feudal property and form of exploitation began to show strain. Further rationalization was then only possible under the great wave of liberal law-giving in the nineteenth century, when the individual was fully discovered and set free from the restrictions of tithes, feudal rents, and coordinated village agriculture – at his own expense, of course. But that takes us beyond our problem here. Broadly speaking, we can say that access of the fiscal state to the village in the sixteenth century moved largely around problems of rights of access to property, and in the eighteenth, on the basis of clearly defined property rights, centered more on raising levels of production/expropriation. But it should be clear that innovation growing out of the logic of the fiscal state took place on a broad front and was not just a matter of increasing taxes. Resistance, therefore, was sometimes frontal in terms of a tax revolt or the like, but was more likely to be partial and involve only some sectors of the population.

To show how varied the ideology could be, we can illustrate the process with two examples of how state officials gained access to village life and how various interests in the population were related to the ideology in different ways. In Württemberg in the second half of the sixteenth century, the prince's officials became concerned with the problems of control of the forest.[6] Sometimes this had to do with a differentiation of rights between village and crown or between village and some ducal institution, whereby villagers were excluded from forests to which they had 'traditionally' had access as the duke began to exploit them to his own advantage. More often, however, concern had to do with the depletion of forest resources as such – under the pressure of population, for one thing – and state officials began to lay down restrictive rules even for village-owned forest land. Recognizing the dependence of the peasant producer on forest for building, firewood, fodder, etc., officials were concerned with maintaining a proper balance in the household economy such that the peasant would remain a viable rent and tax payer. Although rents were seldom on forest products as such, the well-being of a peasant enterprise was determined by the whole set of resources, and the state was concerned with a clear definition of rights to use the varied and complex forest land. At the same time as the state began to intrude in this area, sometimes because of the intrusion and sometimes parallel to it, conflicts developed between peasant proprietors and farm laborers, or between larger peasants and smallholders, or between well-off and poor over access to village forest. The participants fought over the right to gather beechnuts and acorns, to herd geese, goats, pigs, and sheep, to gather grass and kindling, and to cut wood for building and repairing houses, barns, and sheds and for maintaining fences. In this situation, the state then stepped in as a mediator, sorting out the issue of rights to community-held resources by aiding in the closer definition of property. By the eighteenth century, state officials were more clearly involved in the process of optimizing the resource in itself, acting as managers in planting, rotating tree crops, and the like. In this example, one can see how the state was concerned with broad aspects of peasant production and with sorting out rights to village resources. Although the fulcrum of state interest was the peasant farm as an object of taxation, it both innovated social change and continually adjudicated the conflicting interests of villagers. As a result, the ideology was focussed on the peasant enterprise, farm or household, and a discourse of obligation, duty, claim, and right was created around that productive unit, a discourse which slowly changed its tone eventually to emphasize successful management and productivity.

The second example is the *Spinnstube*, a basic village institution, subjected to numerous ordinances and steady comment by state officials. In essence, it was a kind of spinning bee, a winter evening gathering of unmarried women, which combined work and relaxation. Naturally, such assemblies were the focus of intense interest on the part of unmarried village men. Hans Medick has shown that the many ordinances in the sixteenth and seventeenth centuries attempting to control immorality in these gatherings were aimed by-and-large at the vigorous youth culture.[7] The central idea was to make it impossible for young people to arrange marriages on their own and to see that marriage alliances followed the rules of property ownership. By supporting parents and intervening in Spinnstuben activities, the state was concerned with property devolution, inheritance, alliance, and the consequent access to resources. In the eighteenth century, by contrast, economic aspects of the Spinnstube came to the fore. Enlightenment commentators came to see that competition in the Spinnstube for honor among the young women spurred on work and provided a natural selection process for bringing together productive partners. In this example as well, the opening wedge of state contact centered on the issue of obligations and rights derived from institutions distributing access to property. Immorality as an issue was embedded quite precisely in the dynamics of family obligation. In a broad way, the household became a theme here as well, and the authority of the Hausvater was supported at its weakest point – where the problem of transition between generations appeared, when property devolution was at issue. By the eighteenth century, state administrators began to see the possibility of playing the parental role themselves in the interest of greater productivity and a larger tax base.

The fiscal state first created a discourse over the house and householder as a logical step to securing the peasant enterprise on a viable economic footing. A constant barrage of ordinances read in every village and town, either in church or to Bürger assembled for the occasion, promulgated the ideology of the Haus with its Hausvater. They restricted expensive weddings, large outlays at christenings, village dancing, all of the parts of peasant culture which set up among village members horizontal exchanges that could compete with vertical exchanges with the state. The massive attack on peasant culture was aimed at creating an image of the individual as a productive member of a house and cutting many of the ties which bound house inhabitants to their fellows.

In the early modern construction of the individual, the officials of the sacral state also played a central role. It is perhaps rather bold to abstract briefly from a long and complex history, but before the sixteenth century, there seem to have been two crucial turning points which help focus the issues for us here. It appears that the great discovery of the Carolingian period was that people have basic needs.[8] At least this was a central part of the understanding in that period about the nature of church reform. Illich has argued that the churchmen–administrators of the period promoted the idea that certain common needs among men could only be satisfied by professional agents, which in essence was a bid for creating a population dependent on their services. The second stage coincided with the Renaissance, when the final touches were put on the doctrine of individual souls. Pastoral care came to depend on a notion of the soul as having an inherent nature and supported the conception with a series of anti-images, which involved a radical innovation in the ideology of the person. Where there had once been crimes, punishable according to their seriousness, there now appeared individuals with monstrous natures. The heretic, the witch, and the homosexual were recognizable for the first time as intrinsically other, not part of the body of Christ.[9] The simultaneous development of the images and their fluid transitions in meaning can be illustrated with the term 'bugger'.[10] It went from designating 'separated' Bulgarian Christians in the ninth century, to the gnostic sect of Bogumils, to the Albigensian heretics, and finally to people whose natures as sexual beings were 'separate'. The confusion of categories still occurred in sixteenth century Württemberg where villagers referred to sodomy as 'heresy' (Ketzerei).[11]

In the history of the emerging notion of the individual, there are three aspects that should be emphasized here. (1) The ideology arose in a framework of professional pastoral care. (2) The complex set of notions came to be mediated through images of consistently 'normal' and 'abnormal' natures. (3) The point of contact between the officials of the sacral state and the newly defined individual was the house. Illich summarizes the set of connections in his discussion of the Albigensian crusade of the fourteenth century:

> 'The object of the fourteenth-century crusade against heretics in Languedoc was the network of households around Albi, which embraced attractive, *locally* ruled heterodox beliefs. "Cathar" households were perceived as forming infectious cancers within the body of the Church. The inquisition pried into the household to find out if the poison had spread throughout the channels of kinship from a related *domus*. Up until this time, members of households had come to the Church; now the Church moved in the opposite direction, overstepping the house's threshold. The deviant individual became the object of inquisitorial diagnosis and care. Within the heretical household, the theologian sniffed out the bugger, the person smelling of heresy. In this context, the term "bugger" was used in a doubly new way: It imputed a warped nature rather than mere criminal behavior, a monstrosity rather than nature's sinful enjoyment outside the bounds set by God.'[12]

The Reformation, of course, was heir to the notions developed by the late medieval church. In fact, it would not be stretching a point too far to view the Reformation as a revolution in pastoral care. To the extent that this was so, the new conceptions of the individual were of immense service once the first enthusiasm of renewed faith gave way to a long term program of discipline. We have seen how care of souls in Württemberg in the second half of the sixteenth century was centered on the periodic celebration of communion.[13] But villagers attempted to reappropriate the institution and turn it to their own use, emphasizing the insertion of the individual in the set of communal relations. They saw communion as a service which they would come to use when the time was right, which was quite the contrary to the intent of the officials, who considered participation obligatory and used the institution as a tool for putting in practice their program of social and moral discipline, without entertaining the slightest doubt but that the objects of their care needed the proffered services.

The issue that was dealt with by many churchmen at the beginning of the seventeenth century was the relation of external behavior to internal belief. It was felt that while the Reformation had brought true doctrine, a reformation in character was also necessary, and many argued that a true Christian was known by how he lived. A close examination of the theological writings of churchmen–administrators shows that there was a conjunction between the problem posed by the 'sacral state' and that posed by the 'fiscal state'. Johann Valentin Andreae can serve as an example.[14] The central issue for him was the authentic religious experience, which had two distinct sides, right belief and good behavior, for he considered the super-moral religious person if not following right doctrine as a sham.[15] But correct belief could only be demonstrated by a penitent heart and daily practice of a moral life.[16] He argued that purity of religion had been established with the Reformation, but the task of his century was to establish purity of life.[17] His solution was a program of discipline, which began with communion but went beyond that to a morals court, which would control card playing, swearing, lewd singing, idleness, marital conflict, and insolence of children.[18] He saw all of these delicts as disruptive of a proper life centered in the house. Thus at the same time as the needs of state fiscality were moving in the direction of an ideology of the house and good householder, so also this was taken up as a central element of the church. The individual was grasped by Andreae as fulfilling his religious quest only in his household duties, and in turn the well-functioning household contributed to the well-being of the state. Mediating the relationship of individual/house/state was to be the awakened Christian conscience, which was conceived by him as an instrument of moral discipline.[19]

The program which exercised officials of the seventeenth and eighteenth centuries was harnessing the well-ordered house to the needs of the state. Yet there was always tension in the legitimacy requirements of the two sides of state activity. As we have seen in the case of Keil and the pastor he was closely tied to, religion could serve as a source of criticism of the activities of the fiscal state.[20] Or the search for authentic religious experience could run in conflict with the official ideology of the house in the way the pastors damned the Drohmann brothers, who fulfilled the secular officials' definition of the good Christian householder.[21] In fact, the complexity of the issues, overlapping interests, and mutual and conflicting ways of seeing reality characterized relations between the two sets of elites.

The issue for us here has to do with some of the ways the notion of the person was developed inside the two parts of state ideology production and the process by which that notion – or better notions – were introduced. We are only offered fleeting glimpses into particular moments of much more complex discussions, and it is often very difficult to see the implications of the choice of images, words, and metaphors by which people explained or disguised their intentions to each other. What frequently seems to be at issue is an ever developing and ever more precise notion of the individual as an integrated whole, detachable from the matrix of social relations, and definable in terms of a discrete set of needs. In elite culture, the issues were often discussed around the notion of freedom, and each generation offered a different approach to the problem. Indispensable for the discussion were notions of discipline and conscience. To what degree villagers accepted some of the terms of pastoral and official discourse is difficult to say, but we can review the material in the preceding chapters to find some clues. In general, we will find villagers resisting in one way or other a notion of the unique, integrated, more-or-less consistent individual.

It is hard to get away from a notion of the individual to which we have been socialized. Clifford Geertz has remarked:

> 'The Western conception of the person as a bounded, unique, more or less integrated motivational and cognitive universe, a dynamic center of awareness, emotion, judgment, and action organized into a distinctive whole and set contrastively both against other such wholes and against its social and natural background, is, however incorrigible it may seem to us, a rather peculiar idea within the context of the world's cultures.'[22]

It is perhaps too strong to refer to this as the 'Western' conception of the person and not to recognize the enormous historical change and development. As well, it is important to see that the notion Geertz describes has a strongly normative element and is a way of distinguishing 'pathologies' and exercising power. By no means do all sectors of the 'Western' population share the experience of what the value proposes as norm. Yet we can perhaps use Geertz's neat summary as a touchstone in our discussion to contrast the points of view of ruling powers and ruled subjects.

In the sixteenth-century case, we considered situations where the individual was grasped in terms of an inside/outside dichotomy. Villagers talked about the fleeting impressions of emotional fluctuation in terms of the heart. But these were not a series of emotional states proceeding from a dynamic center of awareness but emotions reflecting external conditions. To be subject to attack from someone exercising witchcraft, or to be locked into a tangle with the authorities, or to be thrown into legal dispute with a neighbor or relative meant to have an unsettled heart. By contrast, clergymen were suggesting that one could divorce the external from the internal and that subjective experience could build on a bounded, controllable set of emotions. One could forgive before justice was done and compose the heart despite a situation of conflict. This is an important contrast to a way of understanding inner psychological states as undetachable parts of *social* experience.

Officials were able to consider reconciliation as a subjective act, which could take place in spite of whatever situation of conflict in fact existed. In the dialogue with Hans Weiss, the superintendent dissimulated by suggesting he should reconcile himself with his neighbors, putting the various actors in the drama on a horizontal plane.[23] But Weiss, in refusing to see the matter as a problem of neighbors, immediately stressed the facts of power. The people he was in conflict with were not his 'neighbors' but those with power over him. For him, a retreat into subjectivity was a capitulation to the demands of hierarchy. In fact, running through all of the testimony in the cases dealing with communion is a sense that justice was opposed to the clergy's notion of the person. Reconciliation followed after the reestablishment of proper social relations, not before.

By the early seventeenth century, the ideological construct of the person began to undergo significant revision. The split between subjective life and objective behavior was reconsidered and programmatic elements involving a notion of a consistent personality structure began to emerge. Churchmen–administrators such as Andreae or Arndt tended to undervalue the practice of periodic reconciliation as they centered their interest on the conditions for promoting regularized behavior. In fact, they suggested that there was no significant difference between the way a person acted and his internal spiritual condition. Along with this went an understanding that the individual could stand divorced from the community of which he was a part. As Andreae put it, being a Christian meant being held in contempt by one's fellows.[24] Someone really rooted in his community was someone sunk in sin. Constructed in this way, the person was grasped as positive in so far as he served the needs of house, state, and church, which implicitly for Andreae meant an individual who was prepared to cut himself off from essential ties to his community.

Keil understood that the demands of the state were detrimental to community and modeled the person accordingly in two ways.[25] On the one hand, he refused to believe that the consequences of individual action were for the individual himself. The person was not divorceable from his fellows and his sin could have disastrous consequences for his neighbors. On the other hand, he demonstrated how state activity could lead to individualistic behavior – in the way, for instance, gaming and usury followed from the example of higher officials. Implicit in how he constructed his vision was a counter-attack on a program of discipline. For him, expropriation was the central issue of the age, and he saw in state activity a denial of justice.

The clerical view of the person as individual was mediated in the seventeenth century through two fundamental images: the Christian and the witch. Both models were understood to be anti-communitarian and were in fact mirror images of each other. Both introduced a novel sense of the person into village society. It is difficult to follow in detail the history of popular notions of the witch, since too little close analysis of texts has been done to allow a balanced assessment. But it does seem to be the case that the witch as a consistent, evil person was developed first in elite culture.[26] How far the notion penetrated into village discourse is unclear. But we can see from Anna Catharina Weissenbühler's argument that one could tell that Gall Baum's wife was a witch by her evil face a tendency also to connect the external and internal as consistent with each other.[27] Perhaps therein lies an explanation for the fact that the contagion and seduction models of communication suddenly became so widespread in that society. In village and small town experience, the individual was grasped in community and communication modeled partly on the spoken word. In some way, sharing words with another was to commit oneself to him, to participate in a set of relationships. By grafting on to that experience the notion of a consistent personality, one that does not bend and change shape within shared experience, a unique individual, then the only model available was that of contamination. The word as a source of power when coupled with a notion of consistent evil was easily understood along lines of seduction. Just as God's Word was capable of creating the Christian with sudden force, so the words of the witch were capable of corruption with lightning speed. The witch craze of the seventeenth century can be seen as part of the dialectic between state and population, and one of its effects was to disseminate a notion of the person as detachable from the matrix of local relations. Indeed one of the curious theories developed by Johannes Brenz was that witches were incapable of doing any of the things to other people they supposedly thought they were doing. But because of their inner corruption, they deserved death.[28]

In the conception of a witch as one who simply engages in magic practices, who seeks to exercise one of the alternative methods of power, there is an implicit notion of the person as part of a set of communal relationships. This is understood because the struggle is over one of the goods in the society: property, honor, and the like. In Favret-Saada's image, the struggle arises where there is not room for more than one person in a particular space or position.[29] Such a notion of magic and witchcraft does not necessarily imply an idea of a witch as a consistent being, as a thoroughly evil nature. For that, a theory was developed by state and church officials and became a matter of everyday practice during the period of the witch craze.

Pastor Bregenzer can perhaps be seen as a transitional figure.[30] In the way that he considered his enemies as thoroughly corrupt, he was working with an image of the person as consistent and integrated motivationally. Part of the force of his metaphors proceeded from the fact that he reduced the individual to his position in a particular house and in this he was centrally concerned with some of the main interests of the fiscal state: alliance, property devolution, and organization of the house. In the way that he saw society as broken up into radically conflicting family groups, he was driving towards individualism, while at the same time stressing the house as the locus of individual self-realization. He offers one example of the possibilities inherent in a conjunction of the pastoral and fiscal view of the person, and in his peculiar vision is captured a profound despair for the possibility of justice in this world.

How far the concept of the individual entered into village discourse and remained a continuing element of it is difficult to see. By the eighteenth century, such notions as good and bad householders suggested that some village members worked with notions of consistent personality structures.[31] The inherent usefulness of such conceptualizations in the daily practice of Herrschaft is plain to see. No longer are the problematic images of the witch (outwardly conforming but inwardly corrupt) or the heretic (outwardly pious but inwardly full of poison) relevant. For officials of the fiscal state as part of a culture slowly defining its autonomous set of values, the outward/inward issue no longer presented a problem. External behavior, what one actually produced, was the measure of the contribution to the state. And under this ideological protection, the local exercise of power took place. On the other hand, those who suffered under the arbitrary imposition of that structure found in conscience a countervailing power, a way of suggesting the legitimacy of their claim to justice and of developing a strategy for defending their own definition of their own needs.

In the final episode, discourse over the person moved on to the level of feelings. Canzlei Advocat Bolley thought of the living world as sentient and animals as subject to feelings analogous to those of humans. He contrasted darkness and brutality with enlightenment and sensitivity, thereby suggesting a new dimension in the discussion of the relation of the internal to the external. A central problem for him was to identify and bring to consciousness the different emotions and feelings one was capable of, to refine them, and to run one's conscious existence in terms of the analogous emotional states in other people and animals. The refinement of one's identity took place not in the web of real relations but in the definition of others as containing the same psychological states as oneself. Such a process of self-identification would take place in an educational program designed to train the conscience and reduce corrupting ignorance and superstition. By contrast, villagers, although not happy about the pain subjected on the bull, did not project their own inner states on to the bull and did not define themselves in terms of reflective sympathy. Rather, they were embedded in a practice whereby the individual and the shared meaning of the community were not set off against each other. They understood clearly what Bolley suppressed, that knowledge could not be abstracted from power or from use. Internalization of values is always the internalization of someone else's values – the issue being to know who the parties to the discourse are.

We have only been able to skim along the surface of the problem of the historical construction of reality. We have not found an essential folk culture located somewhere beneath a veneer of civilization or insulated from dominating powers through a series of protective mechanisms. There have been the bits and pieces of a continuing discourse in which relations between people were framed in this or that set of terms, metaphors, or images. We have studied in part the dialectic between reality and people's perception of reality, and observed the reconstruction of new realities in a round of good faith, dissimulation, self-interest, obligation, hope, and despair. We are all used to organizing the history of our civilization around the progressive emancipation of the individual, but we seldom look closely at the paradoxical costs of dependence on those who have brought the message of freedom. That, of course, is the history of the Württemberg village. In the end, however, there does not seem to be any way of drawing up a balance sheet of costs and benefits. It may have been better for villagers to reconcile themselves with their neighbors as the clergy proposed, but we do not have to imagine that villagers did not have effective mechanisms to come to terms with the conflicts involved in daily communal life. It is all well and good to condemn the ignorance and savagery of popular witchcraft beliefs, but we might wonder why the tensions between neighbors had to be distorted through the lens of pastoral care. We may wish to place a value on the well-ordered house, but we must not fail to understand its role in the dynamics of appropriation.

Notes

The following abbreviations are used in the notes:

BWKG	Blätter für württembergische Kirchengeschichte
LKA	Landeskirchliches Archiv, Stuttgart
RGG	Die Religion in Geschichte und Gegenwart, 3rd edn (Tübingen, 1957ff)
RTK	Realencyklopädie für protestantische Theologie und Kirche, 3rd edn (Leipzig, 1896ff)
WA	D. Martin Luthers Werke: Kritische Gesamtausgabe (Weimar, 1883ff)
WHSA	Württemberg Hauptstaatsarchiv, Stuttgart

Introduction

1 For the problems involved in analyzing texts to study peasant culture, see Peter Burke, *Popular Culture in Early Modern Europe* (London, 1978), pp. 65–87, especially p. 66 and pp. 75–9. Burke does not make enough out of the power relations hidden in texts and uses the neutral term 'mediator' rather too freely to describe the redactor of peasant tradition. He is particularly good on the description of the kinds of texts available, their contamination, and the fact that they seldom come from peasants and other members of the popular classes themselves. His description of an 'oblique' approach necessary to analyze them for popular ideas is a penetrating methodological exercise. Carlo Ginzburg also discusses the problem of the study of popular culture through sources generated in dominant culture. He argues for a 'deeply-rooted stratum of basically automonous popular beliefs'. Although his book is essential for anyone studying the issues, I think his view is weak on two counts. He does not provide an understanding of what 'autonomy' could mean given the implications of his otherwise dialectical view of culture. Secondly, he reifies ideas and fails to embed them in a theory of practice. *The Cheese and the Worms. The Cosmos of a Sixteenth-Century Miller* (New York, 1982), pp. xiv–xxii.

2 A good place to begin when thinking about the process of communication in face-to-face societies is Basil Bernstein (ed.), *Class, Codes and Control* (3 vols., London, 1977), vol. 1, *Theoretical Studies towards a Sociology of Language*. He examines the strong metaphorical contents in what he terms 'restricted codes', which are forms of communication arising in particularist situations, context bound, and rooted in local relationships (pp. 175–8). Ginzburg unduly worries about anecdote and does not problematize the nature of communication; *Cheese and Worms*, p. xx.

3 See the issues discussed by Peter Burke, *Popular Culture*, pp. 23–9, 58ff. Although he argues for an interaction between high and low culture, he still tends to see rural culture as slow moving and traditional, acting as a kind of filter for impulses from outside. The level at which innovation can take place inside peasant culture is not discussed thoroughly.

4 On tenure rights in Württemberg, see Wolfgang von Hippel, *Die Bauernbefreiung im Königreich Württemberg*, Forschungen zur deutschen Sozialgeschichte, vol. 1, parts I and II (Boppard am Rhein, 1977), vol. 1, part I, pp. 120–4. The whole volume is a rich source for the institutions of both the original core areas of Württemberg and the territories which were joined to it during the Napoleonic period. Much of the discussion in this section draws on the volume.

5 *Ibid.*, pp. 125–7, 209–13.

6 *Ibid.*, p. 242.

7 Martin Hasselhorn, *Der altwürttembergische Pfarrstand im 18. Jahrhundert*, Veröffentlichungen der Kommission für geschichtliche Landeskunde in Baden-Württemberg, Series B: Forschungen, vol. 6 (Stuttgart, 1958), pp. 6–13.

8 Wolfgang Kaschuba and Carola Lipp, *1848 – Provinz und Revolution* (Tübingen, 1979), pp. 25–6. This volume contains an important theoretical analysis of the peculiar economic development of Württemberg.

9 See Landkreistag Baden-Württemberg (ed.), *Vogteien, Ä-mter, Landkreise in Baden-Württemberg* (2 vols., Stuttgart, 1975), vol. 1, Walter Grube, *Geschichtliche Grundlagen*, p. 14.

10 On the economic expansion and the rise in population in the sixteenth century, see the recent summary of the problems in Peter Kriedte, *Spätfeudalismus und Handelskapital* (Göttingen, 1980), pp. 28–44. The waves of mortality are documented in the Württemberg parish burial registers.

11 See David Warren Sabean, *Landbesitz und Gesellschaft am Vorabend des Bauernkrieges. Eine Studie der sozialen Verhältnisse im südlichen Oberschwaben in den Jahren vor 1525*, Quellen und Forschungen zur Agrargeschichte, vol. 26 (Stuttgart, 1972), pp. 36–48.

12 A study of the size of Württemberg farms in the sixteenth century has not yet been made, nor has there been much investigation into the partitioning

of land upon inheritance. A consultation of some of the cadastres (*Lager-bücher*) suggests that partible inheritance did not yet have the effect it would have in the eighteenth century. Compare the data on one village provided by Paul Sauer, *Affalterbach 972–1972. Weg und Schicksal einer Gemeinde in tausend Jahren* (Affalterbach, 1972), pp. 70–9. On the social structure of Württemberg in the middle of the sixteenth century, see Claus-Peter Clasen, *Die Wiedertäufer im Herzogtum Württemberg und in benachbarten Herrschaften. Ausbreitung, Geisteswelt und Soziologie,* Veröffentlichungen der Kommission für geschichtliche Landeskunde in Baden-Württemberg, vol. 32 (Stuttgart, 1966), pp. 204ff.

13 See, for example, the *Zulassungsarbeit* (thesis) of Ingrid Schulte, 'Ländliches Nebengewerbe in Oberschwaben am Vorabend des Bauernkrieges' (Ms, Bielefeld, 1976).

14 For example, see Franz Irsigler, 'Intensivwirtschaft, Sonderkulturen und Gartenbau als Elemente der Kulturlandschaftsgestaltung in den Rheinlanden, 13–16. Jahrhundert', *Atti della XIe Settimana di Studio, Prato 1979* (Florence, 1982); also his 'Gross- und Kleinbesitz im westlichen Deutschland vom 13. bis 18. Jahrhundert: Versuch einer Typologie', in Peter Gunst und Tamás Hoffmann (eds.), *Large Estates and Small Villages in Europe in the Middle Ages and Modern Times* (Budapest, 1982), pp. 33–59.

15 Kriedte, *Spätfeudalismus,* pp. 13ff, 31ff.

16 Hippel, *Bauernbefreiung,* pp. 242–3.

17 On this issue, see Emmanuel Le Roy Ladurie, *Les Paysans de Languedoc* (2 vols., Paris, 1966), vol. 1, pp. 187–235.

18 See the summary provided by Kriedte, *Spätfeudalismus,* pp. 67–70.

19 The 'poor' as a social grouping should be distinguished from the notion of the 'poor man' or 'common man', which designated the lower groups in the towns and the peasants as such, whether well-off or poor. The issue is raised in chapter 1. Contrast the use of the 'common man' or 'poor common man' during the period of the Peasant War of 1525: Peter Blickle, *Die Revolution von 1525,* 2nd edn (Munich, 1981), pp. 191–5.

20 A partial transcription of the diary of Pastor Wirsing has been made by Eberhard Elbs. The two extant volumes are in the Fürstenbergische Hofbibliothek, Donaueschingen, Hs. Nr. 676a and b. The selection includes the two months of January and June 1573. I want to thank Eberhard Elbs for providing me with copies and allowing me to cite them.

21 Hasselhorn, *Pfarrstand,* pp. 6–16. The pastors as a class of *rentier* in the eighteenth century can be studied by using the *post mortem* inventories located in village archives. Information on the pastors from one village will be given in my future publications on the village of Neckarhausen.

22 For the disastrous fall in Württemberg population, see the village by village reports in the Württemberg Hauptstaatsarchiv Stuttgart (WHSA), A29 (*Kriegsakten* II) Büschel (Bü) 105.

23 Kaschuba and Lipp, *1848*, p. 20.
24 Examples of some of the problems are dealt with in chapter four.
25 Kaschuba and Lipp, *1848*, p. 20.
26 *Ibid.*, p. 19.
27 Kriedte, *Spätfeudalismus*, pp. 15, 117–18. Reactions of peasants to taxation are dealt with in chapter 2.
28 Examples of the problems can be found in chapters 2, 3 and 4.
29 In one of the cases dealing with witchcraft in the period after the Thirty Years' War, two young children had to be placed in a new home. State officials attempted to force various relatives to take the children; WHSA A209 Bü 1467, 18 May 1658. See also 23 Jan. 1657. The theme of children moving to and fro between various relatives occurs often in these documents. At issue in many cases was what responsibilities relatives of different degree had for each other. The state in this period appears to have expected more from distant family than they were willing to offer. Some of the problems are illustrated in chapter 3.
30 See the evidence in chapter 3.
31 This is one of the themes of chapter 4.
32 For examples, see chapters 2, 3, and 4.
33 Material on the distribution of wealth will be offered in my forthcoming book on family and kinship in the village of Neckarhausen.
34 Helga Schultz, 'Landhandwerk und ländliche Sozialstruktur um 1800', *Jahrbuch für Wirtschaftsgeschichte*, part 2 (1980), pp. 11–50.
35 *Ibid.*, pp. 21–4.
36 *Ibid.*, pp. 27–8.
37 *Ibid.*, p. 28.
38 *Ibid.*, pp. 24, 28.
39 Kaschuba and Lipp, *1848*, p. 26.
40 For an excellent summary of the issues with numerous examples, see Heinz Reiff, 'Vagierende Unterschichten, Vagabunden und Bandenkriminalität im Ancien Régime', in *Beiträge zur historischen Sozialkunde*, 11:1 (Jan.–Mar. 1981), pp. 27–37.
41 Königlicher statistisch-topographischer Bureau, *Beschreibung des Oberamts Nürtingen* (Stuttgart and Tübingen, 1848), entry for Beuren, p. 146.
42 *Ibid.*, entries for Neckarhausen, Neckartailfingen, Wolfschlugen, pp. 117ff, 185ff, 222ff.
43 Statistics on the declining size of plots and the increased commercialization of land will be offered in my forthcoming book on kinship and family in Neckarhausen.
44 See my forthcoming book on Neckarhausen (n. 43).
45 Information for this comes from my study of village records from Neckarhausen and will be dealt with in detail in future publications.
46 See my forthcoming book on Neckarhausen (n. 43).

47 An example is to be found in chapter 6.

48 Examples are offered in chapter 5. See also my forthcoming work on kinship and family in Neckarhausen (n. 43).

49 Friedrich Huttenlocher, *Baden-Württemberg, Kleine geographische Landeskunde*, 3rd edn (Karlsruhe, 1968), pp. 83ff. For statistics from the eighteenth century, see WHSA A8 (*Kabinettsakten* III) Bü 85–92.

50, See Grube, *Geschichtliche Grundlagen*, pp. 10–14.

51 Information on officials and their activities comes from the *Gerichts- und Ratsprotocolle, Vogtruggerichtsprotocolle*, and *Kirchenkonventsprotocolle* from the village of Neckarhausen. I also lean heavily for this section on Grube's work, *Geschichtliche Grundlagen*.

52 Grube, *Geschichtliche Grundlagen*, pp. 11–32.

53 *Ibid.*, p. 14.

54 The *Communordnung* is printed in A. L. Reyscher (ed.), *Sammlung der württembergischen Geseze*, vol. 14 (Tübingen, 1843), pp. 537–777.

55 Information on the election of schoolmasters and their position in the village is taken from the various court and council minutes of the village of Neckarhausen.

56 Hasselhorn, *Pfarrstand*, pp. 30ff.

57 Data from this section come from the *Communordnung* of 1758, Reyscher (ed.), *Sammlung*, and from Grube's discussion, *Geschichtliche Grundlagen*, pp. 10–35.

58 *Communordnung* of 1758, in Reyscher (ed.), *Sammlung*, pp. 730–50.

59 A very useful article on the historical development of the concept 'Herrschaft' is to be found in *Geschichtliche Grundbegriffe. Historisches Lexikon zur politisch-sozialen Sprache in Deutschland*, vol. 3 (Stuttgart, 1982), pp. 1–102.

60 For the *herrschaftliche* institutions in Württemberg, the two volumes by Theodor Knapp are still very useful: *Gesammelte Beiträge zur Rechts- und Wirtschaftsgeschichte vornehmlich des deutschen Bauernstandes* (Tübingen, 1902) and *Neue Beiträge zur Rechts- und Wirtschaftsgeschichte des württembergischen Bauernstandes* (Tübingen, 1919; reprint Aalen, 1964). Also useful for the argument here is Hippel, *Bauernbefreiung*, especially for the many details on feudal dues. The modern discussion of Herrschaft is closely tied to the problem of resistance. See the two recent books: Winfried Schulze, *Bäuerliche Widerstand und feudale Herrschaft in der frühen Neuzeit,* Neuzeit im Aufbau, vol. 6 (Stuttgart–Bad Cannstatt, 1980) and Peter Blickle, *Deutsche Untertanen, Ein Widerspruch* (Munich, 1981).

61 Article 'Herrschaft', *Geschichtliche Grundbegriffe*, vol. 3, pp. 64ff, 72–3, 76–82, 85–6.

62 Central to a rethinking of violence and the modern state is the work of Pierre Bourdieu. See, *Outline of a Theory of Practice* (Cambridge, 1977), pp. 40–1, 190–7. Also (with Jean-Claude Passeron), *Reproduction in Education,*

Society and Culture (London, 1977), book 1. Much of my thinking on the subject has been developed in discussions with my colleague, Alf Lüdtke, whose recent book is crucial for further debate: '*Gemeinwohl', Polizei und 'Festungspraxis'. Staatliche Gewaltsamkeit und innere Verwaltung in Preussen, 1815–1850*, Veröffentlichungen des Max-Planck-Instituts für Geschichte, vol. 73 (Göttingen, 1982).

63 See, Alf Lüdtke, 'The Role of State Violence in the Period of Transition to Industrial Capitalism: The Example of Prussia from 1815 to 1848', in *Social History*, 4 (1979), pp. 175–221. On this point I would take issue with Winfried Schulze, *Widerstand*, who argues for a trend towards rationality in handling peasant opposition, especially in the use of juridical institutions. However, he does not analyze the use of courts as one alternative in the apparatus of violence.

64 Article 'Herrschaft', *Geschichtliche Grundbegriffe*, vol. 3, pp. 11ff, 16ff, 36f.

65 The give-and-take in peasant uprisings and resistance movements constantly makes the point. See the discussions in Blickle, *Untertanen*, and Schulze, *Widerstand.*

66 Article, 'Herrschaft', *Geschichtliche Grundbegriffe*, vol. 3, pp. 51f, 98ff.

67 Article, 'Herrschaft', *Geschichtliche Grundbegriffe,* vol. 3, pp. 98ff; Max Weber, *Wirtschaft und Gesellschaft*, 5th edn, 1. Halbband (Tübingen, 1976), pp. 122–30.

68 This two-part model is central to the work of Peter Blickle and is illustrated continually throughout his book, *Untertanen.* Schulze, although he attempts to work out a broad strategy of state activity vis-à-vis the peasantry, never develops a satisfactory understanding of the workings of Herrschaft. See his *Widerstand.*

69 See Blickle, *Untertanen* and Schulze, *Widerstand.*

70 An example is the peasant prophet, Hans Keil, discussed in chapter 2.

71 The literature on community and on Gemeinschaft is enormous. A useful overview is provided in *Geschichtliche Grundbegriffe*, vol. 2 (Stuttgart, 1975), pp. 801–62. A very useful study of village communities and the relevance of the concept of 'community' can be found in McKim Marriott, 'Little Communities in an Indigenous Civilization', in McKim Marriott (ed.), *Village India* (Chicago, 1955), pp. 171–222. See also Julian Pitt-Rivers, *The People of the Sierra*, 2nd edn (Chicago, 1971), chap. 1.

72 This is the implication, for example, in the article 'Person' in *Die Religion in Geschichte und Gegenwart*, 3rd edn, vol. 5 (Tübingen, 1961), p. 234. The discussion of 'person' as constituted within mediated relationships is also valid for 'community'.

73 The same problem appears in Ivan Illich's recent book, *Gender* (New York, 1982). On the issue of 'community' as an analytical concept and 'tradition' as something that needs to be explained, see the useful overview

by Sydel Silverman, 'The Peasant Concept in Anthropology', *Journal of Peasant Studies*, 7 (1979), pp. 49–69, especially pp. 56–7, 63–4.

74 See the stimulating article by Joan Vincent, 'Agrarian Society as Organized Flow: Processes of Development Past and Present', *Peasant Studies*, 6 (1977), pp. 56–65.

75 An excellent discussion of the problem is provided by Clifford Geertz, ' "From the Native's Point of View": On the Nature of Anthropological Understanding', in Keith H. Basso and Henry A. Selby (eds.), *Meaning in Anthropology* (Albuquerque, New Mexico, 1976), pp. 221–37.

76 A very important discussion of the person is provided by Marc Augé, *Théorie des pouvoirs et idéologie. Étude de cas en Côte-d'Ivoire* (Paris, 1975), especially pp. 162–233.

77 Edmund Leach, 'Rethinking Anthropology', in his *Rethinking Anthropology* (London, 1961), pp. 1–27, especially pp. 8–16. A critical reading of Leach's argument is found in Augé, *Théorie des pouvoirs et idéologie*, pp. 162–233.

78 Leach, 'Rethinking'.

79 See *Ibid.*, and Augé, *Théorie des pouvoirs et idéologie*, pp. 162–233.

80 The reference to testing borrowed bread for magic by first feeding pieces of it to chickens has been provided for me by my colleague, Hans Medick, who is working on the Württemberg weaving village of Laichingen; see, Pfarramt Laichingen, *Kirchenkonventsprotocolle*, vol. 1754–64, 24 May 1758. An example of neighbor women, even when they have never had anything to do with each other, joining in on a deathbed communion can be found in WHSA A209 Bü 1467, 8 April 1658.

81 An example can be found in the documents from the village of Neckarhausen where a wife repeatedly accused her husband of witchcraft worked during mealtimes. She refused to let him eat with her and the children. She could only digest food when she ate alone. Every time she ate with her husband, she was subject to magical attack. She would not let a son from an earlier marriage take bread from him. *Kirchenkonventsprotocolle*, vol. 2, 22 January 1769, 25 February 1770, 13 July 1770, 11 January 1771. Another example where a man was suspected of poisoning his wife through magical attack can be found in WHSA A209 Bü 1467, 13 October 1656.

82 An examination of the epithets used in kin relations will be contained in my forthcoming book on family and kinship in Neckarhausen (n. 43).

83 A very important analysis of 'conscience' is at present being undertaken by Heinz-Dieter Kittsteiner. He has kindly given me permission to refer to an unpublished paper, 'Von der Gnade zur Tugend. Zwei Beispiele aus einer Kulturgeschichte des Gewissens'.

84 This perspective is lacking in Geertz's article, 'Native's Point of View'. For an important discussion of the 'person', consult Michelle Z. Rosaldo,

Knowledge and Passion: Ilongot Notions of Self and Social Life (Cambridge, 1980).

85 I am thinking here of Fortes, for example. There are two useful discussions of his way of dealing with belief and action: Marshall Sahlins, *Culture and Practical Reason* (Chicago, 1976), pp. 4–18 and J. A. Barnes, *Three Styles in the Study of Kinship* (Berkeley, California, 1972), chap. 3. A good example of Fortes' thinking on the relationship is 'Kinship and the Axiom of Amity', in his *Kinship and the Social Order* (London, 1970), pp. 219–49. One of the problems with the present investigation of popular culture is that it seeks to get at that culture as if it were a set of ideas, different from but analogous to that of 'high culture'. On the one hand, action and practice are not studied as part of culture. On the other, the ideas and values are not grasped as part of practice but remained reified. This problem, it seems to me, is not overcome in Peter Burke's work, *Popular Culture*. Chapters 2 and 6 above are exercises in the study of culture and practice, belief and action.

1. Communion and community

1 The sources are found in the records of church visitations (*Synodus Protocolle*) in the Landeskirchliches Archiv (LKA) in Stuttgart. They are cited by year, volume (when more than one per year), and folio number.

2 An excellent critical introduction to church visitation practice in the sixteenth century is to be found in Gerald Strauss, *Luther's House of Learning: Indoctrination of the Young in the German Reformation* (Baltimore, 1978), chaps. 12–14. For a useful overview of the context of Württemberg church institutions, see Martin Brecht, *Kirchenordnung und Kirchenzucht in Württemberg vom 16. bis zum 18. Jahrhundert,* Quellen und Forschungen zur Württembergischen Kirchengeschichte, vol. 1 (Stuttgart, 1967), pp. 9–52.

3 LKA *Synodus Protocolle* 1587 II, fol. 203.

4 Hermann Ehmer, *Valentin Vannius und die Reformation in Württemberg,* Veröffentlichungen der Kommission für geschichtliche Landeskunde in Baden-Württemberg, Series B: Forschungen, vol. 81 (Stuttgart, 1976), pp. 77–8; Brecht, *Kirchenordnung,* pp. 21, 47, 51–2.

5 Brecht, *Kirchenordnung,* p. 41. *Kirchen-Ordnung von 1559,* in A. L. Reyscher (ed.), *Sammlung der württembergischen Geseze,* vol. 8 (Tübingen, 1834), p. 254.

6 Ehmer, *Vannius,* p. 77; Brecht, *Kirchenordnung,* p. 39.

7 See below p. 52; LKA *Synodus Protocolle* 1584 II, fol. 216.

8 LKA *Synodus Protocolle* 1587 I, fol. 220. Throughout this book, certain parts of the narrative are displayed as quotations. I am following a convention frequently used by French historians and social scientists and Anglo-Saxon

anthropologists, which allows me to highlight certain materials and to establish the parts of the text for which I will offer a 'close reading'. The displayed portions are not usually quotations but paraphrases closely following the language and rhythms of the original sources. Whenever material from the texts is directly quoted, quotation marks are used.

9   Martin Luther, *Von weltlicher Obrigkeit, wie weit man ihr gehorsam schuldig sei* (1523), in *D. Martin Luthers Werke: Kritische Gesamtausgabe* (WA) (Weimar, 1883ff), vol. 11, pp. 268–9.

10 *Ibid.*, pp. 264–5. This position was also held later, for example, in *Vermahnung zum Sakrament des Leibes und Blutes unsers Herrn* (1530) in WA, vol. 30, part 2, p. 107.

11 Johannes Brenz, *Ob ein obrigkeit über das gewissen handle, wann sie mit gewalt die verfüerischen leerer verweiset,* in Johannes Brenz, *Frühschriften,* edited by Martin Brecht, Gerhard Schäfer, and Frieda Wolf, vol. 2 (Tübingen, 1974), pp. 501–5.

12 *Ibid.*, p. 502.

13 *Ibid.*

14 *Ibid.*, p. 503.

15 *Ibid.*, p. 505.

16 *Ibid.*

17 *Visitations-Ordnung vom 4. Mai 1547,* in Reyscher (ed.), *Sammlung,* vol. 8, p. 70.

18 *General Reskript, betr. die Visitation der Speziale vom 6. August 1597,* in Reyscher (ed.), *Sammlung,* vol. 8, p. 300.

19 Luther's tracts on the Peasant War dealt with the issue of mercy several times, carefully distinguishing the concept from that of compassion. Because of their disobedience, the peasants had earned nothing but punishment. No official had the right to proceed with compassion (*Barmherzigkeit*). However, it was possible to extend mercy (*Gnade*) and not to punish as required by law. To receive mercy, the rebellious peasants had to surrender – otherwise the state had every right not to show compassion. *Ein Sendbrief von dem harten Büchlein wider die Bauern* (1525), in WA, vol. 18, pp. 385–90.

20 Weiss' conflict with authority was by no means an isolated case. In the story of Jacob Heer (LKA *Synodus Protocolle* 1587 II, fol. 209, retold on p. 52), enmity with officials was noted. In the village of Neckarhausen, Jerg Maier was put in jail for swearing at the pastor and refusing to attend communion (*Synodus Protocolle* 1587 II, fol. 218). In Enzweihingen (*Synodus Protocolle* 1584 fol. 230), a man did not go to communion because of quarrels with the village peace officer (*Dorfschütz*). In Neckartenzlingen the recalcitrant Bastian Heim got put in jail for swearing and not attending communion (*Synodus Protocolle* 1582, fol. 176). In Unterensingen, Andreas

Fausel (*Synodus Protocolle* 1582, fol. 177) was not brought to obedience despite the threat of jail. In Neckarhausen Matthias Dettinger (*Synodus Protocolle* 1586, fol. 177) was to be corporally punished and put in jail for blasphemy and non-attendance at communion (see p. 51 below).

21 *Vermahnung*, WA, vol. 30, part 2, p. 131.
22 *Ibid.*, pp. 131–2.
23 Ehmer, *Vannius*, p. 75.
24 Johannes Brenz, *Vermahnung obgemelter argument, so der warheit im sacrament des leibs und blut Christi zuwider sein . . .* (3 September 1529) in *Frühschriften.* p. 453.
25 *Ibid.*, pp. 453–4.
26 *Ibid.*, p. 459.
27 *Kirchen-Ordnung von 1559*, in Reyscher (ed.), *Sammlung*, vol. 8, pp. 195ff.
28 *Ibid.*, pp. 192–3.
29 Reyscher (ed.), *Sammlung*, vol. 8, p. 113, footnote 75.
30 LKA *Synodus Protocolle* 1582, fol. 69.
31 LKA *Synodus Protocolle* 1586 II, fol. 123.
32 LKA *Synodus Protocolle* 1587 I, fol. 251.
33 LKA *Synodus Protocolle* 1586 II, fol. 521.
34 LKA *Synodus Protocolle* 1587 I, fol. 159.
35 LKA *Synodus Protocolle* 1584 I, fol. 220.
36 LKA *Synodus Protocolle* 1586 II, fol. 59.
37 See p. 52, the case of Jacob Heer, LKA *Synodus Protocolle* 1587 II, fol. 209.
38 Friedrich Armin Loofs, 'Abendmahl', in *Realencyklopädie für protestantische Theologie und Kirche (RTK)*, 3rd edn, vol. 1 (Leipzig, 1896), pp. 66–7.
39 *Kirchen-Ordnung von 1559*, in Reyscher (ed.), *Sammlung*, vol. 8, p. 265.
40 LKA *Synodus Protocolle* 1587 I, fol. 138.
41 LKA *Synodus Protocolle* 1586 II, fol. 251.
42 LKA *Synodus Protocolle* 1587 II, fols. 210ff. See p. 52 above.
43 LKA *Synodus Protocolle* 1584 I, fol. 230.
44 *Vermahnung*, WA, vol. 30, part 2, pp. 595–626.
45 'Gedächtnis', in Jacob Grimm and Wilhelm Grimm, *Deutsches Wörterbuch*, vol. 4 (Leipzig, 1878), pp. 1927ff.
46 *Vermahnung*, WA, vol. 30, part 2, pp. 616–17.
47 *Ibid.*, pp. 618, 621.
48 *Ibid.*, p. 617.
49 *Ibid.*, pp. 601–2.
50 *Ibid.*, p. 623.
51 LKA *Synodus Protocolle* 1582, fol. 118.
52 *Vom Missbrauch der Messe*, in WA, vol. 8, p. 517.

53 *Ibid.*, p. 518.
54 *Eyn Sermon von dem newen Testament das ist von der heyligen Messe*, in WA, vol. 6, p. 364.
55 An important new discussion is provided in the unpublished paper by Heinz-Dieter Kittsteiner, 'Von der Gnade zur Tugend. Zwei Beispiele aus einer Kulturgeschichte des Gewissens'. A useful summary of the Western discussion on conscience, putting Luther in context, is M. Kähler's article, 'Gewissen', in *RTK*, vol. 6, pp. 646–54.
56 Article 'Abendmahl' in *Die Religion in Geschichte und Gegenwart* (*RGG*), 3rd edn, vol. 1 (Tübingen, 1957), p. 30.
57 LKA *Synodus Protocolle* 1586, fol. 177. It does not seem to me here that this case deals with anabaptist thinking. At least that is not the kernel of the argument. See the discussion in Franklin Hamlin Littel, *The Anabaptist View of the Church*, 2nd edn (Boston, 1958), pp. 98–101.
58 LKA *Synodus Protocolle* 1587 II, fols. 210f.
59 LKA *Synodus Protocolle* 1587 II, fols. 210f.
60 LKA *Synodus Protocolle* 1584 II, fol. 216.
61 Recent analysis of witchcraft distinguishes between those individuals who actively practice acts which are meant to harm specific individuals (or are thought to) and others who can harm without intent and often with no specific target. The classic statement of the problem is found in E. R. Leach, *Rethinking Anthropology* (New York, 1966), pp. 19–27. An important discussion of the various arguments is found in Marc Augé, *Théorie des pouvoirs et idéologie. Étude de cas en Côte-d'Ivoire* (Paris, 1975), pp. 85–233.
62 LKA *Synodus Protocolle* 1585 II, fol. 202.
63 LKA *Synodus Protocolle* 1582, fol. 117.
64 Ehmer, *Vannius*, p. 52.
65 *Sermon von der heyligen Messe*, in WA, vol. 6, p. 362.
66 Article 'Abendmahl', *RGG*, vol. 1, p. 35.
67 Ehmer, *Vannius*, pp. 61–2.
68 Johann Georg Hartmann (ed.), *Kirchengeseze des Herzogthums Wirtemberg*, vol. 3 (Stuttgart, 1798), p. xxx.
69 *Kirchen-Ordnung von 1559*, in Reyscher (ed.), *Sammlung*, vol. 8, p. 219.
70 The term *Gutherzigen* occurs frequently in the sixteenth-century legal codes. In the Visitation Ordinance of 1547, reference is made to *guthertzige trewmainende personen* (Reyscher (ed.), *Sammlung*, vol. 8, p. 71), who were to assist in the visitation. One of the things they were to do was see that the village magistrates were *unns gutherzig*, i.e. well-intentioned vis-à-vis the Herrschaft (p. 72). The *Hartnackigen* were to be deposed and *Gutherzigen* elected in their place (p. 74). The opposite type were labeled *Vergiffte Neid hertzige Leut* (p. 78). From the context it appears that 'good-hearted' was more than just well-intentioned but involved active support.
71 The plague data comes from the examination of several parish registers for

the region south of Stuttgart. More information will be provided in my forthcoming study of the population of the village of Neckarhausen.

72 Hartmann, *Kirchengeseze*, vol. 3, p. xxx.

73 In fact, it could well be that communion first became a central institution for Herrschaft only with the Reformation. In the late medieval church, it was not an important aspect to religious practice. Carl C. Christensen, for example, has shown in a statistical analysis of pre-Reformation religious art (1495–1520) that the scene of the Last Supper seldom occurred as a theme. In Lutheran art it was absolutely central; *Art and Reformation in Germany* (Athens, Ohio, 1979), pp. 147–51.

2. A prophet in the Thirty Years' War

1 The sources for this study come from a dossier in the series of criminal files in the document collection of the Württemberg High Council (*Oberrat: Kriminalakten (1513–1806)*). They are found in the Württemberg Hauptstaatsarchiv (WHSA) in Stuttgart under the *Bestand* number A209, *Büschel* 1462a, 'Acta die von Hans Keylen zu Gerlingen angegebene Visiones betr. 1648–1653'. There are 167 separate documents in the file. Some of them contain a number, others only a date. References will be in the form: 'WHSA A209 Bü 1462a, 1' (or, e.g., '12 May 1648'). The chapbook from which the verse is taken is found in the file (no. 1) and is entitled: 'Kurtzer Summarischer doch aigentlicher und warhaffter Bericht Was sich den 4. Hornung dieses jetzt lauffenden 1648. Jahrs zu Gorlingen 2. Stund von der Fürstlichen Württembergischen Hauptstadt Stuttgart mit einem Rebmann Namens Hanns Keil laut seiner aussag begeben unnd zugetragen hat'. It appeared during the investigation of Keil and was confiscated by the authorities.

2 WHSA A209 Bü 1462a, 89. From another confiscated chapbook which appeared shortly after Keil's vision, entitled: 'Eyfferiges Bedencken ob die kundt- und wunderbahre Erscheinung einem Mann den 4. Februarii dieses 1648. Jahrs zu Görlingen ... für ein Göttlich wunderzeichen anzunemmen und zu halten seye?'.

3 *Ibid.*, 26. The story has been retold once before but with no attempt to comment on the texts: Dreher, 'Hans Keil, der "Prophet"', *Blätter für württembergische Kirchengeschichte (BWKG)*, 8 (1904), pp. 34–61. Dreher from time to time uses a different text from the one I use, but he gives no information about specific documents in the file. An interesting commentary on the Keil phenomenon is to be found in Martin Scharfe, 'Wunder und Wunderglaube im protestantischen Württemberg', in *BWKG*, 68/69 (1968/69), pp. 190–206. He interprets the signs of wonder as social sanctions. Keil needed some kind of a sign to give him legitimation. Scharfe argues that the population unreflectingly took up the vision as reality. The

function of such events is to integrate the in-group and to exclude the stranger. In what follows, I will argue that a close reading of the text does not lead to a functional explanation of the vision and that the credulity of the population is too much taken for granted. I find Pierre Bourdieu and Jean-Claude Passeron's statement of the problem more satisfactory: 'the apparent relationship between prophecy and its audience must be revised: the religious or political prophet always preaches to the convicted and follows his disciples as much as they follow him, since his lessons are listened to and heard only by agents who, by everything they are, have objectively mandated him to give them lessons'. *Reproduction in Education, Society and Culture* (London, 1977), pp. 25–6.

4 ,WHSA A209 Bü 1462a, 3.
5 *Ibid.*, 23.
6 *Ibid.*, 24.
7 *Ibid.*, 107.
8 See Winfried Schulze, *Reich und Türkengefahr. Studien zu den politischen und gesellschaftlichen Auswirkungen einer äusseren Bedrohung* (Munich, 1979), pp. 255ff.
9 H. Vorgrimler, 'Buss-Sakrament', in Heinrich Fries (ed.), *Handbuch theologischer Grundbegriffe*, vol. 1 (Munich, 1962), pp. 204–17. An older but very useful discussion is to be found in the article 'Busse' in J. S. Ersch and J. G. Gruber (eds.), *Allgemeine Encyclopädie der Wissenschaften und Künste*, vol. 14 (Leipzig, 1825), pp. 142–5. See also the article 'Busse' by J. Köstlin in the *Realencyklopädie für protestantische Theologie und Kirche (RTK)*, 3rd edn, vol. 3 (Leipzig, 1897), pp. 584–91.
10 WHSA A209 Bü 1462a, 1 (4 Feb. 1648). Note that the chapbook referred to in note 1 above is also numbered '1'.
11 *Ibid.*, 2.
12 *Ibid.*, 4, 5.
13 Martin Brecht, *Kirchenordnung und Kirchenzucht in Württemberg vom 16. bis zum 18. Jahrhundert*, Quellen und Forschungen zur Württembergischen Kirchengeschichte, vol. 1 (Stuttgart, 1967), pp. 63–5.
14 Johann Valentin Andreae, *Theophilus*, edited by Richard van Dülmen (Stuttgart, 1973), p. 105.
15 Brecht, *Kirchenordnung*, p. 60.
16 Andreae, *Theophilus*, pp. 104–5.
17 Brecht, *Kirchenordnung*, p. 81.
18 WHSA A209 Bü 1462a, 6 (7 February 1648).
19 *Ibid.*, 7, 8.
20 *Ibid.*, 10.
21 *Ibid.*, 16.
22 *Ibid.*, 19.
23 *Ibid.*, 17.

24 *Ibid.*, 12.

25 *Ibid.*, 34, 37b, 63, 64a, 64b, 88.

26 As frequently happens in such matters, other events took place which were assumed to throw light on the main event – this time literally (*Ibid.*, 18). In the evening of the 12th, as the messenger from Gerlingen approached the Rotenbild gate in Stuttgart, a great lighting up of the sky took place. One soldier reported that a fiery ball appeared in the sky and lasted to 10.30. Another described it as like a moon, which darkened as if a light had been extinguished and then lit again.

27 *Ibid.*, 30.

28 *Ibid.*

29 *Ibid.*, 28.

30 *Ibid.*, 30.

31 'General Rescript, betr. Abwarnung der Gemeinden von den Vorspielungen eines Schwärmers' (14 Apr. 1648), in A. L. Reyscher (ed.), *Sammlung der württembergischen Geseze*, vol. 8 (Tübingen, 1834), p. 325.

32 WHSA A209 Bü 1462a, 37a.

33 *Ibid.*, 52.

34 *Ibid.*, 54.

35 *Ibid.*, 55.

36 *Ibid.*, 53.

37 *Ibid.*, 61.

38 *Ibid.*, 65.

39 Not only did the news spread throughout Württemberg and bring specific difficulty in Gerlingen and surrounding villages for the officials, but there was also another kind of meaning to the rumors that made their way around the edges of the territory. One can already see the political implications to the rumor that the pope and emperor had sent their agents to enquire after Keil – and that from within Protestant Württemberg. However, the following story from Hechingen, a town in a Catholic state bordering Württemberg on the south, shows how such historical moments deepened the confessional differences between territories (*Ibid.*, 74b). 'The duke and his wife called Keil before them to see if he was consistent in his testimony. There came a knocking, and the duchess went to the door but no one was there. When it came again, the duke also was not able to find anyone there. The third time Keil answered only to find the angel standing there. He tried to show the angel to the duke, to whom it remained invisible. The angel told the duke to convert and believe in what was just, for otherwise there would come a gruesome death and the land would be visited with punishment. The duke responded that he was ready to convert to the Catholic faith. At that, the angel told him to give him his hand, but because he could not see the angel, the duke refused. The angel then extended his arm and the duke could see nothing but just half an arm.

He then gave the angel his hand. Since then he has had Capuchins and Jesuits with him.'

40 *Ibid.*, 75a.
41 *Ibid.*, 75c.
42 *Ibid.*, 76.
43 *Ibid.*, 78a.
44 *Ibid.* 84, 85.
45 *Ibid.*, 94.
46 *Ibid.*, 73.
47 *Ibid.*, 115, 122.
48 *Ibid.*, 108.
49 *Ibid.*, 143.
50 *Ibid.*, 166.
51 See the article on Spinnstuben by Hans Medick, 'Village Spinning Bees. Sexual Culture and Freetime among Rural Youth in Early Modern Germany', in Hans Medick and David Warren Sabean (eds.), *Interest and Emotion: Essays on the Study of Family and Kinship* (Cambridge, 1984), pp. 317–39.
52 When Keil's cousin in another village tried having a vision in a vineyard twenty years earlier, he was just told not to be so silly, and nothing came of the matter; WHSA A209 Bü 1462a, 30.
53 *Ibid.*, 151.
54 *Ibid.*, 107.
55 Claude Lévi-Strauss, *The Savage Mind* (London, 1962), p. 18. Hans Medick suggested the analogy of the *bricoleur* to me.
56 In fact he worked on his 'spontaneous' vision for over nine weeks and re-wrote it as many as 'forty times'.
57 Heinz-Dieter Kittsteiner, 'Von der Gnade zur Tugend. Zwei Beispiele aus einer Kulturgeschichte des Gewissens' (unpublished Ms, n.d.). Cited with permission of the author.
58 WHSA A209 Bü 1462a, 30.
59 *Ibid.*, 107.

3. The sacred bond of unity

1 A processual notion of culture has been developed in a series of stimulating papers by Gerald Sider: 'Christmas Mumming and the New Year in Outport Newfoundland', *Past and Present*, 71 (May, 1976), pp. 102–25; 'The Ties that Bind: Culture and Agriculture, Property and Propriety in Village Newfoundland', *Social History*, 5 (1980), pp. 1–39; 'Family Fun in Starve Harbour: Custom, History, and Confrontation in Village Newfoundland', in Hans Medick and David Warren Sabean (eds.), *Interest and Emotion: Essays on the Study of Family and Kinship* (Cambridge, 1984), pp. 340–70.

2 There is a very large literature on witchcraft in the seventeenth century. The latest overview and guide to the literature is Gerhard Schormann, *Hexenprozesse in Deutschland* (Göttingen, 1981). For Württemberg, see H. C. Erik Midelfort, *Witch Hunting in Southwestern Germany 1562–1684. The Social and Intellectual Foundations* (Stanford, 1972).

3 The sources for this chapter are the documents found in a file in the Württemberg Hauptstaatsarchiv Stuttgart (WHSA), A209 (*Oberrat: Kriminalakten (1513–1806)*), Büschel 1481, entitled: 'Untersuchung gegen die 13. jährige Anna Catharina Weissenbühler von Warmbronn wegen Hexerei Verdachts'. In most cases, the date of the document is given in the text, making it unnecessary to cite the source each time.

4 *Ibid.*, 17 (4 November 1683).

5 *Ibid.*, 1 (16 June 1683) and 26 November 1683.

6 Contrast the treatment of consanguineal kin in chapter 5.

7 Sharing food was, of course, a central aspect to communion, especially communion for the sick – discussed in chapter 1.

8 See the analysis of the 'scoff' in Gerald Sider, 'Family Fun'. He centers his analysis on the lack of exchange in this customary party where food is stolen.

9 The term 'relational idiom' is developed by Esther Goody in *Contexts of Kinship* (Cambridge, 1973), pp. 2–3, 41–50, 121–8. She uses the notion to deal with the sharing of cooked food and witchcraft and offers significant parallels to the discussion here.

10 *Ibid.*, p. 23. See also the discussion in Hans Medick and David Warren Sabean, 'Interest and Emotion in Family and Kinship Studies', in their (eds.) *Interest and Emotion*, pp. 11–15.

11 Midelfort, *Witch Hunting*, pp. 158–63.

12 For the distinctions see E. R. Leach, 'Rethinking Anthropology', in his *Rethinking Anthropology* (New York, 1966), pp. 1–27. See also the important work of Marc Augé, *Théorie des pouvoirs et idéologie. Étude de cas en Côte-d'Ivoire* (Paris, 1975), especially pp. 180ff.

13 For example, a man testified that his wife was a witch. 'Das alles aber hat sie nicht erkaufft aber ererbt'; Village of Neckarhausen, *Kirchen-konventsprotocolle*, vol. 1, 24 Aug 1744.

14 From a village informant.

15 WHSA A209 Bü 1467, 13 October 1656.

16 *Ibid.*, 22 July 1658.

17 *Ibid.*, 23 Jan 1657.

18 *Ibid.*, 8 Apr 1658.

19 Midelfort, *Witch Hunting*, pp. 178ff; Keith Thomas, *Religion and the Decline of Magic. Studies in Popular Beliefs in Sixteenth- and Seventeenth-Century England* (London, 1971), pp. 526ff; Alan Macfarlane, *Witchcraft in Tudor and*

Stuart England. A Regional and Comparative Study (London, 1970), pp. 168ff.

20 For example, the incidents related in chapter 4.

21 A good example is provided by Schormann, *Hexenprozesse*, pp. 96–9. See also WHSA A209 Bü 1467.

22 Medick and Sabean, 'Interest and Emotion'. Marcel Mauss, *The Gift: Forms and Functions of Exchange in Archaic Societies* (London, 1969), pp. 55ff.

23 Village of Neckarhausen, *Kirchenkonventsprotocolle*, vol. 2, 15 May 1769.

24 *Ibid.*, 13 July 1770, vol. 3, 5 May 1776.

25 WHSA A209 Bü 1467, 13 October 1656. Village of Neckarhausen, *Kirchenkonventsprotocolle*, vol. 2, 22 January 1769, 25 February 1770, 13 July 1770, 11 January 1771.

26 Laichingen, *Kirchenkonventsprotocolle*, vol. 1754–64, 24 May 1758.

27 Frances A. Yates, *The Art of Memory* (London, 1972, reprint), pp. 6ff.

28 *Ibid.*; Ruth Crosby, 'Oral Delivery in the Middle Ages', *Speculum*, 11 (1936), pp. 88–110. See also the stimulating paper by Franz H. Bäuml, 'Varieties and Consequences of Medieval Literacy and Illiteracy', *Speculum*, 55 (1980), pp. 237–65, especially pp. 249ff.

29 Walter J. Ong, S. J., *The Presence of the Word* (New Haven, 1967), pp. 32f, 223.

30 S. J. Tambiah, 'The Magical Power of Words', in *Man*, N.S. 3 (1968), pp. 175–208.

31 Dale F. Eickelmann, 'The Art of Memory: Islamic Education and its Social Reproduction', *Comparative Studies in Society and History*, 20 (1978), pp. 485–516, especially pp. 494–5, 505.

32 The literature on the Reformation concept of the word is large. A recent useful work is Klaus Haendler, *Wort und Glaube bei Melanchthon* (Gütersloh, 1968).

33 Johannes Brenz, *Frühschriften*, edited by Martin Brecht, Gerhard Schäfer, and Frieda Wolf, vol. 2 (Tübingen, 1974), pp. 280ff, 385ff.

34 *Kirchenordnung von 1559*, in A. L. Reyscher (ed.), *Sammlung der württembergischen Geseze*, (19 vols., Tübingen, 1828–51), vol. 8, p. 243.

35 John Calvin, *The Institutes of the Christian Religion*, edited by John T. McNeill (2 vols., London, 1961), vol. 2, p. 1019.

36 *Ibid.*, 1018.

37 Ong, *Presence of the Word*, pp. 122–31.

38 *Kirchenordnung von 1559*, in Reyscher (ed.), *Sammlung*, vol. 8, p. 181.

39 *Ibid.*, vol. 11, part 1, p. 4.

40 *Publikations-Reskript zum zweiten Landrecht* (1 July 1567), in Reyscher (ed.), *Sammlung*, vol. 4, pp. 168–70; *General-Reskript* (4 April 1584), p. 442; *Mandat* (21 May 1586), p. 450; *Verordnung* (11 November 1608), p. 464.

4. *Blasphemy, adultery and persecution*

1 The file is found in the Württemberg Hauptstaatsarchiv in Stuttgart (WHSA) in the series A214 (*Kommissionen des Oberrats (1579–1817)*), Büschel 335, entitled 'Acta der zu Heubach, Pflugfelden, Mauren und endlich zu Hattenhofen gewesenen unruhigen, und aus dem Herzogthum fortgewiesenen Pfarrer M. Georg Gottfrid Bregenzer betr. 1696–99, 1700–1710'. References will be to the documents by date or title.

2 See Christian Sigel, *Das evangelische Württemberg*, 2nd section, *General Magisterbuch* (vol. 10, mimeograph, n.p., n.d. [1932]), p. 419. There is a copy in the Landesbibliothek in Stuttgart.

3 WHSA A214 Bü 335, 13 October 1696.

4 *Ibid.*, 'Wann ein Schuler seinem Schulmeister alles layds anthät . . .'

5 *Ibid.*, 6 Dec 1697.

6 *Ibid.*

7 *Ibid.*, 4 May 1698.

8 *Ibid.*, 6 Dec 1697

9 See the Introduction, p.13–16.

10 WHSA A214 Bü 335, 4 May 1697. The conflicts over the lesser tithes were frequent for Württemberg pastors; Martin Hasselhorn, *Der altwürttembergische Pfarrstand im 18. Jahrhundert*. Veröffentlichungen der Kommission für geschichtliche Landeskunde in Baden-Württemberg, Series B: Forschungen, vol. 6 (Stuttgart, 1958), pp. 9–12.

11 WHSA A214 Bü 335, 4 May 1697.

12 *Ibid.*, 12 July 1699, 24 July 1699, 1 August 1699.

13 *Ibid.*, 7 November 1705.

14 *Ibid.*, 6 February 1706.

15 *Ibid.*

16 *Ibid.*, 1 February 1706.

17 *Ibid.*

18 See the comparative essays in Gisela Völger and Karin von Welck (eds.), *Rausch und Realität* (2 vols., Reinbek, 1982), vol. 1, pp. 134–362.

19 A useful discussion of the context in which my argument here is to be placed is: Hartmut Lehmann, *Pietismus und weltliche Ordnung in Württemberg vom 17. bis zum 20. Jahrhundert* (Stuttgart, 1969), pp. 22–65.

20 Each of the following testimonies and Bregenzer's answers are found in: WHSA A214 Bü 335, 6 February 1706 (protocol from 1–4 February 1706).

21 *Ibid.*, May 1705.

22 *Ibid.*

23 *Ibid.*, 6 February 1706 (protocol from 2 November 1705).

24 *Ibid.*

25 *Ibid.*, 11 February 1705.

26 *Ibid.*
27 *Ibid.*, 22 February 1706.
28 *Ibid.*, 22 August 1710.
29 A good example of eighteenth-century pietist exercise is Karl Ph. Moritz, *Anton Reiser, Roman* (Frankfurt, 1979).
30 See the sharp insights provided by Martin Scharfe for the nineteenth century in *Die Religion des Volkes. Kleine Kultur- und Sozialgeschichte des Pietismus* (Gütersloh, 1980), pp. 62, 65, 88.
31 See Edward Shorter, 'Illegitimacy, Sexual Revolution and Social Change in Modern Europe', *Journal of Interdisciplinary History*, 2 (1971–2), pp. 237ff. Data for a Württemberg village will be provided by my study on Neckarhausen; meanwhile, see my 'Unehelichkeit: Ein Aspekt sozialer Reproduktion kleinbäuerlicher Produzenten. Zu einer Analyse dörflicher Quellen um 1800', in Robert Berdahl, *et al.* (eds.), *Klassen und Kultur. Sozialanthropologische Perspektiven in der Geschichtsschreibung* (Frankfurt, 1982), pp. 54–76.
32 This point was suggested to me by Eric Wolf.
33 See Emmanuel Le Roy Ladurie, 'Family Structures and Inheritance Customs in Sixteenth-Century France', in Jack Goody, *et al.* (eds.), *Family and Inheritance. Rural Society in Western Europe 1200–1800* (Cambridge, 1976), pp. 37–70. The great study of French customary law is: Jean Yver, *Égalité entre héritiers et exclusion des enfants dotés* (Paris, 1966).
34 For Württemberg see Rolf-Dieter Hess, *Familien- und Erbrecht im württembergischen Landrecht von 1555*. Veröffentlichungen der Kommission für geschichtliche Landeskunde in Baden-Württemberg, Series B: Forschungen, vol. 44 (Stuttgart, 1968).
35 See Jeanne Favret-Saada, *Die Wörter, Die Zauber und Der Tod* (Frankfurt, 1979), pp. 32ff (published in English as *Deadly Words: Witchcraft in the Bocage* (Cambridge, 1980)).
36 WHSA A214 Bü 335, 'Geistliche Schützen-Kunst und Schützen-Zunfft'.
37 Still a useful book on 'enthusiasm' is Ronald Knox, *Enthusiasm. A Chapter in the History of Religion* (New York, 1961). For Arndt, see Constantin Grosse, *Die alten Tröster* (Hermannsburg, 1900), pp. 177–97. See also the article on Arndt in *Realencyklopädie für protestantische Theologie und Kirche*, 3rd edn, vol. 2 (Leipzig, 1897), pp. 108–12.
38 Johann Arndt, *Vier Bücher vom wahren Christenthum* (1610) (Lüneberg, 1653), *Vorrede*.
39 *Ibid.*
40 *Ibid.*, book 1, p. 33.
41 *Ibid.*, p. 44.
42 *Ibid.*, p. 48.
43 WHSA A214 Bü 335, 'Theologica Apologia'.

44 On Stegmann, see the article in Johann Heinrich Zedler (ed.), *Grosses Vollständiges Universal-Lexikon*, vol. 32 (Leipzig, 1744, reprint Graz, 1962), pp. 1471–2, for a list of his works and a short biography. WHSA A214 Bü 335, 'Aus D. Josua Stegmanni pp. Rintel: seinem Nutzlichen unndt Geistreichen Tractat vom wahren Christenthumb etc. Excerpta . . .'
45 Arndt, *Vom Wahren Christenthumb*, Book 1, pp. 33–4.
46 *Ibid.*, Book 4, pp. 110ff.
47 See the article, 'Hermeneutik', in *Die Religion in Geschichte und Gegenwart* (*RGG*), 3rd edn. vol. 3 (Tübingen, 1959), pp. 242–62. Also, the article, 'Typologie', vol. 6 (Tübingen, 1962), pp. 1094–8.
48 Article 'Typologie', *RGG*, vol. 6, p. 1095.
49 Article 'Hermeneutik', *RGG*, vol. 3, pp. 251–2.

5. The conscience of the poor

1 The file studied in this chapter is found in the Württemberg Hauptstaats-archiv in Stuttgart (WHSA), Series A214 (*Oberrat Commissionen (1579–1817)*), Büschel 476, entitled, 'Acta, die wegen des 9. Julii 1733 todgefundenen Pfarrers Breuningers zu Zell in Anno 1743. zu tag gekommenen bedenckliche Umstände betr. 1733–48'. Documents will be cited by number.
2 *Ibid.*, 5.
3 *Ibid.*, 8.
4 There are numerous examples in the village court records in the village of Neckarhausen. They will be discussed in detail in my forthcoming study.
5 Sometimes the process acted as a kind of purge. A guilty individual would take someone to court for libel, well knowing that he would lose. Once he was found guilty and had stood his punishment, he could no longer be taunted with his delict without in turn being able to demand satisfaction.
6 An important analysis of the nature of village discourse is to be found in Regina Schulte, 'Infanticide in Rural Bavaria in the Nineteenth Century', in Hans Medick and David Warren Sabean (eds.), *Interest and Emotion: Essays on the Study of Family and Kinship* (Cambridge, 1984), pp. 77–102.
7 A detailed examination of the ideology of 'house', 'household', and 'householder' will be contained in my forthcoming study of family and kinship in Neckarhausen. Meanwhile see the critical comments in my 'History of the Family in Africa and Europe: Some Comparative Perspectives', *Journal of African History* 24 (1983), pp. 163–71.
8 WHSA A214 Bü 476, 13.
9 Mauchard then quoted Gen. 49.5–7.
10 WHSA A214 Bü 476, 14.

11 *Ibid.*, 2.
12 *Ibid.*, unnumbered, dated 12 August 1733.
13 *Ibid.*, 46.
14 Georgii began his plea against the Drohmanns by quoting Nahum 1.2–3; *Ibid.*, 31.
15 *Ibid.*, 58.
16 The Swabian term *brutal* meant rude, insolent, uncivil, presumptious. It was often coupled with words. In fact, the term *Brutalium* was a rough way of referring to the mouth: 'Ich schlage dich aufs Brutalium' (I will punch you in the mouth). See Hermann von Fischer, *Schwäbisches Wörterbuch* (6 vols., Tübingen, 1904–36), article 'brutal'.
17 See my forthcoming work on family and kinship in Neckarhausen.
18 The discussion here is based on my study of marriage and *post mortem* inventories from the village of Neckarhausen. See also Rolf-Dieter Hess, *Familien- und Erbrecht im württembergischen Landrecht von 1555.* Veröffentlichungen der Kommission für geschichtliche Landeskunde in Baden-Württemberg, Series B: Forschungen, vol. 44 (Stuttgart, 1968).
19 An analysis of the land market will be contained in my study of kinship and family in Neckarhausen.
20 See the discussion in the Introduction, p. 35.
21 WHSA A214 Bü 476, 58.

6. *The sins of belief*

1 The poem comes from Karl Steiff, *Geschichtliche Lieder und Sprüche Württembergs* (Stuttgart, 1912), no. 288, pp. 1009–10, and is entitled 'Die letzte Hoffnung Demokratie' or 'Wie reimt man das zusammen?'. It was composed in October 1850. The original contains many verses, each involving a rhymed wordplay which is left blank and then substituted with a harmless phrase. In the original stanza, the missing word is *Sparren*; that is, Napoleon (III) has a screw loose. In my translation, I have rather ineptly rhymed 'bull', 'fool', and the missing word, 'normal'.

> Beutelsbach, Zwiefalten, Napoleon,
> wie reimt sich das zussammen?
> In Beutelsbach begrabt man den Farren,
> In Zwiefalten sind die Narren,
> und Napoleon hat einen – sparsamen Geist.
> So reimt sich das zusammen.

2 Hugo Moser, *Schwäbischer Volkshumor. Neckereien in Stadt und Land, von Ort zu Ort,* 2nd edn (Stuttgart, 1981), pp. 346–7. The original term is *Hommelhenker.*
3 Württemberg Hauptstaatsarchiv in Stuttgart (WHSA) Series A214 (*Kom-*

missionen des Oberrats (1579–1817))), Büschel 810, entitled 'Commissarische Untersuchung wegen lebendig Begrabung eines Farren zu Beutelsbach.'

4 *Ibid.*, Protocol dated 24 October to 5 November 1796 and report dated 7 November (document 10 A).

5 For an overview of the regulations and ordinances, see A. L. Reyscher (ed.), *Sammlung der württembergischen Geseze,* vol. 14 (Tübingen, 1843), pp. 1110–11.

6 WHSA A214, 10 December 1796 (document 13).

7 *Ibid.*, 7 January 1797 (document 15).

8 *Ibid.*, 29 September 1801 (document 19).

9 *Ibid.*, 20 August 1801, 22 September 1801 (documents 21, 22).

10 *Ibid.*, 14 September 1801 (document 23).

11 *Ibid.*, 14 September 1801 (document 25).

12 *Ibid.*, 1 October 1801 (document 25).

13 *Ibid.*, unnumbered and undated.

14 Vanessa Maher called my attention to this point. See the essays collected together by M. F. C. Bourdillon and Meyer Fortes (eds.), *Sacrifice* (London, 1980), especially J. W. Rogerson, 'Sacrifice in the Old Testament. Problems of Method and Approach', pp. 45–60, and S. W. Sykes, 'Sacrifice in the New Testament and Christian Theology', pp. 61–83.

15 In fact, he was a very old man, dying just after the first investigation at the age of seventy-nine. The new pastor was appointed in December 1796. *Schwäbische Merkur* (23 November 1796), p. 347; (26 December 1796), p. 375.

16 In Neckarhausen, for example, a boar was first purchased for the village in the 1860s. The growth in the number of pigs kept by villagers and attention to breeding came as a result of farming new root crops after the agricultural revolution.

17 The example is taken from an investigation into the criminal activities of a Schultheiss in the village of Neckarhausen during the first decade of the nineteenth century; WHSA A214 Bü 746.

18 Useful reading on knowledge as power inside a community and the necessity for strategies of concealment and dissimulation can be found in Juliet Du Boulay, *Portrait of a Greek Mountain Village* (Oxford, 1974), pp. 179–229. What she says about communication among villagers is also relevant for that between the inside and outside.

Conclusion

1 Fritz Redlich, *The German Military Enterpriser and his Work Force. Vierteljahrschrift für Sozial- und Wirtschafts-geschichte,* Beiheft 47 (2 vols., Wiesbaden, 1964).

2 For a review of the literature on peasant revolts in Europe and their relevance for state development, see Winfried Schulze, 'Europäische und

deutsche Bauernrevolten der frühen Neuzeit – Probleme der vergleichende Betrachtung', in his (ed.), *Europäische Bauernrevolten der frühen Neuzeit* (Frankfurt, 1982), pp. 10–60. See also his work on central European revolts: *Bäuerliche Widerstand und feudale Herrschaft in der frühen Neuzeit,* Neuzeit im Aufbau, vol. 6 (Stuttgart–Bad Cannstatt 1980).

3 See Dietrich Gerhard, 'Amtsträger zwischen Krongewalt und Ständen: ein europäisches Problem', in his *Gesammelte Aufsätze,* Veröffentlichungen des Max-Planck-Instituts für Geschichte, vol. 54 (Göttingen, 1977), pp. 71–88; J. Russel Major, 'The Crown and the Aristocracy in Renaissance France', *American Historical Review,* 69 (1963–4), pp. 631–45; Hans Rosenberg, *Bureaucracy, Aristocracy and Autocracy. The Prussian Experience 1660–1815* (Cambridge, Mass., 1958), pp. 1–25.

4 Based on my study of court protocols from the village of Neckarhausen.

5 Two useful works on the fiscal state are: Rudolf Braun, 'Taxation, Sociopolitical Structure, and State-Building: Great Britain and Brandenburg-Prussia', in Charles Tilly (ed.), *The Formation of National States in Western Europe* (Princeton, 1975), pp. 243–327; Gabriel Ardant, 'Financial Policy and Economic Infrastructure of Modern States and Nations', in *Ibid.,* pp. 164–242.

6 For this section see some of the conflicts found in the document collection A206 (*Oberrat: ältere Ämterakten (1550–1748)*) in the Württemberg Hauptstaatsarchiv in Stuttgart (WHSA), Büschel 1341a, 1348, 1364, 3871, 3929, 3966, 4233, 4941, 4942, 4950, 4971, 5091, 5099.

7 Hans Medick, 'Village Spinning Bees. Sexual Culture and Freetime among Rural Youth in Early Modern Germany', in Hans Medick and David Warren Sabean (eds.), *Interest and Emotion: Essays on the Study of Family and Kinship* (Cambridge, 1984), pp. 317–39.

8 See Ivan Illich, *Vom Recht auf Gemeinheit* (Reinbek bei Hamburg, 1982), pp. 30–48, especially p. 33.

9 Ivan Illich, *Gender* (New York, 1982), pp. 148–57; Jeffrey Burton Russell, *Witchcraft in the Middle Ages* (Ithaca, 1972), pp. 50, 60, 65, 93, 110, 170.

10 Illich, *Gender,* pp. 147–52.

11 See the entries from the village of Neckartailfingen in the collection of *Urfehden* (A44) in WHSA.

12 Illich, *Gender,* p. 152.

13 Chapter 1.

14 Johann Valentin Andreae, *Theophilus,* edited by Richard van Dülmen (Stuttgart, 1973).

15 *Ibid.,* p. 83.

16 *Ibid.,* pp. 57, 89, 109.

17 *Ibid.,* pp. 35, 107.

18 *Ibid.,* p. 105.

19 *Ibid.*, p. 35.
20 Chapter 2.
21 Chapter 5.
22 Clifford Geertz, ' "From the Native's Point of View": On the Nature of Anthropological Understanding', in Keith H. Basso and Henry A. Selby (eds.), *Meaning in Anthropology* (Alburquerque, New Mexico, 1976), pp. 221–37, here p. 225.
23 Above, p. 40.
24 Andreae, *Theophilus*, p. 135.
25 Chapter 2.
26 Russell, *Witchcraft*, p. 170.
27 Above, p. 98.
28 H. C. Erik Midelfort, *Witch Hunting in Southwestern Germany 1562–1684. The Social and Intellectual Foundations* (Stanford, 1972), pp. 37–8.
29 Jeanne Favret-Saada, *Die Wörter, der Zauber, der Tod. Der Hexenglaube im Hainland von Westfrankreich* (Frankfurt, 1979), pp. 104ff (published in English as *Deadly Words: Witchcraft in the Bocage* (Cambridge, 1980)).
30 Chapter 4.
31 Chapter 5.

Glossary

Amt	district (*pl.* Ämter)
Amtmann	district official
Amtsschreiber	district clerk
Beisitzrecht	right to residence without privileges accorded to Bürger
Bürger	enfranchised inhabitant of a village or town; adult married male
Bürgermeister	chief financial officer of a village or town; sometimes a second Bürgermeister had charge of community property (*sing.* and *pl.*)
Bürgerrecht	residence privileges of a Bürger
Bürgerschaft	collectivity of Bürger
Canzlei Advocat	legal official of chancery
Contribution	war tax
Deputierte	*ad hoc* village deputies
Dorfschütz	village policeman
Feind	enemy (*pl.* Feinde)
Feindschaft	enmity
Feldschütz	police officer for agricultural land
Freund	friend (*pl.* Freunde); affinal relative
Freundschaft	friendship (rare); relatives; affinal relatives
Gemeinde	village or town community, collectivity of Bürger
Gemeinschaft	community
Gericht	court
Gerichtsherrschaft	lordship or authority arising from the right to exercise justice
Gerichtsschreiber	court recorder, clerk of the court
Gerichtsverwandte	juror, member of the Gericht; *see* Richter
Geschrei	rumor, clamor, stir

238

Geschwätz	gossip
Geschweyh	sister-in-law
Gesellschaft	society, association
Gevatter	godfather; expresses the relation between the godfather and the parent
Grundherrschaft	lordship over land, landlordship
Haus	house; expresses the juridical and economic whole
Haushalter	householder, head of a Haus
Hausvater	male head of a Haus
Heckenpfleger	administrator of a poor relief fund in Leonberg
Heiligenpfleger	administrator of the poor relief fund
Herr	lord
Herrschaft	lordship; authority; domination; state
Incipient	apprentice in the office of the district clerk (Schreiberei)
Knecht	servant
Landschaft	parliamentary institution in Württemberg
Landtag	*see* Landschaft
Leibeigene	bondsman; serf
Leibherr	personal lord over Leibeigene
Leibherrschaft	personal lordship over Leibeigene
Oberamt	Württemberg administrative district
Oberamtmann	chief administrative officer in an Oberamt (*see* Vogt)
Oberrat	High Council in Württemberg
Obrigkeit	magistrates
parteiisch	biassed, partisan
Pförchmeister	administrator of sheep-folding
Rat	council, council member (*pl.* Räte)
Rathaus	village or town administration building
Richter	juror, member of a Gericht
Ruggericht	annual or semi-annual village court
Sage	rumor, discourse, opinion; tradition
Schreiber	clerk, secretary
Schreiberei	office of the clerk
Schultheiss	chief administrative officer of a village
Schutz und Schirm	protection
Schwager	brother-in-law
Schwärmer	enthusiast, fanatic
Schweher	father-in-law
Scribent	journeyman clerk

Söhnerin	daughter-in-law
Spinnstube	spinning bee, evening gathering to sew and spin
Stabsbeamte	official exercising jurisdiction in the name of the duke, e.g. Vogt
Stadt und Amt	a Württemberg administrative district, (*see* Oberamt)
Stadt- und Amtspfleger	financial officer of a district
Stadt- und Amtsschreiber	district clerk
Substitut	sub official in the district Schreiberei
Superintendent	deacon; chief church official of a district
Untervogt	deputy Vogt
Verwandte	relatives; blood relatives
Verwandtschaft	group of relatives; blood relatives
Vogt	chief administrative official of a district (*pl.* Vögte)
Vogtruggericht	annual or biennial court of a Vogt held in a village
Waldmeister	administrator of forest land
Weisspfennig	silver coin; tax
Wildschütz	game-keeper
Zehntherrschaft	lordship over tithes

General index

court, *see Gericht*
cousin, 96, 98, 101, 108, 110, 132–3; *see also Base*; *Vetter*
crossroads, 174, 177–8, 184, 191
culture, 94, 95, 111; elite, 208, 210, 228n1; folk, 212; high, 4, 91, 215n2, 221n85; oral, 110–11; peasant, 2–3, 205, 214n1, 215nn2–3; popular, 2, 35, 73, 84, 91, 135, 175, 199, 214n1, 221n85
cursing, 63–8, 72, 87, 90, 107, 138; *see also* swearing

dancing, 123, 125, 131, 134
daughter-in-law, *see Söhnerin*
Dettinger, Mathias, 51–2, 223n20
devil, 40–2, 77, 97–9, 101–2, 125, 131, 133, 159, 171; mark of, 101–2, 107
devotion, *see Andacht*
Dilleny, *Scribent*, 122–4
discipline, and communion, 39, 73, 119; and conscience, 89; and *Herrschaft*, 42, 69, 198; from God, 78, 86; of community, 112; program of, 71–3, 77, 79, 111, 206–8, 210
discourse, analysis of, 199; as contrasted to ideas, 36, 195–6, 198; idiom of, 110; levels of, 208, 210–11; oral, 102, 104, 111–12; over the household, 204; over the person, 212; *see also* community, discourse
domination, 59, 106, 142, 198; and class, 67; and practice, 173; apparatus of, 25, 120; as an aspect of texts, 2–3; concept, 24; contrasted to self-administration, 14; state, 8; symbolism of, 62, 150; *see also Herrschaft*
Dreher, Pastor, 225n3
Drohmann, Friederich, 145, 156
Drohmann, Hans Jerg, 144, 207; acquittal, 161; activities during night of murder, 156–8; as object of gossip, 147–9, 153–6, 160, 166; character, 149–52, 155, 162–5, 170–1, 207; relations with Geigers, 154, 158, 166–9; relations with Hans Jerg Bauer, 155–6, 164
Drohmann, Michael, 144; acquittal, 161; activities during night of murder, 158–9, 161; as object of gossip, 147–9, 153, 156, 166; character, 149–52, 155–6, 160, 172–4, 171, 207; relations with Michael Bauer, 159
Du Boulay, Juliet, 235n18

Du form of address, 116–17, 121, 124

Ehebrecher, 137; *see also* adultery
Elbs, Eberhard, 216n20
Ellwangen, Michael, 178–9, 184
enemy, 31–2, 38, 52–4, 78, 113–14, 117–18, 133, 142, 160–2; *see also Feind*
Enlightenment, 198, 204
enmity, 31, 38–9, 47, 52, 54, 114, 129, 162; *see also Feindschaft*
envy, 28, 30, 32–4, 40–1, 47, 54, 56–7, 108–9, 142; *see also Neid*
exchange, 49, 100, 107, 109, 191–2, 205
exorcism, 69, 79
exploitation, 110, 136, 202
expropriation, 4, 5, 7, 73, 93, 200, 202–3, 210
extortion, 64–6, 92

face-to-face relationship, 3, 27
fama, 173
family, 129, 137–8, 217n29
father-in-law, 154, 165, 167, 239
Fausel, Andreas, 222n20
Favret-Saada, Jeanne, 211
fear, 35, 109, 163–5, 171
Feind, 31, 138, 170, 238; *see also* enemy
Feindschaft, 31, 52, 152, 163, 166, 238; *see also* enmity
Feineysin, Hans Michael, 96, 98, 100–1
Feineysin, Maria Catharina, 100, 101
feudal, classes, 7; dues, 218n60; exactions, 8, 20; property, 202; relations, 21, 201; rent, 5, 7, 14
financial records, *see* accounts
Fink, *Scribent*, 122–5, 127
food, 103; as idiom, 100, 102; as metaphor, 100–1, 110; as poison, 100–1, 110; shared, 97, 100, 109, 229n7
forgiveness, 38, 48, 52
fornication, 64, 66–7, 71, 123, 127, 129
Fortes, Meyer, 221n85
freedom, 208, 212
Frend, 31, 138, 154, 170, 238
Frendschaft, 129, 136, 153, 169, 238; *see also* friendship; kin
friend, *see Freund*
friendship, 17, 162; *see also Freundschaft*
Funckh, Joachim, 79

Gallasin, *see* Baum, Madalena
gaming, 66

Index of places